Harnessing the Wind

THE ART OF TEACHING MODERN DANCE

Harnessing the Wind
THE ART OF TEACHING MODERN DANCE

JAN ERKERT
COLUMBIA COLLEGE CHICAGO

Human Kinetics

50694833

Library of Congress Cataloging-in-Publication Data

Erkert, Jan.
  Harnessing the wind : the art of teaching modern dance / by Jan
Erkert.
     p. cm.
Includes bibliographical references (p.).
  ISBN 0-7360-4487-6
  1. Modern dance--Study and teaching. I. Title: Art of teaching modern
dance. II. Title.
  GV1783 .E75 2003
  792.8'071--dc21

                              2002015806

ISBN 0-7360-4487-6

Acquisitions Editor: Judy Patterson Wright, PhD; **Developmental Editor:** Patricia A. Norris, PhD; **Assistant
Editor:** Lee Alexander; **Copyeditor:** Cheryl Ossola; **Proofreader:** Jennifer L. Davis; **Permission Manager:**
Dalene Reeder; **Graphic Designer:** Fred Starbird; **Graphic Artist:** Dawn Sills; **Photo Manager:** Leslie A.
Woodrum; **Cover Designer:** Jack W. Davis; **Photographer (cover):** William Frederking; **Art Manager:** Kelly
Hendren; **Illustrator:** John Matthews; **Printer:** Versa Press; **On the cover:** Dancer Carrie Hanson

Printed in the United States of America   10 9 8 7 6 5 4 3 2 1

Human Kinetics
Web site: www.HumanKinetics.com

United States: Human Kinetics
P.O. Box 5076
Champaign, IL 61825-5076
800-747-4457
e-mail: humank@hkusa.com

Canada: Human Kinetics
475 Devonshire Road Unit 100
Windsor, ON N8Y 2L5
800-465-7301 (in Canada only)
e-mail: orders@hkcanada.com

Europe: Human Kinetics
107 Bradford Road
Stanningley
Leeds LS28 6AT, United Kingdom
+44 (0) 113 255 5665
e-mail: hk@hkeurope.com

Australia: Human Kinetics
57A Price Avenue
Lower Mitcham, South Australia 5062
08 8277 1555
e-mail: liahka@senet.com.au

New Zealand: Human Kinetics
P.O. Box 105-231, Auckland Central
09-523-3462
e-mail: hkp@ihug.co.nz

In memory of my father, James Erkert,
who viewed the world with the logic and patience of an engineer;
and my mother, Ruth Erkert, who lived her life with grace, curiosity, and wonder.

Contents

Part II   Class Preparation   21

Preface

Harnessing The Wind: The Art of Teaching Modern Dance is a philosophical guide to the *art* of teaching modern dance, integrating somatic theories, scientific principles, and contemporary aesthetic practices. This book is for any teacher or dancer in the contemporary dance field who, at the end of class, questions what was accomplished that day. It purposely does not provide a set of easy recipes; rather, it encourages lively internal conversation and dialogue among students and colleagues. It asks you to make conscious choices about what, why, and how you teach.

This book will not teach you to teach; the art of teaching is learned through practice in the classroom—making fast decisions, placing hands on students, and finding the right rhythms. But if you are a dance student in a college program taking your first pedagogy course, this book will provide you with the information and theory necessary to begin the task of teaching. If you are a seasoned teacher, this book will inspire new questions, confirm your intuition, and hopefully, introduce new possibilities.

Dance teachers have a long history of learning through experience. Historically, the apprentice system has been our training ground. After logging thousands of hours in class, the dancer becomes a teacher. But the time has come to ground experience with theory. Analytical knowledge confirms intuitive choices and challenges old beliefs. This powerful combination of theory and intuition will help teachers train smart dancers who are ready to handle the demands of contemporary dance.

In each of the fourteen chapters, the main text addresses important issues of dance training. In recent years, somatic practices and scientific research have yielded an explosion of information about movement training, so discussions about anatomy, kinesiology, and somatic approaches are included. This information provides new teachers with a solid theoretical base and provokes experienced teachers to investigate their practice further. Too much theory at one time can be overwhelming, so take one chapter at a time and sit with it for a while. Compare the information to your experience. What rings true for you? What is worth exploring in more detail? What is useful in the classroom? The book's structure progresses as you might, from the first thought of teaching a dance class to the closing applause.

Part I, Philosophy, asks the question, "What am I teaching?" Rooting our teaching in a clear philosophical point of view is the beginning of the journey. Chapter 1, Dancing Roots: Technique, defines the role of technique. By looking back at our dance ancestors and conducting a deep, personal investigation of movement, we develop a unique point of view about dance training. Technique should enhance individuality, not erase it; it is within the individual that artistry begins. Chapter 2,

Flying Souls: Artistry, explores the delicate job of nurturing the artist during the quest for technical control.

Part II, Class Preparation, is where the planning process takes shape. A clear vision allows us to develop strategies and goals that are both realistic and comprehensive. Chapter 3, Sculpting Dreams: Goals, lays the groundwork for building a progression of movement skills. Rituals provide consistency in order to honor traditions and truths. Principles of neurological learning and movement reeducation are explored in chapter 4, Centering Minds: Rituals, helping you to create an environment where students can search for center. Chapter 5, Gathering Power: Conditioning, offers information about anatomy, kinesiology, and somatic practices that will enable you to safely incorporate conditioning principles into dance training and produce powerful, resilient dancers. In a technique class, dancers learn by doing, and shaping movement phrases kinesthetically enhances movement learning. While this is a physical art, chapter 6, Shaping Phrases: Dancing, asks you to consider elements of phrasing upon entering the studio. To sequence exercises effectively, the dance teacher must consider a vast array of possibilities, such as conditioning, dynamics, and patterning. In chapter 7, Weaving Light: Sequencing, graphs and planning guides are provided to help you compose a successful class.

Part III, Class Presentation, is where the spontaneous skills of teaching come into play. The delicate art of pacing requires teachers to keep muscles warm while delivering information. Chapter 8, Time Flowing: Pacing, discusses the importance of delivering a class that flows. Learning to see and sense enables a teacher to develop a good eye and gentle touch. Chapter 9, Body Listening: Corrections, provides information about reflexes, alignment, and touch, so that your corrections will enhance student performance and confirm the student's innate wisdom. Chapter 10, Space Moving: Images, explores the power of images in movement learning. Based on theories stemming from somatic practices, you will learn why images work. Understanding the unique relationship between music and dance unlocks the doors to musicality and phrasing. Chapter 11, Silence Sounding: Accompanists, addresses the skills necessary to successfully collaborate with musicians.

Part IV, Professional Concerns, embraces important issues surrounding the teaching professional. In chapter 12, Energy Talking: Communication, scientific and educational theories are explored to illuminate the relationship between mind and body particular to the process of learning to dance. Dance training is a rigorous activity putting stress on both body and mind, and students may cope by developing dangerous obsessions or injuries. In chapter 13, Excellence Training: Health, you will learn how to recognize problems and intervene when necessary. Teaching dance is a rigorous career demanding tremendous vitality. Chapter 14, Youth Spinning: Vitality, addresses ways to maintain a healthy body, a curious mind, and a fresh spirit.

Two additional features of the book will help you dive deeper into your exploration of teaching. Each chapter is followed by an investigation and a reflection.

Because teachers must embody what they teach, the investigations provide guided suggestions for experimentation and observation. These short exercises culminate each chapter and cover a range of activities including writing, drawing, chart making, observing, and experiential processing. The investigations are for anybody, from student to professional. The in-class investigations are designed to encourage teachers to develop new practices within the classroom. These might also be assigned to a student teacher. Take one investigation a day and relish it.

Take a list from one chapter and dwell on it for a year. Return to them again and again and see how your teaching practice has evolved.

Teaching dance is inseparable from life, and so the personal reflections unveil the intangible things we teach such as breath, centering, playfulness, presence, and openness. The reflections are to be read and savored in the studio with a cup of coffee, before class to remember why you are there, or at night curled up in bed. Share them with a friend, a non-dancer, a spouse, or a lover. Perhaps the reflections will help others understand your dancing life and the rigors of this demanding art form.

Accompanying each chapter and reflection are photographs by Erika Dufour, William Frederking, and Rod Murphy. These photographs of dancers who have graced Chicago stages remind us why we are working so hard in the classroom. The illustrations by John Matthews provide a visual stimulus while illuminating the text.

Last, the appendixes include a syllabus for modern technique, a level-placement guide, an assessment report, and evaluation forms. Developed by a faculty team at The Dance Center of Columbia College Chicago, they can be used as resources and guides to your own practice.

Acknowledgments

*J*umping off a cliff is a far easier task than writing a book. Little did I know what I was getting into when I entered the world of words. As I plunged into deep waters, a vast community of people came to my rescue. I owe great thanks.

I begin with my husband's son, Mark Lewy, and his gracious wife, Ana, for providing the perfect place to start: a beautiful castle in the rolling vineyards of Spain. When I returned from Spain I printed out what I had written; I could now hold in my hands the results of my labor. But whom could I turn to that would sort through this rough, rough draft? Carol Bobrow carried the perfect credentials: a dear friend and a dance teacher with a passion for reading cookbooks. She gave me confidence when she said the book was like listening to her own thoughts.

Writer and dancer Maggie Kast was next to grace the book. A gentle soul with a sharp intelligence, Maggie imparted the power of nouns and verbs. Editor Maureen Jansen ruthlessly covered it with red ink, correcting all the grammar I didn't learn in grade school. Joseph Reiser, a composer and author, said it read more like a memoir—and he said I wasn't famous enough to have a memoir. I thank him for his harsh honesty. Joannie Kaufman, Ginger Farley, Anna Paskevska, and Beth McNeil provided unique points of view. Selene Carter and Scott Oury expertly pinpointed holes. I thank Irene Dowd for an intelligent, thorough, and generous critique via phone waves. Judy Wright believed in the manuscript from the start; I knew working together would not be dull when she threw off her shoes and jumped into a dance class, nylons and all. My editor, Pat Norris, offered invaluable insight, helping me to wrestle down computer programs as well as words and thoughts. Lee Alexander and Cheryl Ossola worked magic with my words.

Who taught me how to teach? Of course, my students, and I thank them for their patience. I especially want to thank Michiru Onizuka-Kempen for her passion when I was losing mine, former student Robyn Gravenhorst, who did some fine detective work, and Chansri Green for taking the book on a test-drive. I owe a great debt of gratitude to those dancers who graced my life and my dances. Juli Hallihan-Campbell, Lezlee Crawford, Louise Green, Jen-Jen Lin, Peter Rothblatt, Cecily Sommers, Michael McStraw, and Tim Veach were physicists of movement. Mary Johnston Coursey and Sandra Sucsy reveled in forgotten sensations. Julie Worden, Christine Bornarth, and Anthony Gongora knew and lived ecstatic presence. Chia Yu Chang, Mark Schulze, and Carrie Hanson provided the whole picture to the fragments of my knowledge. Finally, the company of my dreams—Paul Cipponeri, Robbie Cook, Erica Gilfether, Krenly Guzmán, Suet May Ho, and Kim Nelson—was a magical love poem. A great debt of gratitude goes to all.

I thank Jyl Fehrenkamp and Deborah Siegel for helping select photos, and the dancers in the photographs for working so hard and looking so good. Elizabeth Chang, Krenly Guzmán, Christopher Nelson, and Margaret Morris provided graceful bodies and generous spirits for the illustrations.

I don't envy my dance teachers. As a student I was slow, rebellious, and rigid. I thank my first dance teacher, Evelyn Kreason, for lessons in her garage where I thought I was studying toe tap due to a missing comma, and Christopher Flynn from the Joffrey Ballet for limiting me to pliés and tendus. I thank the University of Utah crowd for introducing me to modern dance: Elizabeth Hayes, Shirley Ririe, Loabelle Mangelson, Joan Woodbury, Dr. John Wilson, and Bill Evans. Never letting anyone get away with anything, Shirley Mordine opened my world to weight and space even though it took tears to get there. Each of the following artists gave me a morsel that made me chew for decades: Suzanne Linke, Akira Kasai, Viola Farber, Carla Maxwell, June Finch, Mary Anthony, Margaret H'Doubler, Ralph Lemon, Trisha Brown, Jawole Willa Jo Zollar, Joe Goode, Chuck Davis, Wally Cardona, Barbara Mahler, Jeff Curtis, Bill T. Jones, Doug Varone, Bebe Miller, Margaret Jenkins, Ellie Klopp, and Rennie Harris. Bonnie Bainbridge Cohen, Lisa Clark, Kim Nelson, and Beth Stein opened the doors to the wisdom of somatic practices. My body thanks healer Papillon and yoga teachers Tom Quinn and Suddha.

Musicians Richard Woodbury, Claudia Howard Queen, Winston Damen, Laurence Hobgood, Michael Kirkpatrick, Lucinda Lawrence, Pennington McGee, Toby Twining, Doug Brush, and Bob Garrett stretch my limbs when they put hands and mouths to task.

Opportunity is everything, so I thank each person who called me on the phone with a job. Special thanks go to Pat Knowles, who observed me teaching a group of unruly children and called the next day with an invitation to teach at the University of Illinois. I wonder what she was thinking. I got to experience hot places like Texas and Taiwan thanks to Susan Douglas Roberts and Ming-Shen Ku, and the coldest places on earth thanks to Linda Shapiro and Emmy Thompson. Maria Inez Camou introduced me to the tango in Montevideo, and Miguel Mancillas, Adriana Castellanos, Athenea Baker, and Marta Ketchum shared the flavors of Mexico despite my ill attempts at Spanish.

Opportunity is one avenue of support; the other is financial. Several key people have given me both. Bette Rosenstein understands both artistic process and needs, and gives generously of time, money, and love. Sandy Gerding taught me that I could have whatever I wanted; I just needed to define it.

From the top-floor studio of the Dance Center of Columbia College, I look out over the horizontal expanse of Lake Michigan as it butts up to the vertical explosion of skyscrapers. But it is more than the space without; it is the space within that generates excitement. I am indebted to our chairperson, Bonnie Brooks, for engineering release time and supplying the next to the last word, and I thank Columbia College Chicago for a Faculty Development Grant to work on the manuscript. The faculty—Bonnie Brooks, Dardi McGinley-Gallivan, Shirley Mordine, Deborah Siegel, Eduardo Vilaro, Erica Wilson Perkins, and Richard Woodbury—challenge my thinking daily. I thank Pan Papacosta for recharging my interest in physics.

At the end, I thank my family. My sister, Susan Jackson, an indomitable spirit, has become my best friend even though she liked to hit me when we were young. My engineering brother, Tom Erkert, provides a steady force of unconditional love. My niece Carrie Jackson Cioffi's joy and confidence buoy my faith in the next generation of women. Thanks to Larry for creating peaceful gardens and Shawn for the big bear hugs. Von, Nicholas, and Jonathan have been trying really hard to teach me about computers and Pokeman, and they're gradually realizing I am a tough student. Robin Lewy says I taught her how to breathe, but little does she know she taught me the same skill. I strive to be like my young friend Zac Osgood; his courage, love, and humor in the face of adversity are the embodiment of grace.

My granddaughter Nora's passion for feather boas, tutus, and sequins reminds me why I do this. I thank Eloi for teaching me how to tell stories. Camilo's gentle touch and open heart remind me of his father, David—I take comfort in the great chain of genes. A big thank-you goes to Kyle for allowing me to hold him underneath the wind chimes. Finally, I thank my husband, Bernt, for adoring me. I find home intertwined in his strong limbs and sturdy heart.

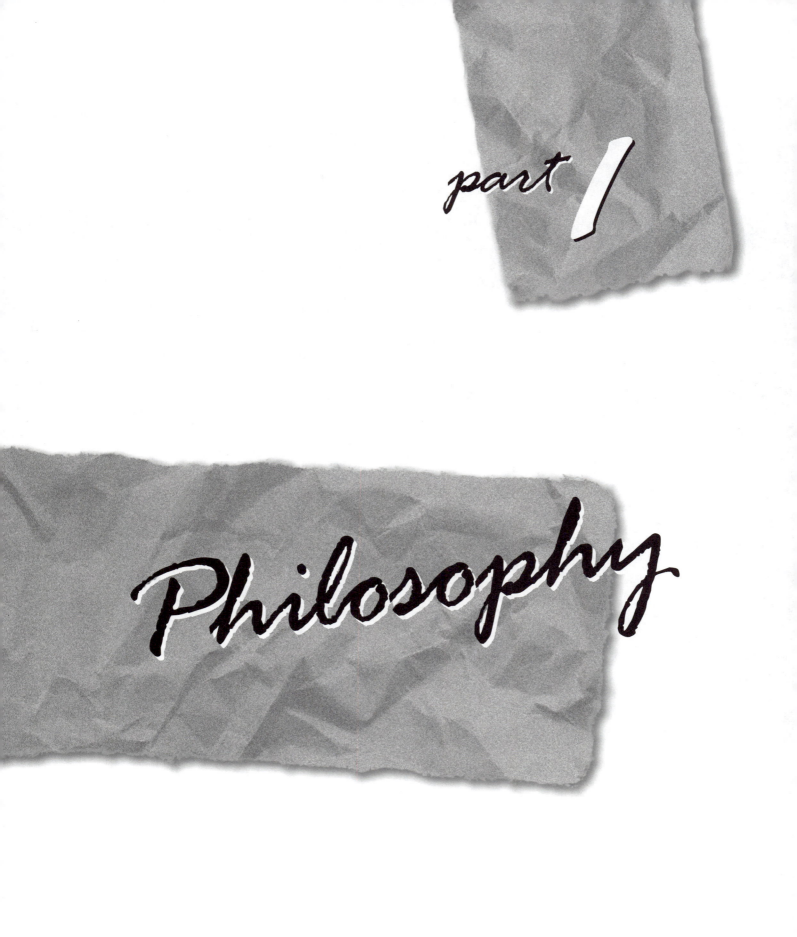

part *1*

Philosophy

William Frederking, photographer; Sabine Fabie and Mark Schulze, dancers.

chapter 1

Dancing Roots
TECHNIQUE

A feather blows in the wind. As it floats down gracefully, eyes follow its erratic yet gentle dance. It occasionally catches an updraft, suspending its flight for a moment before finally succumbing to the pull of gravity. Tossed by fate, the feather is completely at the will of the wind. Envious of such delicate freedom, I hike up a mountain to go paragliding. Preparing to run off a cliff, I meditatively straighten the strings connecting the harness to the sail and meticulously fasten the belts and straps securing my legs and pelvis. As I wait for just the right gust of wind, trusting in the sheets of fabric laid out behind, I take a tentative first step. When I feel the sail gather the wind, I run with all my might. At last the sail billows with the full force of the wind, and I am lifted off the mountaintop. I glide above the trees and feel oddly secure and confident dangling from strings and straps. The sail is immediately responsive when I shift my weight to turn and pull the strings to catch the updrafts. Whether I desire to soar upward or return to earth, the harness channels the force of the wind, controlling every moment of my journey. Wind and gravity are at my command, and I return to earth lightly and safely.

TECHNIQUE

For the dancer, technique is a harness that provides the necessary control to fly and spin, allowing the dancer to rebound in and out of the earth with unseen wings. What makes up the harness in dance technique?

- *Point of View.* Technique provides a philosophical point of view in the investigation of movement principles, based on the traditions and wisdom of dance ancestors.
- *Artistry.* Technique supports ecstatic presence, the uniqueness of each individual.

*F*or the dancer, technique is a harness that provides the necessary control to fly and spin, allowing the dancer to rebound in and out of the earth with unseen wings.

✆ *Goals.* Technique provides a progression of movement training with clearly defined goals.

✆ *Rituals.* Technique offers rituals supporting neurological learning and movement reeducation, honing skills and bringing focus to the body and mind.

✆ *Conditioning.* Technique builds resilience in the body and the mind, enhancing adaptability, mobility, stability, and responsiveness and enabling the dancer to withstand the physical rigors of the art form.

✆ *Dancing.* Technique shapes the skills of dancing through movement specific to dance.

✆ *Sequencing.* Technique presents a sequence of exercises that effectively combines dance skills and progressive motor learning in concert with scientific principles.

WISDOM OF ANCESTORS

The process of shaping a philosophical point of view begins with a look backward at the family tree. In China the symbol of a teacher is a bell, because a bell continues to ring in a student's heart. As a teacher makes the numerous decisions demanded in a dance class, there will be the little bell of one teacher and the louder-than-life gong of another. Past teachers whisper, "Pull up; breathe; shoulders down; trust yourself." Without your realizing it, your words, images, and tone of voice begin to model a beloved or not-so-beloved teacher from the past. Those teachers struck a chord because there was something shared—a philosophical viewpoint or a passion. Ancestors ring loudly.

Technique is based on traditions. Like the wisdom of ancestors, dance is passed down mouth-to-mouth and body-to-body. But technique is more than a tradition. Folk dance is a tradition but not a technique. A folk-dance class is similar to a repertory class; the dance is learned, but there is no system of training that prepares the dancer to do the dance. Like folk dance, technique stems from tradition, complete with historical and cultural knowledge, but it is also a system of training.

This system of training must provide the formal study of dance skills. Quiet, slow internal work is beneficial for movement reeducation, but this movement is not dance technique because there is an assumption of prior or additional dance training. Unless these practices are woven into the progressive learning of dance skills, they are better defined as *retraining* programs. Dancers must learn to dance by practicing the skills of the art form. But wait—what are those skills?

Defining skills is tricky. Modern dance is not as codified as ballet. Uniqueness and rebellion are part of the defining philosophy of modern dance. Born out of rebellion, a revolutionary spirit drives each generation. Historically, choreographers not only invented a way of putting together all the theatrical elements but also created

Uniqueness and rebellion are part of the defining philosophy of modern dance.

a new way of moving, preparing dancers to perform their choreography. Isadora Duncan threw away corsets and tutus, allowing her torso to be free. Doris Humphrey played with gravity, and her dancers learned to fall. Merce Cunningham bent torsos with new variations in time and space. Choreographers invented new techniques propelled by choreographic exploration. Is a new technique needed for every choreographer?

Today's generation of teachers has been trained by a variety of teachers working out of numerous styles. Most dancers today have not apprenticed with one master for their entire training. Today's teachers reach beyond the *classic* modern techniques of Graham, Cunningham, or José Limón. They are exploring an *eclectic* technique, selecting whatever they consider best from various sources. Rather than relying on the classic techniques, these teachers are building innovative approaches to technique, incorporating old materials and adding new technologies and theories. These new hybrids will take dance into the future.

But creating a good harness is difficult, as Graham, Limón, and Cunningham found out. These techniques have become classics for a reason. They stem from a clear philosophical point of view and they are brilliant in their design. Eclectic approaches can lack the glue that holds technical concepts together. Sometimes new technologies are exciting but need the test of time. Whether teachers are working with a codified technique or inventing and weaving new approaches into ancient wisdom, developing a clear point of view is paramount.

POINT OF VIEW

Dance teachers develop a point of view over time by listening to the wisdom of ancestors and to the truths of personal experience within the body. If a teacher relies only on the messages of past teachers and does not explore truths viscerally, her approach becomes didactic and shallow. If she listens to inner experiences and does not translate them to external, universal truths, her teaching becomes egotistical. Dancers establish a point of view by knowing themselves in relation to the history and practices of the art form.

Each teacher's personal journey is intrinsic and distinct. Past training enters the picture. A teacher who has a rich musical background will see dance through the window of musicality and phrasing. One with gymnastics training will teach dance through a lens of momentum and energy. Personality and learning styles also influence vision. A mind that enjoys architecture and structure will most probably favor form and clarity: A person steeped in human relationships will move toward emotional content. Each person has a specific lens based on past studies and personality. But the search continues.

Exploring Physical Truths

Establishing a *point of view* is rooted in core realities of the muscle and heart, spirit and bones, gravity and momentum. To know these requires research and physical

A spiraling movement.

exploration. Teaching the concept of spirals begs for an exploration of spirals until the mind and body embody them. Is the spiral important because dance ancestors said so or because it is physically, viscerally, and intellectually experienced? Investigating in the studio leads to questions: "Where does a spiral initiate from? Does it start in the tail and move upward, or in the eyes and move downward? Which is better? Is there a *better way* or do they create different truths?" The body provides answers, and with answers come more questions. Is a universal truth being revealed, or something peculiar to an individual body? A quest for truth inspires questions rather than answers.

Classic or Eclectic Approach?

An inquisitive teacher of a classic modern technique deconstructs the style and explores the viewpoint of the founder. After thoroughly understanding the *truths* of the founder, teachers incorporate their own filters, adding personal insight to the founder's message. If this homework is not done, only the shell of the style will be taught. Students studying Graham technique often replicate the shapes quite well, but the intent of the movement remains a mystery. Mary Anthony, a former Graham dancer, instructed students in her classes to lie down on the floor and breathe out until there was no breath left. She commanded them to exhale some more, and again more. As the students forced the last bit of air out of their lungs, their bodies naturally began to form the classic Graham contraction. In her own way, Anthony communicated the source of the contraction. By communicating the intent of movement she empowered her students. Now they could use the power of a contraction to transcend the limitations of style.

Right or Wrong?

Students have the tools necessary to seek their own path if they understand both the teacher's and the style's points of view. There is a right way and a wrong way in technique, but right and wrong are determined by a particular *point of view*. To release weight in the torso is wrong in ballet; it is right in modern class during a fall to the floor. If students understand the philosophy behind the right and wrong, they can make choices about the use of these principles for their own goals and creative exploration. Then technical training can enhance rather than limit.

Developing a point of view is messy. It is not fast, nor is it ideal. Students may hunger for black and white, good and bad, but dancing is not that easy. It takes hundreds of questions. Bonnie Bainbridge Cohen, founder of Body-Mind Centering™, embodies her knowledge, but many times during workshops she would answer questions with, "I have no idea; let's explore." It is perfectly fine not to have the answers. The thrilling part of teaching is the willingness to be curious.

Investigations

1. Dance ancestors: Who were your teachers? Write a journal entry about your favorite teacher. Which values do you share with that teacher?

2. Create an object that helps you build a philosophy—a chart, a graph, a painting, or a sculpture.

   ▸ This object must contain the elements of dance (space, time, and energy). You can break them down in any way possible. For instance, you can use as elements motion, meter, spatial directions, dynamics, and accent. Organize the elements in such a way that the most and least valued are expressed in some way. Saul Steinberg's famous *View of the World From 9th Avenue,* which appeared on the cover of *The New Yorker* in 1976, expresses a proud personal bias. Seen from a New Yorker's perspective, the city takes a majority of the foreground and the rest of the United States is relegated to the background. Your object should express your particular history, personality, and bias. Do you love space and hate rhythm? Then make space huge, and rhythm only a tiny square at the end of the page. Which element do you need to understand first to get to the other ideas? Allow your personal preferences to enter the picture. Do not try to find a logic or pattern to space, time, and energy. This reveals your bias.

   ▸ The way you organize your ideas is crucial. Make a graph, a three-dimensional globe, or a circle. Bring in umbrellas, food, or other objects, creating a metaphor for how you view dance. For instance, if you organize your thoughts by stream of consciousness, you might draw a river, allowing the dance elements to flow on a circuitous route. If you are methodical, perhaps a chart such as the periodic table in chemistry is a better model. Teaching is about organizing ideas. The more you understand your own system of logic, the easier it will be to structure your classes.

   ▸ Do this exercise once a year or once every decade. How does it change?

3. Develop a point of view.

   ▸ What do you know about a spiral? What don't you know? Find examples of spirals in nature. Find them in photographs, shells, drawings, and toys. Are there any poetic quotes about spirals? How do these objects relate to what you physically know about spirals in movement? Which parts of the body act in a spiral? What is different about a spiral that is initiated from the bottom up, or from the top down?

   ▸ Create two exercises or movement patterns that explore aspects of spirals gleaned from your research. Support the movement exercises with visual aids or a quote.

In-Class Investigations

1. Base a whole class on the concept of spirals. How would you structure the class? How could each of your comments focus on the spiral?

2. Teach spirals in different classes: technique, improvisation, anatomy, composition, or writing. How does the information change and shift depending on the student population? Is the subject richer after you've explored it in so many different forms?

Reflection: BREATH

The dance teacher expounds, "We do not have to think to make our hearts beat, or our lungs take in and expel air. Thank God. At the rate I forget my keys, I would be dead by now." Feeling very witty, she is caught off guard when a student asks, "Then why are you always telling us to *breathe*, when it's impossible not to breathe?" The teacher thinks to herself, *I have no idea.* She begins her quest.

William Frederking, photographer; Sandra Sucsy and Mary Johnston-Couvsey, dancers.

In an Ashtanga yoga class, the great master places the dance teacher next to the best breather in class. She follows the dutiful yogis as they begin a deep snore in unison called *ujjayi* breath. The good breather next door makes sounds like an ocean wave. Marveling at his breath, she realizes it is beginning to sound close. Too close. Looking around to see if he somehow entered her body, she realizes her own breath is making the snoring sound. As if she were swimming through rapids, the breath washes her insides.

While the teacher is sitting at home and pondering the existential meaning of breath, the plumber comes in to fix some pipes. "It all has to do with the plumbing. Everything comes in and everything goes out through the pipes. When the pipes are clogged, the house shuts down."

Never satisfied with a simple answer, the teacher travels to Hawaii to study the whales. Whales use 90 percent of their lungs instead of the measly 10 percent humans sip on. On the beach the hula dancers' big bellies expand and contract with ease. She looks toward the whales and tries to imagine one wearing a corset. Diving underwater with the gentle beasts, she luxuriates in a suspended peace without struggle. Suddenly, she explodes back up to the surface gasping for air. She will need to work on the other 80 percent.

That night in a dream the teacher sees a newborn baby, blown in fresh from the breath of God, transform into an aged, gnarled woman lying on her deathbed. Waking up in trauma, her breathing turned upside down, she gulps in air while screaming and exhales while reaching outward. She commands herself to breathe, and her lungs function as a regulator: slowing the heart, expanding the liver, and relaxing the stomach.

Suddenly the teacher understands: Breath is the pipeline to the internal world; the first and last breaths are bridges to other worlds. She goes back to class, waiting for a student to ask that question again.

William Frederking, photographer; Christine Bornarth and Anthony Gongora, dancer

chapter 2

Flying Souls
A R T I S T R Y

Air brushing the skin, muscles coiling and springing, blood pumping, and the mind focusing—anyone who has ever danced knows the sensations. This ecstatic presence can be found in an elderly, fat man waltzing at a wedding, a child spinning in her bedroom, a rebellious teenager moshing at a rave, or a sophisticated professional dancer performing onstage. The dance teacher provides the environment so that this sensation may be cajoled to turn up at every moment in every class. When it emerges, the teacher keeps it alive by drawing full awareness to its existence. Found in the calm of a plié, in the absolute and total concentration of a relevé, or in an exploding combination at the end of class, ecstatic presence is immediately apparent. By recognizing it and drawing attention to it, the teacher encourages each person to seek its constant presence.

The underlying passion for ecstatic presence is unique to each person. For one dancer the rich emotional language of a gesture sends chills up his spine; another finds excitement in the extreme intellectual and physical rigor of the art form. Some people dance because it communicates something inexpressible in words. Reasons for dancing change over time. A young dancer might be completely enthralled with the pure physicality of muscles moving. A mature dancer might shift to other dimensions, seeking out the spirit of heart and bones. This chapter will discuss broadening our notion of technique, incorporating improvisation into the technique class, and the importance of playfulness and solitude in developing dance*artists*.

DOING AND UNDOING

Theater director Eugenio Barba speaks of technique: "Artistic discipline is a way of refusal. Technique in theatre and the attitude that it presupposes is a continual exercise in revolt, above all against oneself, against one's own ideas, one's own resolutions and plans, against the comforting assurance of one's own intelligence, knowledge, and sensibility." (Cardone 2002, 16) Artist Robert Rauschenberg lends a quote to Deborah Hay in *My Body, the Buddhist,* "Thoughts are filters that get clogged by history, habits, and ambitions blocking the flow of uncharted responses to unmeasured now." (Hay 2000, 97) Students are often bound by "history, habits and ambitions." With locked minds and joints, they need a revolution against themselves in order to breakdown the rigidity of their neuromuscular patterning. In order to create space for new possibilities, stillness and play might be the right prescription.

There is an ongoing process in training that includes both doing and undoing, stripping to the essence of being, then putting it all together again. And just when it's all put together, the stripping begins again. A constant process of doing and undoing is at the core of training. The smart dancer is not *erasing* idiosyncratic habits; the habit is a part of the body's memory, stored in the neurological hard wiring. The smart dancer unhooks the wiring in order to build a broader set of choices. The great basketball player Michael Jordan has a habit of hanging his tongue out every time he hangs in the air. Whereas in basketball the tongue doesn't matter, in dance the face has to be free for expression and focus. In technique class, the dance teacher would bark at Jordan, "Nix the tongue; not every choreographer wants a panting bull." In time Jordan would learn to have choices. By separating movement and habit, he could stick out his tongue for comic effect when he chose to do so, but he would not have to rely on it to make a basket.

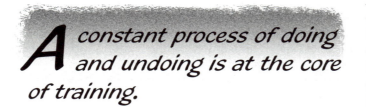

A constant process of doing and undoing is at the core of training.

Great actors are chameleons, adapting their personalities to new characters by understanding the power of their own voices, faces, and bodies. Susan Sarandon can play a wild woman in *Thelma and Louise* and a nun in *Dead Man Walking.* Anthony Hopkins is chilling as a psychopathic killer in *Silence of the Lambs* or sadly destitute as a butler in *Remains of the Day.* John Wayne is always John Wayne.

However, it is crucial to honor the habit, not degrade it. If the habit is labeled *bad,* it will be locked away in a closet never to be used again. A good actor clears himself of his idiosyncratic little tic so that he can be free to make choices about his voice, physicality, or energy. If valued and not forgotten, the little tic left behind in acting school becomes the core of a rich character some day. A great actor or dancer carries the essence, not the baggage, of his ego. This stripping yet validating is a delicate balance. Stripped too far without validation, the student arrives in the professional world generic, a clean slate with no internal voice. But if nurtured properly, the technically trained dancer emerges with the capability of many voices.

In an interview in *Contact Quarterly*, butoh artist Min Tanaka speaks of exiting your own persona to be free as a performer. "It's a step to get free. If you are always only you, this is very limiting. By bringing somebody else into you, you can get much more freedom. Because you cannot be that person, you have to come out from the person to yourself. To get free means to be in that person for a while, to be more yourself. You have your body and yourself. When you go in front of the people for dancing, you should bring a prepared body. In this body you have to have another body ready. This must be." (Vermeersch 2002, 25)

TEACHING THE REAL TRUTH

Learning opposite points of view on each side of the continuum is key to fostering a dance*artist*. Physicist Niels Bohr states very simply, "The opposite of a true statement is a false statement, but the opposite of a profound truth can be another profound truth." (Palmer 1998, 62) Teaching technique as a series of polarities encourages versatility and choices. F. Scott Fitzgerald wrote, "The test of a first-rate intelligence is the ability to hold two opposing ideas in mind at the same time and still retain the ability to function."

Performing is full of dualities—internal focus and external awareness, giving everything or nothing, stillness versus movement—and technique class must prepare the dancer for these nuances. In *My Body, the Buddhist,* Deborah Hay describes the dualities of an entrance onstage in her dance *Exit.* "When the music starts the dancer hears an appeal to exit. In so doing, she notices she is also entering. The two experiences are as inseparable in life as they are occurrences in her body. The weight of the past mingles with the weightlessness of becoming. The combined consciousness of these two equally moving events splits her into tremors of responsiveness, and she hasn't even taken her first step." (Hay 2000, 74)

In dance, there is weight on one end and lightness on the other. It is most common to hear modern teachers emphasizing weight and "down," and ballet teachers emphasizing lightness and "up." Both want the same thing. Both want the ability to bound into the air effortlessly and both need to recognize gravity to do so. The more weight is truly understood, the more effortless the rebound. Working with extremes teaches choices and limitations. How much can you release weight before there is a loss of control? Without value judgments on the trueness or rightness of any one concept, future dancers and choreographers have the ability to choose whether to play with a balloon filled with water or helium.

Movement can be broken down into thousands of dualities: flow/form, effort/shape, yin/yang, intellectual/visceral. For purposes of discussion, let's look at flow/form. Based on experience and ancestry, some teachers arrive at the conclusion that flow is the essence of dance, so they begin teaching by emphasizing flow. These teachers are generally concerned with gravity, weight, connectivity, and energy. But ultimately, the flow-based teacher does not forget form, it is the end result—flow arrives at form. The form-based teacher emphasizes shape, clarity, and line in order to find flow. They both work towards balance, they simply enter the room through a different doorway.

The weight and lightness of a plié.

ODD CHOICES

Today, contemporary choreographers are utilizing dancers to invent movement, create partnering, and help shape the choreography. They want inventive dancers that are facile, smart, and engaged in the world. Dancemakers rely on the dancers' physical imaginations, throwing out images and seeing their responses. They want to see unique solutions to choreographic problems. If all a dancer can do is repeat something from technique class, then technique has done them a vast disservice. Matthias Kriesberg writes about Stefan Wolpe, a German avant-garde composer, and his quest to find something unique: "During the 1950s, classical composers leaning toward serialism were intent on practicing rigorous, comprehensive control in their music. Wolpe dissented: 'A few of us wish to liberate our scores again,' he wrote in 1956, 'so that improvisation will return, where overall control is suspended for a moment,' to 'admit something stranger into the work of art.'" (Kriesberg 2002, 26) Technical skills alone are clearly not enough; strength and resiliency are just a prerequisite.

The strange and quirky dance*artist*.

To foster something "stranger" in a dance*artist,* we must look at perceptions of aesthetic beauty. One of the main purposes of technique is to increase efficient motor patterning, so it is easy to jump to the belief that grace is beautiful and awkward is not. But what if a choreographer wants awkward, raw, angry movement? What if a choreographer does not want smooth edges? By engaging dancers in aggressive, awkward, and raw physical movements in technique class, dancers will be taught to value these choices as well. If technique teachers get locked into flowing, pretty movement as the right way to move, dancers will end up looking pretty, nice, and boring.

The early modern dancers' technique was raw, but their passion and quirkiness were astounding. In the article "Choreographing a Life," educator Susan Stinson says, "I look back at films of the early Martha Graham company and realize that our undergraduate students today are more technically advanced than those early modern dancers. What have we lost by continually pushing the technical expectations of what it takes to be a dancer? Can we imagine something different? Can we imagine giving up some demand for technical expertise that we now know is possible, and gaining something that we might value even more in our art?" (Stinson 2001, 31) Perhaps one of the goals of technique should be strange quirkiness.

Supporting discovery will unearth the great artists of tomorrow. Steve Paxton, one of the founders of Contact Improvisation, speaks of his journey to discovery in a note to White Oak Dance Company.

It is the job of the dance student to first bring the unconscious movement of their body into the realm of consciousness. Next, to form the movements into an array of possibilities, a dance technique, which is useful for choreographers to pattern into the new, albeit customary dance of their culture. For the student and the culture it is a precious legacy: the steps, their organization, and the way we learn them.

Cultural legacies, however, can be confining. My inquiry was not so much about escaping the legacy of dance as discovering the source of it. Where was something pre-legacy, pre-cultural, pre-artistic? Where was ancient movement?

This was the fascinating question of those days for me, and remains my interest. The answer of course, was right under my nose.

I placed the chair in the space, and began to stand. (Lepkoff 2001, 37)

ROLE OF IMPROVISATION

Today's technique teachers can help by broadening students' perceptions of what technique is, but technique cannot provide this delicate balance alone. During rigorous technical training, students must have the opportunity to explore their own movement and validate the uniqueness of their own voices. The study of improvisation encourages unique movement choices and opens up the movement palette. Improvisation reinforces technique. While technique removes the rough surfaces, improvisation cherishes the coarse textures. Experience in improvisation allows the dancer to consistently sort out what is ego, what is idiosyncrasy, what is worth keeping, and what needs to be hugged, folded up, and put away in the old cedar chest for use later on. Improvisation creates a dynamic counter-play in the dance of adding and subtracting. Mary Starks Whitehouse, considered to be the founder of the improvisational form Authentic Movement says, "Learning how to move, based on imitation, is not the same as discovering, with help, one's own movement. Without access to this layer of discovery, the dancer often performs beautiful but quite unalive patterns of physical action that do not move the audience." (Whitehouse 2002, 22)

A panel of adjudicators at a college festival had to select students for scholarships to attend summer festivals. They were allowed to observe students executing only a ballet barre and a jazz combination. One panelist began pacing up and down the studio, muttering in an exasperated voice, "We are missing Nijinsky—we will never find Martha." He was right; too many students are lost by overvaluing technique. Teaching in a program with open enrollment, many students enter with no technical background; but they possess savvy street smarts and an inventive sense of dance. If viewed in a technique class, they would be dismissed automatically. But when they are set loose in an improvisation class, their regular nightlife activities (usually improvising in the clubs or on the streets) are riveting to watch. Success in improvisation class gives them confidence to attempt the arduous road of technical training.

> *Technique removes the rough surfaces, but improvisation cherishes the coarse textures.*

PRACTICE SOLITUDE

If dance training is to nurture dance*artists,* teachers must encourage dance students to practice solitude, either through meditation practices or simply by being in a room alone. Deborah Hay asks in *My Body, the Buddhist,* "How many dance students dance alone uninterruptedly for at least forty minutes daily, outside of rehearsing, choreographing, or physically stretching? Why is this not a four-year requirement for every college dance student? How else can a person develop an intimate dialogue with the body?" (Hay 2000, 1) Dance is a social art form; we take class together, we rehearse together, but the dance*artist* is nurtured with solitude. During rigorous technical training, solitude informs.

Looking Inside

In *BodyStories: A Guide to Experiential Anatomy,* Andrea Olsen says, "One of the most thoroughly neglected areas of body education is the awareness of what is happening inside: the dialogue between inner and outer experience in relation to the whole person. We spend much of our time involved in outer perception through the specialized sense organs of sight, sound, taste, smell, and touch. We are generally less involved in developing our capacities for inner sensing, which is the ability of the nervous system to monitor inner states of the body. How and why do we progressively close down our capacity for body listening?" (Olsen 1991, 11)

Ruth Zaporah, founder of Action Theater, speaks about the importance of meditation.

> *I was a philosophy student in college, and in 1968 I began an ongoing exploration and practice of Buddhist meditation—at the time, Zen; more recently, Dzogchen. Both practices—meditation and improvisation—work on the mind, the former without physical action, the latter with. Both are about being open to the present moment and what it offers. Both cultivate a quiet, non-chattering mind, a mind of acceptance rather than doubt and resistance. Both cultivate awareness as a way to step back from concept, leaving an open perceptual field undiminished by immediate naming. What do I mean? Your hand is outstretched and the palm is up. Instead of immediately applying a concept such as begging or imploring, the action is experienced as sensory, nameless. In this sense, every moment is its first impression, before naming reduces it to a thing. In my mind, meditation and improvisation are always talking to each other, informing and affecting the way I go about both. (Zaporah 2002, 51)*

Looking Outside

Furthermore, teachers must encourage students to look outside the world of technique for inspiration. Great artists and founders of new movements in dance seek not what is in front of them, but what is behind them. Min Tanaka speaks of his mentor, Tatsumi Hijikata, one of the founders of butoh: "Hijikata loved to work with carpenters, wallmakers, and fish sellers. He felt their bodies were beautiful, and he asked them to move starting from the movement of their life. This created many interesting and beautiful things. The carpenter lives twenty years with his specific body for a specific purpose. The body is full of experience. The body doesn't show technique, because the movement is natural for them, but they have technique, a huge technique, I am sure." (Vermeersch 2002, 23)

Seeking inner guidance and outward inspiration is the stuff of a dance*artist,* a soul soaring in its own strangeness.

Investigations

1. Observe a dance class. Was there a moment of ecstatic presence? If so, when was it? Did it occur during the pliés, tendus, or main combination? What was important about that moment: the energy, the commitment, or the flow? Did the teacher do anything to extend this moment?

2. Go into a room once a day without any agenda. Write about the experience.

3. Observe people in the world who move for a living: waitresses, carpenters, assembly-line workers, and fishermen. What are their technical skills?

4. Play with children. What movement does it inspire?

5. Write about your own journey to becoming a dancer. What process of stripping and rebuilding did you experience? What did you strip away? What did you put back together? In what way were you different after this process? What else do you wish to strip away or put back together?

In-Class Investigations

The following are improvisation exercises to incorporate into technique class.

1. Warm-ups. Each of these exercises can be done in five minutes as a pre-class activity.
   - Allow 8 counts for each body part. Reduce to 4 counts. Reduce to 1 or 2 counts. Instruct students to use each body part with awareness of the following:
     - Skin (wiggling, soft, open, receptive)
     - Muscles (strong, elastic, pumping blood)
     - Bones (internal structure, clarity, weight)
   - Allow 16 counts to fold into the floor (back to bed), 16 counts to stretch and yawn and come back to standing (waking up). Repeat in 8 counts, 4 counts, 2 counts. (This allows students who are hungering for more time in bed to get their wish while they begin the process of folding and unfolding joints in a way unique to their own body.)
   - Working in partners, move in and out of the floor while holding hands, touching back to back, or leaning on each other. (This provides human contact and weight play.)
   - Walk through the space on or off the beat. Encourage awareness of the space, the beat, classmates, direction changes, body joints, space between people, levels, and alignment.

2. Teach triplets. Allow the students to improvise with turns and spatial patterning while keeping a triplet pattern. If they can accomplish the above, add movement in and out of the floor.

3. Fly across the floor once doing an improvised dance. Ask the students to repeat it with as much detail as they can remember from seeing it only once. Then ask one student to be the leader, another the follower. The leader goes across the floor in an improvised movement pattern; the follower repeats as much as possible. (This builds movement-memory skills.)

4. Ask one person to observe a movement phrase performed by a classmate. Ask that person to perform the phrase with all the nuances, weight, and idiosyncrasies of his or her partner. Ask them to imitate you, the teacher. (Be ready for some pretty accurate and revealing information from your students. They have spent a great deal of time watching you!)

5. After a class has rigorously perfected a movement phrase:

   ► Take away the counts; let students perform it in their own time. (This is an important step in training students to differentiate phrasing from metric timing.)

   ► Take away the spatial patterning, allowing students to spontaneously change range and directions.

   ► Invite students to use the material for an improvised duet.

   ► Provide differing images or emotional intent for the same movement pattern, thus encouraging variance in energy and dynamics.

Reflection: PLAY

Ancient Chinese Recipe for Movement Training

- First 18 years of life: Play, run, climb mountains.
- Second 18 years of life: Channel the energy of the body by studying a form, preferably tai chi chuan.
- Third 18 years of life: Study some more.
- Fourth 18 years of life: Study less, have more fun.
- Fifth 18 years of life: Slow down, move less, meditate.
- Sixth 18 years of life: Sit still and let other people think you are dancing.

William Frederking, photographer; Brian Brooks, dancer. Courtesy of Deeply Rooted Dance Theater.

Twentieth-Century American Recipe for Movement Training

- Before 6 months: Walk with the aid of a jumper.
- First 3 years of life: Try out for baby gymnastics.
- Second 3 years of life: Sit still at a desk.
- Third 3 years of life: Perfect skills in ballet, jazz, tap, hip-hop, kung-fu, and cheerleading.
- Fourth 3 years of life: Study hard, work like a dog.
- Fifth 3 years of life: Study harder, get injured.
- Sixth 3 years of life: Stop dancing.

When registering freshmen in college for dance classes, I inquire, "What is your movement-training history?" I long for the answer, "I played."

part **II**

Class
Preparation

chapter 3

Sculpting Dreams

G O A L S

A physical education teacher sets a goal: Be able to do 100 push-ups by the end of a term. It's clear and measurable. But how do you set goals for art-istry? Can you evaluate the qualitative intent of a push-up? Dance*artists* resist and run with terror from anything that looks like measured assessment. Perhaps it's easier for artists to think about dreams. Dreams entail flight and fancy. Dreams are open to variation and change. Michelangelo had a vision when he began molding David's body. Before touching the clay or stone, the abstract sculp-tor Henry Moore had dreams of something big, thick, and round. Dreams create clarity. This chapter will address the creation of goals over time: a semester, a term, a course, a class. It will also address the progression of learning toward those goals. How does one break movement down into smaller, comprehensible units? How do the goals shift when working with beginners or professionals? How are student goals woven into class goals? Expectations may change because of the shifting nature of dreams. Perhaps it is unrealistic to build a 100-foot sculpture integrating many media if this is your first time working with clay. Dreams become unrealized daydreams if they are not periodically evaluated. So finally, this chapter will address evaluation. In the end, did Michelangelo like *David?*

VISION

The dream of traveling to Rome is very different than going to Independence, Iowa. Students need to know how to pack their bags. Goals are the architectonics of success. They help define structure by building on one another. Increasingly larger goals encompass smaller goals. What is your vision of the ultimate dancer? Should a student who becomes a master under your tutelage coordinate move-ment effortlessly? Work knowledgeably with efficient alignment? Be strong and flexible enough to jump to any height and conform to any shape? Execute move-ment with clarity, integrity, and precision? Adapt to any style, whether it be Bob Fosse or butoh? Transform souls with delectable artistry? Reaching for the moon is commendable, but now it is necessary to start back on Earth and build a series of steps leading upward.

Martha Graham once said that it takes 10 years to train a dancer. It is hard to organize 10-year chunks. Most dance classes are set up in shorter time spans: a four-year college program, a yearlong study, a semester, a six-week intensive workshop. Four-year programs have the luxury of defining their vision through the establishment of a curriculum. Not only will students take modern dance technique, but also jazz, ballet, African, anatomy, history, music, composition, somatic studies, and a host of other activities. Dance teachers work within a larger organization: a school, a festival, or a private studio. They must share or at least understand the mission of the larger organization. Whereas the larger goals define the institution, the smaller goals define the course covering a time span of a week to a year. The organization decides to stay within Europe; the teacher now has to decide if it will be Italy or Finland.

DESIGNING A SYLLABUS

The first contact with students is usually written communication. The class is advertised in a flyer. A college student peruses the course descriptions in a catalog, looking for a course that does not require reading or writing. The teacher communicates why the course is being offered and what will happen in it. What will students gain? Will they be stronger and more confident? Will they be able to waltz with their girlfriends?

In higher education, the syllabus is used to communicate detailed information on the first day of class. A contract between teacher and student, it lays the groundwork so that there are no false expectations. Whether working autonomously in a studio or within a prescribed college curriculum, a teacher who articulates the key components of a syllabus will clarify vision, goals, and expectations.

Rationale

The syllabus begins with a rationale explaining why the class exists. The student needs to know why it's important to travel to Rome when all they do there is speak a foreign language. The reasons may vary depending on the targeted population for the class. If the class is being taught in a high school, the student may wonder, "Why should I study modern dance if I want to be a hip-hop dancer on MTV?" If the course is part of an international dance festival, the reasons might be more specific to style and philosophy.

Description

A description of what will happen in the class is crucial to overcoming faulty expectations. If a student expects to fly to Rome and you are taking a boat, there will be many conflicts along the way. A simple statement might be, "The class begins with floor exercises to strengthen and stretch the muscles. Progressing to standing exercises, students practice elements of space (direction, levels, and planes), time (rhythm, accent, and speed), and energy (qualities and dynamics). The class culminates with movement traveling across the floor. A professional percussionist accompanies the class." Specifics might include stylistic influences (a Limón-based class) and the emphasis of the class (soaring and gliding versus anatomical precision). If the description is used in a flyer as a marketing tool, it can be tweaked to sizzle and sell by using sexy adjectives and juicy verbs. But bare bones, the student needs to know what will happen in class.

Topics

Topics are the content of the course. What are you teaching? Are you teaching a tendu, or is the tendu a vehicle for something else? Alignment, centering, movement retention, or elements of space, time, and energy might be some of your answers. More specifically, it is helpful to develop a list of dance terminology. Ballet has developed a clearly defined list of steps over the last 500 years. Modern dancers resist codifying terminology. A bison in one class might be a funny jump with a lower back curve in the next class. But some terminology is specific to each teacher's class. *Contraction, release,* and *bison* might be part of the terminology list for one teacher, whereas *connectivity, breath, head* and *tail, homologous, homolateral,* and *contralateral* might be crucial on another teacher's list.

Objectives

Last are the objectives. "At the end of this course the student will be able to . . ." do what? Dance is a physical activity, and every student comes in with different strengths and weaknesses and will progress at their own rate. How can a teacher guarantee any of these goals will be accomplished? Return to the long-term dream, the vision. After years of discussion, the faculty at The Dance Center of Columbia College came up with six major goals to be accomplished in a four-year program: coordination, alignment, conditioning, clarity, adaptability, and artistry. Beginning with this broad brushstroke, it is now possible to make smaller goals based on the level being taught. To do this we must take a look at learning movement through a series of progressive steps (See appendixes A and B).

PROGRESSION OF MOVEMENT SKILLS

A naturally gifted dancer is teaching a beginning class. Her dancing is seamless; she effortlessly coordinates movement patterning. She demonstrates a difficult roll into the floor that involves tucking the foot under. The students struggle with the movement and one asks over and over, "How do you do that?" She says with exasperation, "I don't even begin to know how to break that down; you just do it." Immersion in the dancing is one method—just as with learning a language, you just get in there and do it. The student struggles and finds his own problems and connections. But the *art* of teaching resides in the ability to break things down into simple, understandable units. In an advanced class one can assume many things, but beginners demand that the teacher know how to pare things down to the basics. What are the building blocks of movement?

> *The art of teaching resides in the ability to break things down into simple, understandable units.*

Developmental Movement Patterns

To understand the origins of movement we must turn to babies, the great masters of movement learning. Infants yield, reach, pull, crawl, creep, stand, and fall. Truly remarkable, they innately know what needs to happen first before they are ready for the next step. They push ahead, then go backward for a while. Developmental movement patterns are the stages infants go through as they learn to move. Many founders of somatic practices such as Body-Mind Centering, Bartenieff Movement Fundamentals, and Feldenkrais turned to the study of developmental patterns and reflexes to evolve their theories. These building blocks of movement are very useful to dance teachers. They tell us where to begin. Three neuromuscular patterns are necessary to movement: homologous, homolateral, and contralateral.

Homologous

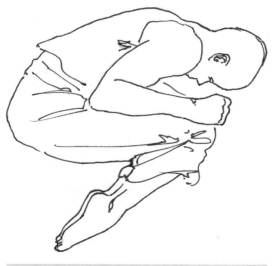

Homologous movement.

A baby begins her movement life out of the womb by lying on her back or belly and rocking. The back-and-forth motion, created by pushing with her feet or pulling with her hands, helps the infant distinguish top from bottom. These flexion and extension, folding and unfolding movements in the sagittal plane are called homologous patterns. Imagine a baby standing on your lap (with your help) and jumping up and down on your knee. Beginning dancers need an abundance of practice in this pattern, which approximates the movement of a frog or kangaroo. Starting class with rocking, folding, extending, pushing, and pulling stimulates these instinctive beginning patterns. Simple pliés, relevés, jumps, and slides in parallel across the floor are an upright version of this pattern.

Homolateral

Homolateral movement is coordination of the same side. Babies learn to differentiate right from left when they creep using the same arm and leg to reach forward. Imagine a salamander or a fish moving side to side to propel itself forward. In anatomy, these are patterns of abduction and adduction in the lateral plane. Making angels in the snow or lying on your back and swishing back and forth stimulates this pattern.

Contralateral

Contralateral movement is usually the last and most sophisticated pattern a baby learns. This cross-patterning coordination is practiced every day when we walk or run, or anytime there is opposition between the arms and legs. A sequential spiral of the spine underlies this pattern. This is the core to all locomotion movements, and it integrates both homologous and homolateral patterns. Often students arrive at a midpoint in their training when the upper body and the lower body are both efficiently coordinating movement, but separately; the upper body doesn't know the lower body. Contralateral movements connect the upper and lower body

| Homolateral movement. | Contralateral movement. |

through sequential spirals. Graham wisely made the contraction and spiral the center of her technique. Irmgard Bartenieff studied the way a child turns from his back to his belly or vice versa. The child will look where he wants to go and then reach his hand across his body to turn himself. The Bartenieff X-roll is a spiraling contralateral pattern. Lying on the back and reaching one arm across the body on the upper diagonal initiates a pull that turns the body over. (A leg can initiate the movement on the lower diagonal.) The roots of coordination patterning and alignment problems are apparent in this deceptively simple exercise. Contralateral or cross-patterning can be practiced throughout the class while lying, sitting, standing, walking, running, skipping, or leaping. Contralateral patterns bring wholeness and three-dimensionality to movement.

A good teacher senses where the students are and what they are ready for. Understanding the movement building blocks assists a teacher in knowing where to begin and how to structure a satisfying sequence of movement exercises.

Level Progression

When setting goals for each level, the developmental stages of life can be used as a guide. Beginning dancers emulate the playfulness and curiosity of a child. Intermediate students spend a bulk of their time learning the tough skills of technique, repetition, and discipline. As their intellectual knowledge surpasses their physical skills, they get frustrated, much like teenagers. Then adulthood arrives, and advanced dancers must make personal choices about how they will use their newfound skills. As wise elders of society, professional dancers return to the playfulness of a child.

Beginners

Starting with raw movement, beginning dancers return to the first five years of life. They revisit the three beginning coordination patterns practiced as a baby:

homologous, homolateral, and contralateral. They run and skip and enjoy their physicality. They improvise. Subtle details are not relevant. They build their musculature, working on strength and stretch. They work in simple rhythms, learning to get on the beat and know what a beat is. Beginners have high passion, and their physical growth happens in leaps and bounds. With the right images and directives, their bodies will make the right neurological choices. They realize that heightened spatial awareness is necessary to avoid hitting their classmates. They learn that discipline every day can be a drag. Slowly it dawns on them that getting a good night's sleep is crucial to their ability to get through class the next day. A beginning teacher needs a gentle heart in the body of a drill sergeant.

Intermediates

Intermediates crave the refinement of adulthood, but they move with the awkwardness of a child. Their bodies need endless repetition; yet just like teenagers, they get bored and frustrated during long plateaus with little apparent growth. This level takes a demanding yet patient teacher. Intermediates are beginning to have a relationship with the space and people surrounding them. Their focus lifts, and they become more engaged with the external world, expanding physical forms. Their musculature is strong and facile enough that they can make smaller, more detailed changes. The raw energy of the beginner is shaped by a conscious use of space, rhythm, and musicality. They learn that they can suspend the leap a little longer if they reach through space. They can get there faster with rhythmic accents. There is a lot of drama at this stage of learning as they plow through the highs and lows of physical accomplishments.

Advanced

When young adults leave home for the first time, they are both cocky and insecure. Mind and body are not quite yet one. Advanced dancers' bodies have progressed to this level, but their confidence is far below what they can actually accomplish. The teacher is wise to invite daring behavior after all the careful, tedious, intermediate work. Patterns that demand dynamics, rhythmic attack, and precision stimulate excitement and growth. Advanced dancers are ready to refine their energy and to phrase movement with musicality. They are more efficient and so movement becomes more effortless in a larger kinesphere. Further expanding their physical potential, they crave challenges, so complexity is welcomed. Their eyes are not only out in the world, but they begin to realize they can change the world.

Professionals

At first, professional dancers often experience a period of loss. Class isn't as hard anymore; they don't even sweat as much. Professionals perform movement so easily with deep connections that their muscles relax. This is the beauty of professional dancers. They possess an amazing ability to move, jump, and leap with little apparent effort and without the bulky muscles of youth. What is the new challenge?

Simplicity challenges. Simplicity brings extreme concentration back to their practice and allows them to rediscover details overlooked in their earlier training. They can spend an hour on a simple arch. Complexity is in rehearsal; it is not necessary in class. They work on performance skills, making choices about whether to stare into the audience's eyes or to flirtatiously take their gaze away. Improvisation is also crucial, allowing the professional to develop a rich and personal movement vocabulary. Professional dancers are wise enough about their bodies to seek out whatever they need outside of dance class. For some this means a regimen of Feldenkrais, swimming, and weight lifting. For others it means yoga, Pilates, and Contact Improvisation. Learning new forms provides the professional a chance to be awkward and curious again. They return to the beginning of the life cycle.

A teacher's goals should match the natural flow of the learning cycle. Stressing nuances with beginners frustrates both student and teacher. Beginning students are not ready to perform movements requiring intrinsic control. An intermediate teacher must repeat and repeat and repeat. And if the students become impatient, the teacher must find a way past the frustration. An astute advanced teacher challenges students with complexity, subtlety, or dynamics. Professionals require a teacher brave enough to be simple. (See appendix B)

Course Objectives

How to translate students' developmental needs into course objectives? Beginning-level goals should be large and encompassing:

- A student will display a sense of balance in adagio movement.
- A student will be able to leap without undue strain.

Intermediate students will focus on *clarity* of forms and rhythms. Goals will include more attention to details and specifics:

- A student will be able to sustain balance and flow of energy in adagio movement.
- A student will be able to leap while articulating feet.

Advanced students are willing to take risks, to stretch beyond their spatial kinesphere. Goals should emphasize range, complexity, and dynamics:

- A student will perform a long, sculptural adagio with energetic variations.
- A student will maintain height in a leap and land with efficiency while maintaining alignment.

The professional is working on artistry. Goals should encompass phrasing and nuance:

- A professional will perform an adagio with a sophisticated sense of phrasing.
- A professional will perform a leap with clear intent and rhythmic nuance (see appendix B).

PRINCIPLES AND STRATEGIES

Technique is not about *getting* the movement combinations; it is about what the combinations or exercises can teach us. The movement sequences are a vehicle, not an end goal. It is important to ask, "What principle is being taught, and is it threaded into the class?" For example, one student teacher used a fouetté-type movement throughout her class. She explained that she was teaching a fouetté. Looking beyond the step, why was the fouetté important? She replied, "I am most concerned with the spatial clarity of direction changes." Perhaps her class could be based on the *spatial clarity of direction changes* with the fouetté as an example. This would encourage work on focus, clarity of form, and spatial patterning. Movements would spring from a concept and not just be limited to a step. "Oh," she said, with lightbulbs going off, "that would change everything."

Principles

A principle can be physical, mental, or emotional. In educational terms these principles are called psychomotor (physical), cognitive (mental), or affective (emotional). Physical skills are the *doing* of movement. A student demonstrates rhythmic patterns, proper alignment, varied dynamics, or locomotor movements. Cognitive skills are the *knowing* of information, such as the ability to recognize three developmental movement patterns, five locomotor movements, or five positions of the legs in ballet. Affective skills are the *feelings,* the ability to move with confidence or personal investment.

A teacher's job is to create connections between the physical, cognitive, and affective. If the affective goal is concentration, a teacher must ask what physical skills are needed to attain it. Demanding beginnings and endings to every movement helps a class learn concentration. A brilliant teacher, Suet May Ho, knew how to create those connections in her work with disadvantaged schoolchildren in Chicago. She worked on balance by instructing the children to balance a large peacock feather in their open hands. They were learning an affective skill by solving a physical problem.

Many artists teach in a community setting. In one day a teacher might see preschoolers, K-12 students, business people, senior citizens, and professional dancers. Pick one principle to explore, but change the level of expectation for each group. For example, you can work on changing directions by having the seniors in wheelchairs change their eye focus, the preschoolers play a game of hide-and-seek, and the professionals explore the subtlety of shifting weight. Presenting the same idea gives focus to planning and allows different ages to bring insight to the problem. At the end of the day, the teacher is enriched by multigenerational input.

Every day in every class, a dance teacher works on everything. But focusing attention on one principle or concept, such as spiral, shifting weight, or confidence, yields much deeper results. Identifying a principle to teach each day gives clarity to movement patterns, class structure, and corrections.

Everything flows from the main principle in the planning process. If breath is to be the principle, the main movement combination is built on breath rhythms and the sequencing of exercises flows out of breathing. Perhaps the class begins with partner-breathing, then moves into large swinging movements that intensify breathing patterns. The teacher and the class build momentum as each exercise deepens the understanding of breath. With minds focused, there is no struggle to figure out what to correct. Breath guides the teacher's comments: "Use the diaphragm," or "Take a longer inhale at the top of the leap to suspend the leap."

Setting Strategies

Once the principle is established, the job ahead is to develop creative strategies that promote understanding of the movement principles. Strategies are a series of little steps toward the goal (the chosen principle) that set up a progression of physical, cognitive, or affective skills. The strategies selected and the order they are placed in reveal a personal philosophical approach (the point of view) to teaching and learning.

Let's use level changes as an example of a movement principle. What do students need to know, physically or mentally, in order to accomplish level changes? One teacher (from a flow-based technique) decides that inherent in the task of going to and from the floor is understanding the relationship between weight and gravity. This leads to an exploration of falling. Another teacher (from a form-based technique) decides the key element is to understand a contraction and have the strength to lower to and rise from the floor in different forms. Each teacher has the same goal but a different process of getting to the goal. Each process has its merits, but what is most important is creating strategies. What are the steps that will lead the class there—to the other side?

The following are examples of principles and strategies at work:

Changing levels.

⑤ To explore the principle of three-dimensionality in an advanced class, the strategy was to immerse the students in spatial curves. They accomplished the curves, but weren't getting *internal* three-dimensionality. It seemed the camera angle was right but a zoom with a telescopic lens was needed. Three-dimensionality of the lungs was explored by breathing into all five lobes. Working in partners, the students felt the depth, width, and length of their lungs. As they did spirals in their warm-up sequences, they imagined their lungs spiraling deeply from within. They went back to the spatial curves and were able to perform them with a deep and rich sense of three-dimensionality.

⑤ A group of advanced students lacks confidence. What do students need to know *physically* in order to build confidence? The strategy is to design a movement combination that works with direct force, accents, and large range. The class begins with loud karate yells as the students take jabs at each other. Each exercise emphasizes high energy. Low energy is used only to give a moment of balance to the class. The goal is to see students delightfully exhausted and confidently dancing at the end of the class.

⑤ A beginning class has learned the difference between run and hop. They are ready to learn more complex movements, such as slides, leaps, and gallops. What do students need to know in order to execute these steps? Under-curves and over-curves are strategically placed in class. Pliés, relevés, foot articulation, and spatial shifts of weight are emphasized to reinforce the actions of slide and leap. The beginning of class emphasizes building strength in the foot, knee, and hip joints. The main movement combination sails through space with alternating slides, leaps, and gallops.

⑤ An intermediate class is progressing. They are very clear in all their shapes and forms, but they lack elasticity in their movement. What do students need to know in order to accomplish elasticity? There could be several answers; strategies are peculiar not only to the teacher's point of view, but also to the students themselves. Perhaps it is simply a matter of flexibility, in which case more stretches are added to the beginning of class. Careful observation provides the missing information. The students do not understand the oppositional forces of push and pull. They lack an understanding of the spatial reach that pulls the body into space and the powerful thrust of a push from center to hip to heel to floor. The next day the class begins with coiling pushes into the ground.

A model: flow-based teacher creates a principle and strategies for beginning students.
The principle: level changes, to learn how to move in and out of the floor.
The strategy: to explore the weight of the body falling in space.

1. There is a natural fear of falling. Students need to address their fears and understand how to bypass the righting reflexes that are stimulated when falling.
   ► Play trust games to experience the sensation of falling. Students are encouraged to yell, scream, and laugh as they face their fear of falling.
   ► Take the class on a field trip to an amusement park. Ride all the rides that suspend or toss the body through the air. Scream like crazy.
2. When falling, the body can counterbalance the weight: The head leans one way to counterbalance the weight of the hip leaning the other way. Counterbalancing allows the body to control a fall's speed.
   ► Working in partners, students face each other holding hands. Leaning away from each other as they stand and sit, they counterbalance each other's weight.
   ► Present numerous warm-up exercises developing counterbalance techniques, such as lateral leans and stretches, to build strength and flexibility in the torso.
   ► Present the classic Limón side fall (a counterbalance) into the floor.
3. A fall that leans in one piece (imagine a tree falling) has much greater speed and force than a counterbalanced fall. Have students practice leaning forward and falling. Instruct them to run just as they are about to fall to the ground. At first, limit the combinations to falling without taking the body to the floor. As students develop strength and skills, add falls to the floor. Present in various speeds.
4. Suspension before a fall creates physical and rhythmical control.
   ► In body swings or tendu-tombé exercise, encourage students to suspend before they fall by engaging in a spatial reach.
   ► Ask the musician to add rubato or a ritard just before the fall, challenging the dancers to suspend the spatial reach.
5. Righting reflexes become disoriented when going upside down and falling. Practicing upside-down, handstand-like movements helps the body learn to function in new relationships with gravity. Incorporate push-ups and arm-supported movement into the warm-up to develop strength in the upper torso.

6. The body needs to become familiar with all the folding and unfolding possibilities of the spine, arms, and legs (pretzels, squats, etc.) to maneuver the level changes.

   ► Present a beginning warm-up descending into the floor and ascending out of the floor, developing folding and unfolding movement patterns.

   ► Stimulate reach and push-and-pull patterns by simulating the playfulness of a child.

   ► Present lying and sitting warm-ups to encourage familiarity with all positions in relationship to gravity.

In-Depth Teaching

What becomes a principle for class one day may end up lasting a week, a semester, a year, or a lifetime. Many artists spend a lifetime exploring one small aspect of a principle —like Monet painting hundreds of haystacks in order to understand light or Cunningham investigating the relationship of the body to space and time. These artists help us discover the whole within the part. Educator Parker Palmer compares this process of in-depth teaching to a hologram in which every piece of information is contained within the whole. He says, "In every period of history, there is an event that, when deeply understood, reveals not only how historians do their work but also illumines the general dynamics of that epoch. In the work of every philosopher, there is a pivotal idea that when deeply understood, reveals the foundations of his or her system or nonsystem of thought." (Palmer 1998, 123) The computer age has brought us unbelievable breadth—information is available to us at the touch of a button, so more than ever, today's teacher needs to take the students on a journey downward, into a hole that communicates the whole. Once a hole is dug, there is no end to the amount of dirt to be excavated, creating a journey to Rome or perhaps the moon.

RECONCILING INDIVIDUAL DREAMS WITH CLASS GOALS

Every class creates its own unique dynamic. The 9:00 A.M. beginners are spitfire and energy. Even the mention of passionate sex doesn't wake up the 12:00 P.M. intermediates, and the adult class at 6:00 P.M. is so timid the voice dare not be raised. Classes take on a certain character that allows generalizations to be made and class goals to be established. But inside each class is a range of individuals with very different needs. How do you balance goals for the class with goals for the individuals? The student wants to go thrift shopping and the teacher wants to go to Neiman Marcus.

Dance students write about their dreams. Elisa, who can't coordinate her body to save her, wants to work with children with special needs. Harry wants to dance with the Ailey company. Akisha wants to open a dance studio. They are all standing in front of the dance teacher, who must challenge each one in the way they need to be challenged. Should Elisa be pushed to get the coordination patterns? It is informative for the teacher to know that she does not want to become a professional dancer, but get it she must, because if she is encouraged to struggle through her roadblocks, she will better understand the struggles of her future special-needs students. Harry gets the movement patterns easily but lacks discipline. He needs to perfect each detail; the Ailey company's artistic director, Judith Jamison, would not accept anything less. Akisha wants to open a dance studio, but she can't remember movement patterns. She is going to have to remember 100 different dance patterns in her future dream life: one for the babies' recital, one for the teens, one for the tappers, and one for the jazz class. Knowing student goals helps in designing the focus, but it doesn't lessen the responsibility to challenge each student.

Often, an individual's needs conflict with those of the class. An energetic student in a lethargic class is welcomed because she pulls all the other students forward. But if she can only work at full throttle, it does her a disservice to encourage her to do so. Talking with her outside of class, giving her permission to tone down at times, helps to balance individual and class goals.

Should dance teachers approach recreational dancers differently than they do the professional-track student? Professional dancers need to work like hell on *balance,* because they will be onstage with hundreds of people looking at them. Their egos and their futures are on the line. The adult beginner does not need balance to sell radio advertising the next day. But they both need balance in their lives, and the pursuit of physical balance is as crucial to the nondancer's mental balance as the professional's career is dependent on the accomplishment of it. The teacher needs to be as serious in the demand for balance from the nondancer as from the professional. The degree of accomplishment may be different, but the passion to pursue it must remain the same.

> *The pursuit of physical balance is as crucial to the nondancer's mental balance as the professional's career is dependent on the accomplishment of it.*

EVALUATION

Setting goals provides clarity. Evaluation provides answers to the gnawing questions that haunt the teacher's dreams at night: Have you accomplished what you set out to do? Are your strategies working? Are your goals attainable or are you being too unrealistic? Have you damaged your students for life?

Methods for Gathering Information

Evaluation can be carried out in numerous ways. It can be a process of rigorous measurement or anecdotes gathered from students. It can take the form of quiet self-reflection in a journal or involve objective, outside professionals. Whatever the method, ask whether your goals have been accomplished. If not, why not? This ever so humbling process allows a good teacher to become a great teacher.

Videotape

Videotape is extremely useful in evaluating dance because it compresses time. By taking a video at the beginning and end of the term, it is possible to compare skills. It is hard to remember how bad students were at the beginning of the course. Watching the first day of class renews your confidence; the students did learn something after all! Outside professionals can offer objective information. Invite a colleague or a mentor to view short clips from the first and last day. Prepare a form that clearly lists your class goals, and ask the panelists to rate improvement from beginning to end. Discussion elicits valuable information about which strategy paid off and which did not. (See appendix C)

Student Evaluation

Evaluation from students is helpful but should be managed to elicit the right information. Finding out if the class liked you may satisfy your ego, but finding out whether students were challenged or thoroughly warmed up is more valuable information. If your goal was confidence, ask a direct question: "Has your confidence increased?" If you prepared a vocabulary list, a quiz might tell you whether they understand, at least intellectually, the material covered. It is also helpful to ask students to evaluate their participation. The response, "Because of sleep deprivation, I was unable to generate any energy at 8:00 in the morning," can be weighed against "I didn't feel challenged." It's a two-way street (see appendix D).

Guest Artists

Well-taught students should be *adaptable* to new styles and approaches. One of the best ways to evaluate real learning is to watch students take class from another teacher. If they understand a spiral only in context of a particular form, then true learning has not taken place. But if they can successfully transfer the idea of spiral, alignment, or weight shift to another style or approach, then deep learning has been accomplished. Invite a guest artist or colleague to teach class and see what learning has taken place.

Analysis

Did the goal and strategy work? Perhaps *clarity* was the primary movement principle, so the class spent a majority of time perfecting forms and rhythms. By asking a specific question about clarity in the evaluation, you can find out if the goal was achieved. But evaluation should include the big picture: Did the emphasis on clarity enhance other skills? Did the work on clarifying spatial forms improve strength? Is alignment any better?

The teacher who believes that students can't move with ease because they lack strength and flexibility puts beginning students in boot camp. A majority of time is spent executing sit-ups, push-ups, and yoga stretches. "Are they stronger?" is an important question in the evaluation. Students or outside evaluators most likely will respond with a resounding "Yes!" However, returning to the big picture, ask whether this strengthening work helped students move with ease. As the students move awkwardly across the floor, it is clear that they are stronger, but they did not integrate their strength into dancing skills. By analyzing the big picture, you learn valuable information about the viability of your strategies.

If the expectation was that by end of the term beginning students would be able to perform a series of mixed locomotor movements, ask if you accomplished the goal. If not, why not? Analysis leads back to planning. Careful analysis may lead to discussions about expectations, curricular changes, and teacher preparation, thus enhancing and improving teaching practices. Confident that you are on the right track, you can return to dreams of a luscious vacation in an Italian villa to see Michelangelo's *David* (see appendixes C, D, and E).

Investigations

1. Write a description of your favorite professional dancer. What do you value in a performing dance artist?

2. Write about a time you accomplished a goal, inside or outside of dance. What happened on the way towards that goal? What did you learn from the journey?

3. Prepare a syllabus.
   ► Write a rationale. Why is this class important to a student?
   ► Write a description. What is the student going to do in the class?
   ► Write a list of topics. What are you going to teach?
   ► Write a vocabulary list. Which terminology is important for students to know?
   ► Write a list of objectives specific to the level being taught.

4. Watch a baby move. Write about your observations. What correlates with learning technique?
   ► Experiment with homologous patterns. What technical exercises are based on these flexion and extension patterns in the sagittal plane?
   ► Experiment with homolateral patterns, moving like a salamander. Create patterns that emphasize same-sidedness. How does this feel to your body? What is stimulated in your imagination?
   ► Experiment with contralateral patterns, walking with opposition of arms and legs. Try walking with the same arm and leg forward at the same time. How does this feel? What is helpful about cross-patterning?

5. Address each technical skill below. How would each of these be introduced to a beginner? How would the introduction change with intermediate or advanced students?
   ► Leg extensions
   ► Rhythmic clarity
   ► Spatial clarity
   ► Alignment

6. Make up one lesson plan and adapt it to preschoolers, adult beginners, professionals, and senior citizens.

7. Create a list of strategies for the following principles:
   ► Spirals
   ► Confidence
   ► Musical phrasing
   ► Five locomotor movements

In-Class Investigation

1. Videotape your students executing these skills at the beginning and end of your course. Invite a colleague to observe the videos and engage in a discussion on the progress of your students.
   ► Adagio
   ► Locomotor movements
   ► Movement combination
   ► Jumps and leaps

Reflection: PRESENCE

Stage presence is rooted in the ability to be present, a difficult goal to attain.

Right now it is 3:00 A.M. and I am sitting on the couch with my laptop computer. My cat is settling onto a window ledge next to the couch. It is hot and muggy, my skin is sticky, and there is a steady stream of sound coming from the crickets outdoors. I pour hot ginseng tea into the cup

Erika Dufour, photographer; Paul Cipponeri, Krenly Guzman, and Robbie Cook, dancers.

at my side. I am writing a story about presence, so I have given myself a rule: Write only about this moment, right now, period. This is a difficult task because by the time I write about the period I just typed at the end of the sentence, it is already past.

It is August 28, 2001, and now it is 3:03 A.M. I am sitting on the couch with steaming hot tea, but I have not yet taken a sip because it is too hot. I cannot sleep tonight, rather this morning, because too many images ... my cat walks over the edge of my shoulder ... it hurts when she walks on my shoulder because I injured my shoulder yesterday morning and now I will be unable to perform tomorrow. She contemplates jumping down. No, she decides to sit down close to me. My shoulder hurts; there is ice on it, giving a cold sensation to my hands, which are typing right now. It is the middle of the night, the tea is still too hot to drink, but it creates a cloud of steam drifting across the computer screen on this sweaty, muggy night. I am awake in the middle of the night because I am haunted by an image that made me fall in rehearsal yesterday ... the damn cat won't stay put. The sounds of the crickets are fading, but I hear a man walk by with a dog. It was the bark in the sound track that made me remember being cornered by a dog. I was five years old and ... my hands are numb so I remove the ice pack. A car drives by, the cat meows, and the birds are signaling that night will soon change into day. I pick up a cup of tea and bring it to my lips; it smells like mint.

William Frederking, photographer; Suet May Ho, dancer.

chapter 4

Centering Minds
R I T U A L S

Rituals provide a repeatable routine to connect body, mind, and spirit. Whether elaborate or simple, rituals are a part of every culture and art form. In the Chinese tea ceremony, the family teapot is brought to the table so that one does not forget the faces of the past. Elements of the earth, water, and tea are central to the ceremony. Water and tea, like gravity and the body, hold simple truths, and the ritual reminds us that these truths must be reckoned with. The tea secretes a bitter flavor with its first exposure to water. Understanding the nature of tea, the server knows to throw out the bitter first cup. The Chinese begin the tea ceremony the same way every time, with a bow of the head. Repetition gives comfort to a mind scattered by life; yet each day, the drinker returns to the sameness different, bringing to the ceremony varying moods and needs. The ritual provides both consistency and the opportunity for fresh thought. A place of quiet meditation is needed in order to maneuver the elaborate labyrinth leading toward the inner being. A dance class is a ritual, providing an environment where one searches for the soul. This chapter will cover the historical models for rituals, the importance of repetition, centering rituals, and special classes such as a master class, audition, or pre-performance class.

> **A** dance class is a ritual, providing an environment where one searches for the soul.

RITUALS OF ANCESTORS

The 9:00 A.M. African master class taught by a company from Senegal begins with 16 jumps with the legs tucked up, 16 jumps touching the toes in second position, and 16 scissor-kick jumps. Learning a traditional dance follows this. In ancient times a warm-up probably included plowing fields and running to the village to dance. Most dancers drive or take trains to the studio; their contemporary bodies need something more. Teachers may feel they are reinventing the wheel when building a ritual, but there are historical models to refer to. The overall compositional form of a class is greatly influenced by the philosophy, style, or the individual founder of a technique. Let's look at three traditional rituals, the family teapots.

Ongoing Ritual

The base of an ongoing ritual is the pulse; the class follows simple exercises presented quickly, without explanation. Rhythms are often given in a downward or upward progression, such as 16 counts, 8 counts, 4 counts, 2 counts, or the reverse. Simple movements become more complex as the speed increases, like in an aerobics or African class. This type of structure builds deeply into kinesthetic memory, creating spiritual cleansing and building cardiovascular endurance. It is difficult within this form to give corrections, build in spatial complexities, or to address the plasticity of the nervous system. But if a teacher is aware of these drawbacks, she can address them in other ways. Perhaps she does a lab class every other week that dwells on specific corrections, or uses an assistant to make hands-on corrections during class. African classes build spatial complexities by adding complex arm patterns to simple leg patterns, constructing traveling phrases over a stationary rhythm, or layering syncopation onto an ongoing pulse.

Idea-Based Ritual

The *idea* itself (movement principle) is the thread to this class structure. Mary Wigman, and perhaps Isadora Duncan, utilized this approach to teaching. Wigman would present a class in which the entire class pulsed. The next day the entire class might focus on turning. Wigman classes deepened kinesthetic memory. The ritual of pulsing for 90 minutes gives the body a rich sense of the elasticity of bouncing, but knees and ankles leave the class screaming. Wigman classes were built to be extreme. By teaching jumping one day and walking the next, Wigman provided a path to learning based on polarity. These lessons sink in. Classes that emphasize one skill in one session change day to day, so one cannot practice the skill on a daily basis. An aware teacher might counteract these drawbacks by asking students to come to class already warm or by presenting this type of class only one day out of five.

Codified Ritual

In a codified technique, the structure remains consistent. Ballet went through a process of codification over a period of hundreds of years by numerous teachers and dancers. Other techniques, such as Graham and Cunningham, have been shaped primarily by their founders. Ideally a codified structure gives the teacher an excellent road map. Without the worry of building new roads, the teacher can concentrate on the principles behind the movement. A good codified structure provides a very thorough and systematic warm-up as the progression of each exercise builds on the previous one. Each of the dance skills particular to the style is addressed daily, such as turning, jumping, and adagio. Understanding the history and the reasoning behind the structure and style is crucial to teaching a codified technique. The structure can become an empty shell if the teacher does not embody a deep knowledge of the founding philosophy.

Eclectic Blend

The beautifully built structures of the classic modern techniques often combined approaches. The movement principle is threaded through a codified warm-up in a Nikolais class. For example, if the lesson is on spatial curves, the curves are integrated into a set warm-up sequence. Adding a spatial walking pattern to the beginning of class and a spatial curve to the arm movements in the floor warm-up leads to a pattern based on curved spatial paths at the end of class. A Cunningham class is usually structured around a complex ending movement pattern. A master of structural design, Viola Farber would add a stylistic turn to a warm-up arm exercise, or a peculiar shape to a warm-up back exercise. By the end of such a class students will have built a deep kinesthetic memory for the ending movement combination. Less time is spent learning the pattern and more time is spent dancing. Today's teachers continue to experiment with weaving ongoing rituals, idea-based rituals, and codified rituals to form new methodologies for structuring class.

FLOOR OR STANDING

When planning a class, one of the first questions is whether to start on the floor or standing. A determining factor of this decision will be each teacher's unique history. A Limón-trained dancer will feel more comfortable standing. A dancer immersed in somatic practices will probably start on the floor. But there are larger truths to look at, and gravity is key. Consider gravity when lying on the back on the floor. Gravity flows from belly to back. When standing, the weight pours down through the skeleton to the pelvis, legs, and finally the feet. There are two advantages to changing this relationship in a technique class.

Advantages of Floor Work

One advantage is that muscles completely change their function depending on their relationship to gravity. For instance, a forward leg extension standing up is very difficult. Crank the leg up, and gravity's pull is exhausting to counteract. In this case, the hip flexors are the prime movers of the leg. However, the same forward leg extension becomes much easier when lying on the back. Beyond 90 degrees, gravity actually helps the leg move closer to the torso. The hip flexors can relax because they are no longer responsible for moving the femur (thigh) bone. Thus it is much easier to accomplish the same leg extension lying on your back than standing up. *Easier* isn't always what is wanted, but if a student is doing all the *wrong* things standing up (the hip and spine alignment falling apart as they execute the movement), it is useful to do the same movement on the floor. Reducing the effects of gravity allows the student to kinesthetically grasp the sensation of a proper leg extension. The abdominal muscles are another example. Teachers are forever chastising their students to use their stomachs. (Note that the stomach is an organ. The muscles in the belly are the abdominal muscles. It is preferable to use the term *abdominal muscles.*) The abdominal muscles may work, but do not have to contract to keep the body standing. When lying on the back, suddenly everything becomes work for the abdominal muscles because they have to fight gravity to do just about anything. If building strength in the abdominal muscles is the goal, floor work is optimal.

The second advantage to using the floor is a curious one. A baby's first movement experience is generally maneuvering on the floor. Adults spend a lifetime practicing movement standing up. When the body is horizontal to gravity, it has the unique opportunity to return to its first movement memory. Revisiting its original blueprint, the body is fresh and receptive, just like a baby. The body has not linked the habit of raising the shoulders every time the leg moves. The floor provides opportunity to learn new motor pathways more efficiently. It is no mistake that so many somatic practices are based on floor work.

Integration of Floor and Standing Work

The skill of a dance teacher is to integrate floor work back into standing work. When students don't see the connection between floor and standing work, it can be frustrating. Reinforcing the connections verbally and kinesthetically helps the students link floor and standing movements.

Prepare two types of warm-ups: a standing warm-up that moves in and out of the floor, and a floor warm-up that moves in and out of standing. Using both structures provides a refreshing change for students and encourages the plasticity of the nervous system. If teaching the same students five days a week, alternate the warm-ups. If teaching two days a week, present a floor class in the fall and a standing class in the spring.

Modern technique is partially defined by its emphasis on movement that rolls to and from the floor. Doris Humphrey fell into the floor, and ever since, choreographers have exploited this level change. These transition movements between floor and standing are a key to understanding modern technique. How do joints fold and extend? How does gravity interact with the falling body? What connectivity is necessary to spring in and out of low crouches and high jumps? How one answers these questions defines personal as well as stylistic preferences.

A physicist friend said he couldn't stand watching dance; he saw it as a pointless exercise of dancers continuously trying to outwit gravity and failing. Watching dancers go up and down, up and down, created a boring scenario with no variation. But to dance teachers, gravity provides a fascinating place to experiment.

REPETITION

Repeated over days, weeks, months, years, and decades, a ritual is a doorway into the body, a prayer. But how much should exercises and patterns change day to day, week to week, and year to year? Days gradually get longer, until suddenly it is summer. The tides move out, revealing secrets in the sand. The sequence of exercises should shift like sands over time. The question of how much and how fast is a delicate art that consumes the daily practice of planning class. There are some important scientific principles that will help teachers make informed choices. In the opening chapter of her groundbreaking book *Human Movement Potential: Its Ideokinetic Facilitation,* Lulu Sweigard states, "Movement is a neuro-musculoskeletal

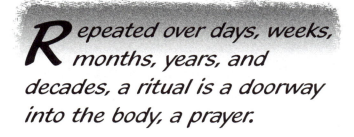

Repeated over days, weeks, months, years, and decades, a ritual is a doorway into the body, a prayer.

event. The nervous system initiates movement and controls its patterning. It stimulates the muscle, the workhorse, into action to move the skeleton, the machine for movement. There can be no efficiency in movement, nor can there be realization of the full potential for movement unless all three components—nerves, muscles, bones—perform with optimal facility." (Sweigard 1974, 3) Movement involves all three systems, but the nervous system is key to movement training; the muscles are simply *workhorses* moving the bones.

Role of the Nervous System

For each movement, the nervous system creates a series of highways. A ballet student taking a modern class will observe a movement that looks a bit like a pas de chat and her map will dictate a pas de chat. The brain goes back to what it knows. That is why ballet dancers look like ballet dancers when taking a modern class, and modern dancers look like modern dancers when taking a ballet class. But then, if the student is smart and inquisitive, he will look further and notice that the movement is not exactly a pas de chat, but has an unusual dip in the middle. At first try, he will be very awkward because there is no blueprint to follow. But after he performs it 100 times, a new road is added to the old map. This road is smaller and more distinctive. Technique is the process of building as many roads as possible, the smaller and more detailed the better. This allows choices and subtleties in the way we travel. If only a limited amount of choices are repeated and repeated, the road will be deep, making it ever so hard to take a detour.

Plasticity of the Nervous System

Remaining conscious of neurological patterning, teachers must keep two things in mind when balancing the continuum of old and new over time: the need for repetition and need for new information. If there is no repetition, the nervous system will not be able to create a highway. If the information is always the same, the highway will be dug in like a trench and the nervous system will lose its plasticity.

Variations in Patterning

Repetition of a sequence of exercises over time establishes consistency in the body and mind. If the overall structure is changed too often, students are robbed of an important ritual. By following the same basic sequence, students learn how to pace their energy through the class. They know they can give all their energy to a moving pattern because it will always be followed by a deep stretch. They know they will have two exercises in a row to warm their feet and ankles. The exercises may vary, but the students know what is coming.

In a ballet class or a Cunningham class, the sequence acts as the old, worn, familiar blanket. A shiny new toy is presented within the exercise itself. The fifth exercise may always be a foot exercise, but each day it is a little different. One day it is faster, another day slower; one day complex, another day simple; one day in a six phrase, another day in mixed meter. New information can be added gradually or suddenly to give balance. Perhaps a new arm pattern is added to an old leg pattern, or a new spiral sequence is added to the flat-back sequence. Day to day, there is subtle variation. Month to month, the sequence adjusts to emphasize a growing concern for details or rhythm or whatever the class is emphasizing. With each new term or year, the structure gets tweaked or overhauled as new ideas are brought in and old ones are discarded.

Another variation occurs in the balance between the warm-up material and the longer dance phrases. Often teachers like to build a movement combination over time, presenting an eight-count phrase one day, another phrase the next. By the end of the week, a fairly long movement combination is put together. This is very effective if the same students are in class every day. Another layering technique is to build the main movement combination throughout the week, while beginning to sneak small, new concepts or patterns into the warm-up. These will come to fruition the following week.

A Set Warm-Up

A *set* warm-up is when the sequence and the exercises remain exactly the same over time. The set warm-up can be very effective; it digs deep grooves. Students will become accomplished at its very specific movements; however, they will be unable to use the skills in new situations. Varying the tempo, the spatial dimensions, or the dynamic energy each day honors the need for fresh information in a set class. Slight changes are imperative to helping the neuromuscular pathways stay plastic and receptive to new information. When using a set warm-up, it is important to present fresh, challenging movement combinations daily.

Moving On

One of the most important questions in teaching dance is how long to stay with the same things before moving on? Accomplishment and frustration are good guides. When students have accomplished a skill, it is time to move on to the next challenge. Accomplishment is fairly easy to assess. When students have *not* accomplished a skill, stay with it until they are either blue in the face or frustrated beyond belief. Moving on without demanding the satisfaction of accomplishment is a disservice to students. Teachers get bored with material far faster than their students because their neurological roads are well developed. However, student frustration needs to be read carefully. It may signal that it's time to switch gears, or it may mean that the teacher has to muster the audacity to say, "One more time," for the thousandth time.

A LABYRINTH TOWARD CENTER

Boardsailing is a sport with a board and a sail. Standing on the board and holding onto the sail, one manipulates the forces of nature. The upper body listens to the wind. The lower body listens to the water. The center of the body coordinates the forces of the wind and the water. Dance class is a ritual that hunts for the ever-ellusive center, and the dance teacher builds a maze to support the search. Let us look at two very different models for centering. These two models require one to adopt a different mind-set, different ways of looking at the body and its relationship to the world. One yin and the other yang, both create a way of approaching centering. In the early 1970s Dr. John Wilson taught a kinesiology class at the University of Utah. (Bill Evans, the renowned teacher, and Andrea Olsen, author of *BodyStories: A Guide to Experiential Anatomy,* were in this class as well.) Wilson proposed two metaphors for seeking center.

Geometric Model

Think of Leonardo da Vinci's beautiful drawing of a body with axes and planes and circles drawn through it. This model looks at the body through geometry. With a strong sense of bilateral symmetry, the torso and the limbs move with the stabilizing force of the core. Working methodically on each plane to establish a firm connection to the core creates a strong relationship to linear space. Curves are found within the lines. The simple pattern of en croix (in the shape of a cross) reinforces this logic. The limbs move through all three planes—sagittal (forward and back), lateral (side to side), and transverse (rotation in and out)—while one side stabilizes the body. By moving the limbs around the core, the dancer *finds center,* and is now ready to begin the movement through space during center floor.

Biometric Model

The biometric model is based on biology instead of geometry. This model explores how joints are arranged in relationship to the center of gravity. Olsen developed Dr. Wilson's theory further in *BodyStories,* calling it the Arthrometric Model. (*Arthro* is the Latin root for joints.) This model views the body from the front, imagining a

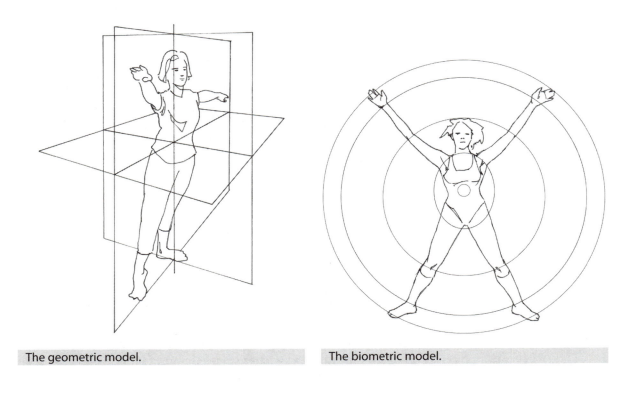

The geometric model.

The biometric model.

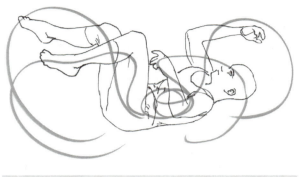

Navel radiation.

series of concentric rings radiating outward. The center contains the core, where cartilaginous joints of the spine provide all three planes of motion. Next are the large ball-and-socket joints (hips and shoulders), setting the direction. In the next ring, the one-plane hinge joints (elbows and knees) provide range. Edging outward, the multi-plane wrist and ankle joints absorb shock; and last, details are refined by the one-plane fingers and toe joints.

In the somatic approach Body-Mind Centering, Bonnie Bainbridge Cohen speaks about navel radiation. Picture a starfish and imagine taking all food, all sustenance, through the belly button. At one point in everyone's life, this happened. The fetus drinks in life through the umbilical cord in the womb. Everything radiates out from this center. There are six limbs all connected to this core: the head, tail, arms, and legs. As a six-pointed starfish, everything connects through the center.

The biometric model and navel radiation are slightly different, but both look back not only to our fetal beginnings but also to our evolutionary past, creating a very different maze than the geometric model. Tai chi chuan, Contact Improvisation, and Bartenieff Fundamentals are examples of these mind-sets searching for center. The center of the body rolls, tosses, and moves through spherical patterning, and the limbs gradually find the core.

Different Mind-Sets

Each of these philosophical approaches enters centering through a different set of doors, and a teacher uses them to his advantage. Immerse ballet dancers in the mind-set of the biometric model or navel radiation. Students will complain that they feel off center, off balance, off *off,* because it feels more like flying a plane than driving a car. A plane and a baby in utero have the ability to turn right and left *and* tilt and dive. If facing a group of improvisers, immerse them in the rigor of geometry. Give them geometric images as they stabilize one side while moving the other. They will complain that they feel rigid and bound. Tell them it takes awhile to learn how to drive a car. Another methodology is to enter one doorway during the floor warm-up—perhaps a series of rolls that allows the limbs to find center—then switch to another doorway for the standing work—perhaps a geometric-based barre.

SPECIAL CLASSES

Holidays explode with rituals, which in time become traditions; special china is used when all the relatives descend on the house. The Catholic Church, known for elaborate rituals, musters up a few more bells, candles, and flowers to remind us of the miracles of birth at Christmas time. Rituals are tailor-made for special occasions: Prior to a wedding, Muslim women receive elaborate henna paintings on their hands; in Chinese weddings, women change dresses all night long to signify wealth. Catapulted out of the everyday ritual, a teacher spices up and tailor designs classes to create a master class, audition class, or pre-performance class.

Master Classes

Like Hansel and Gretel dropping birdseed onto the snow, the mantra of a master class is to leave one thing behind, again and again. Simplicity reigns; after all, a master should be able to reduce all the clutter to one prized possession. If it's too complex, students spend most of their psychic energy getting the combination and adapting to new movement, a new teacher, and new rhythms instead of embracing the concepts underlying the movement. Without the luxury of time, repetition plays an important role. What type of class supports simplicity and repetition—and birds going to bed with a full stomach?

Slice-of-Life Master Class

The slice-of-life class is a taste—a tiny spoon—of rum raisin ice cream. If students want a full scoop they will have to come back. Perhaps the taste includes only the raisin—the rum is left as an enticement for later. Following a familiar structure, the teacher builds a class based on what is done every day; but for this class, each combination or exercise should have less material, allowing time to experience the movement. If the main movement phrase is integrated into the warm-up, the students will spend less time learning the combination and more time grasping the concepts. When you spend a lifetime pursuing an approach to movement, presenting only a taste of it is harder than it sounds. It is easy to assume too much when you spend most of your time surrounded by your own students or company members. For a slice-of-life master class it is most helpful to think in terms of teaching a beginning class, whether the students are beginners or not. It is not important to impress with the complexity of your material, just the richness of the basics.

Start-at-the-Beginning Master Class

Paring it all down, a teacher arrives at breath. The seemingly simple, yet complex, act of breathing is where it all begins. The class lies down on the floor to concentrate on inner awareness, lungs, and breath. Students place their hands on the chest and listen to the lungs moving the body. Slowed down, they ask hundreds of questions and make new discoveries. The teacher makes a daring choice to follow their curiosity. The students experiment with moving the breath from one chamber to the next; they hyperventilate and laugh. End of class. They didn't dance, they didn't sweat, and they didn't do a grand battement. Does it matter?

Etudes Master Class

One chance, one hour, one brief encounter, one flash in the pan: I was to teach a master class at the American College Dance Festival. Master classes are tricky because, like a blind date, you have no way of knowing who will be there or what their needs will be. You spend hours in front of the mirror, trying on various outfits, practicing your hellos, and thinking about witty things to say. Finally you choose the pink-and-purple-polka-dot hat because it is memorable.

Two very simple concepts, yield/push and reach/pull, underlie all movement. Dancers leap into the air and fall apart without the supportive push of the grounded heel, or they push into the ground and sputter without the aid of an integrated reach. Developmentally, the baby experiences yield and push before the more sophisticated pattern of reach and pull. But at this stage of the game, it is the conversation between the two that supports the dancing body.

Classical etudes, which are short studies that reinforce technique, don't sound like playing scales—the music rings out. So I begin to build a small movement etude based on yield/push and reach/pull. Each section incorporates another aspect of the concept. The first phrase begins simply, with a push in the heels and a reach of the head. The next phrase emphasizes the reach of the head and tail in different directions. Each phrase of the choreography builds on the next. Consciously including shifts of weight, feet articulations, deep squats (pliés), and spinal patterns, I choreograph the etude to move through all the joints and properly warm up the body. If certain sections are slowed down, even stretches are possible.

Dancing—the ecstatic presence—needs an ongoing flow, so I will ask the musician to keep playing. But this will create other problems. Without time to stop and explain I will have to "dance" the comments, show in my body the push and pull. Visual elements will help. Yield and push—I find a toy with a suction cup, a spring, and a monster head. The suction cup yields to the ground and a spring pushes upward. A child's train illustrates reach and pull. The child pulls the rope that pulls the engine, which in turn pulls the rope that pulls the next car, all the way down to the caboose. Once the whole train has been engaged, it moves through space. The reach pulls the body sequentially; threads of energy connect from top to bottom.

With so many new things to address, repetition will be the teacher. Children learn songs through repetition. "Row, row, row your boat" is sung over and over until the words, rhythm, and melody are clear. Then a new phrase is added: "gently down the stream." There is a return to the beginning: "Row, row, row your boat gently down the stream." Now a new phrase is added: "Merrily, merrily, merrily, merrily." Once again: "Merrily, merrily, merrily, merrily." Back to the beginning. "Row, row, row your boat, gently down the stream / Merrily, merrily, merrily, merrily, life is . . . life is, life is, life is." Back to the beginning.

Class begins, and phrase one is practiced again and again. Time to observe; they are not yielding before the push. Reducing the phrase to three counts, they practice yield, yield, push (just "your boat, your boat, your boat"). Time to integrate it back into the first phrase. The concepts deepen with each repetition; it is time to move on to the next phrase, which uses the push to transfer weight—untraditional tendus warming up the feet. Return again to the beginning—phrase one and two are done together. In an hour and a half, without stopping, the class danced the entire etude, about 10 phrases. Every time the students returned to the beginning their breath became richer and bolder; their outer expression, their reach into the world became fuller—an evolution inward and outward at the same time. This blind date elicited chemistry, and hopefully the pink-and-purple-polka-dot hat will be remembered.

Audition Class

A teacher needs to think carefully about the goals when planning an audition class. Finding the best performer is very different than finding the best technician.

A Company Audition

How is it possible to weed out all the possibilities and find the one who will satisfy the dancemaker's needs? Start at the end: What and who do you want? Do you want a six-foot-tall woman who will fit the costumes? Don't waste everyone's time;

ask the dancers to walk across the floor, pick all the six-foot-tall women, and send everyone else home. Do you want a dancer with technical control, flashy legs, and big smiles? Have them do a run, run, leap; it shows everything: form, spatial intent, rhythmic clarity, technical skill, and presence. Do you want a collaborative partner, someone who sparkles and makes you sparkle? Take the finalists out to lunch and have a chat; ask them about their favorite animal. Do you want an interesting improviser, a person who provides unique solutions? Ask them to talk about their lunch while running and leaping. A walk, a run, a leap, a lunch—and watch them put it all together.

A Level Placement Audition

When auditioning for level placement, it is crucial to ascertain the full range of each student's skills in order to place them in the correct level . A passionate mover will look great moving across the floor but fall apart in a balance exercise. Concentrate on four combinations, each with a specific goal.

- An adagio with emphasis on form and balance.
- A simple locomotor movement to observe coordination skills and spatial intent.
- A movement combination with level changes for rhythmical clarity and pick-up skills.
- A run, run, leap for ease in elevation and performance presence.

Pre-Performance Class

The focus of a pre-performance class is to prepare the individual and the ensemble for the stage, mentally, physically, and psychically. Mature performers often create their own idiosyncratic rituals. (I remember watching a very well-known soloist asking for a coffee can before the show. First she wiggled for five minutes, then she lay down and took a 30-minute snooze. Waking up on the 5-minute call, she discreetly peed into the coffee can just before sailing onstage.) A group of coffee cans might just do the trick, but most of the time a bit more is needed.

Internal support is a good beginning. After all, if the performers are brave enough to venture onstage, forgoing a lucrative career waiting tables, they need to muster every part of their internal psyches. A moment of improvisation with eyes closed allows the performers to listen to their muscles and get the personal kinks out. As formal class begins, familiar exercises are useful—thinking too hard before a show clutters the brain waves with useless patterns and unnecessary tension. With the unknown lurking just around the corner, a familiar ritual calms the body. Nurturing breath at the beginning supports breath later, just as the adrenaline hits. Something just energetic enough—a speedy foot exercise or a full-body swing—breaks the sweat. Now it is time to get up on the leg with a simple adagio/balance exercise. (Unfortunately, this always seems to coincide with the lighting designer's light check. As the lights flash on and off from side, top, and bottom, the dancers curse their inability to stand on two legs, let alone one—mixed agendas never work.) It is now time to draw attention to the space. Ideally, warm-up class is onstage, for the performers need to weave their energy into the space. Exercises that move through space allow the eyes to seek the floor, the ceiling, the audience, the wings, and each other. A long dancing combination does not service the performer; instead, rely on simple triplets, skips, and slides. Performed together in duets, trios, and perhaps in unison, simple dancing builds communal energy. At the end of class, a moment of play is grand. One group used to love to play tag; screaming and laughing, they exorcised their nervous energy. Another group used to compete to see who could do the best one-minute rendition of the entire show. Reels of laughter stimulated their humanness. Taking five breaths together in a circle with the stage manager, stage crew, musicians, or other performers provides a spherical blanket of support for the task ahead.

From tea rituals to keeping a kosher house, rituals beg us to pay attention. The awe and mystery does not reside in the ritual itself but in the attention to everyday life it demands of us. In a book about healing called *Kitchen Table Wisdom,* Dr. Rachel Remen says, "Ritual doesn't make mystery happen. It helps us see and experience something, which is already real. It does not create the sacred; it only describes what is there and has always been there, deeply hidden in the obvious." (Remen 1996, 284) It is like going through the motions of a tea ritual and suddenly being filled with thanks because you realize you are thirsty.

Investigations

1. What personal ritual do you repeat day after day and year after year? How are you different each time you perform the ritual?

2. Watch an African class, a ballet class, and a modern class. Write down the sequence of exercises. How are they the same and how are they different?

3. Observe a dance class over time. What changes and what remains the same, day to day and week to week?

4. Plan standing and floor warm-ups:

   ► Make up four exercises lying on the floor that are similar to standing exercises (for instance, a développé forward). Experiment with exercises on the back, belly, or side. How does gravity change the experience of the exercise?

   ► Make up four exercises exploring the way the body moves through different levels. What principles are important when making these transitions?

5. Work with a mind-set of the geometric model, biometric model, or navel radiation.

   ► Plan a full class based solely on the mind-set of the geometric model. Create a series of exercises for the warm-up in which the core stabilizes and the limbs move.

   ► Plan a full class based solely on the mind-set of the biometric model. Create a series of exercises for the warm-up in which one radiates out from center, the center moves, and the limbs find the core.

6. Plan a master class, an audition class, a pre-performance class. How are they different?

In-Class Investigations

1. If you usually present a standing warm-up, create a floor warm-up that parallels the standing work, and vice versa. Experiment with how you interchange them. What works?

2. Experiment with the amount of repetition in your class. When adding more repetitive sequences, what do you observe? When adding more variations, what do you observe?

Reflection: DISCIPLINE

When Grandpa died, Mom found thousands of journals in his basement. Writing down what he did every day for 50 of his 90 years, he started each entry with "Woke up, had oatmeal with one spoon of brown sugar." Working in factories as a tool and dye maker, Grandpa's life was full of rituals, but at night, unbeknownst to anyone, he was an inventor.

Erika Dufour, photographer.

When I was a child, I loved to go to ballet class. Tortured by too many choices in my young life—which doll to bring to bed and who to play with—I could count on pink tights, hair buns, and ballet barres. There was deep satisfaction in raising my arm to begin pliés, always at the beginning, with no exceptions. By dégagés—always the third exercise—sweat began to trickle down my back, and by frappés my breathing deepened. The stretch always came after the hard work of the développés and the record always jumped at exactly the same place in the pirouette. Smells of young sweat, chalky rosin, and hairspray mingled with the teacher's cigarette, which he happily lit up after barre. In the center there were new movements to try, but in time they too had an aching familiarity. Mom would always appear in the doorway at grand jetés, checking in to see if through all this repetition something in my dancing was changing.

During puberty, I would wake up as a child and go to bed as a woman. With my body exploding with change each day, the familiarity of dance class suddenly became insufferable. I couldn't bear the thought of one more tendu.

After years of wear and tear as a professional dancer, injuries took their toll. Hobbling into the dance studio to watch class, I was envious of every moment.

Now, upon returning to class, I notice the subtle differences in my joints between yesterday and today. The muscles and lungs are older now and maybe wiser, having found no shortcut whatsoever. My dancing doesn't change much, but it doesn't matter anymore. During pliés I let my mind wander.

One day shortly before he died, Grandpa found an old pancake griddle just the size of his behind in the trash. He went down to his basement and there were sounds of whistling, sawing, and a little swearing. He came up with a smile on his face. "Look here what I fixed up for myself." He had attached the pancake griddle to the cane so whenever he got tired he pulled the griddle down and sat on his cane. He spent many happy hours in his garden watching the birds. His imagination seemed to expand with age. My mother swears it was the oatmeal.

Gathering Power

CONDITIONING

chapter 5

A s the thoroughbred strains for the finish line, gathering power, it takes our breath away with the beauty of its sheer athleticism. The horse is bred and trained to run. The athlete, whether horse or human, wants to jump higher, turn better, and run faster. Scientists are discovering more about the body every day, and athletes have been deeply influenced by scientific analysis. Their success is measurable; they continue to break records as their training improves. Martha Graham called dancers "athletes of god." Yet dance has been slow to incorporate scientific information. Why? Will it upset traditions, history, or the art? Perhaps there is fear that the athlete will supersede the artist. Because of the fancy pyrotechnics that at times substitute for art onstage, some say this has already happened. But research in sport training has provided useful information on many subjects that dovetail with dance*artists'* goals, including movement efficiency, injury prevention, performance excellence, and longevity in the field. Dancers need not be afraid of the information, just selective about how it is used. This chapter will focus on principles from anatomy and kinesiology and their application to dance technique.

RESILIENCE

Margaret H'Doubler began the first dance program in higher education at the University of Wisconsin. She would whirl in to teach technique class with anatomy books, kinesiology charts, and skeletons. At the age of 80, she was remarkably resilient, both mentally and physically. Resilience means to spring back, to rebound, to return to the original form or position after being bent, compressed, or stretched. After a five-hour, brutal rehearsal, a well-trained dancer should be able to bounce back the next day, ready for more. Physical conditioning makes the body resilient and able to withstand the rigors of a dance career.

The classical definition of a conditioned body includes the big four: strength, flexibility, muscular endurance, and cardiorespiratory endurance. To improve these areas, the stress level needs to increase continuously. This is called progressive overload.

How does a traditional technique class condition students? At first glance, we see that conditioning occurs, but let's take a closer look. To increase strength, the muscle must experience more weight or resistance. Is weight consciously added during the course of training? Not unless a dancer gains weight. In order to increase flexibility, the muscle needs to stay at the lengthened state for at least 30 seconds. Longer stretches may occur, but 30 seconds is a long time when there is much to do. Endurance is built by increasing the amount of repetitions. Perhaps 16 tendus are accomplished one day instead of 8, but there is no conscious plan to increase repetitions over time. And to increase aerobic capacity, the heart must be working at or above the target rate for at least 20 minutes. It is rare when a technique class goes that long without stopping. So in terms of the big four of conditioning, technique is not accomplishing the job. If not conditioning, what is happening in a technique class?

A majority of time is spent on neuromuscular coordination, building pathways to enhance efficient movement and develop the core elements of artistry: spatial awareness, rhythmic clarity, and dynamic variation. Although technique class is not ideal for pure conditioning, the reality is that dancing strengthens dancing. Muscles adapt to what they practice. One could spend hours hanging over and stretching the hamstrings in a passive stretch, but this practice would not necessarily make a better grand battement because the muscle has to learn to stretch with speed within the given form. In an article on warm-up in the *Journal of Dance Medicine & Science,* the authors state, "Maximal strength, speed-strength, and strength-endurance are the most common categories of strength, which is determined by the concerted activity of many muscles. This intermuscular coordination should be optimized during warm-up by rehearsing the motor pattern of the activity to be performed." (Volianitis, Koutedakis, and Carson 2001, 77) Thankfully, the core of technique class should still be dancing.

CONDITIONING IN DANCE PRACTICE

Obviously, some sort of balance needs to be reached. If all four conditioning principles were included, a technique class would need to be four hours long with no time spent on rhythm, weight, or alignment. At the same time, students are not served well if they burst into the world of dance unable to meet its demands. The solution lies in a two-fold approach.

Cross-Training Practices

Although advising students to cross-train seems to avoid the issue, it is an important first step in recognizing the limitations of technique class. Students have varying needs, all of which cannot possibly be addressed within a dance class. A teacher must be able to observe carefully, analyze the strengths and weaknesses of the individual accurately, and offer suggestions for supplemental work outside the dance class. Yoga, Pilates, Gyrotonics, weight training, and aerobic work are immensely beneficial to dance students at the right time and in the right place. Cross-training benefits athletes because it allows them to confront their weaknesses. This not only improves performance but also prevents injuries. An inflexible student prevents the impending doom of a torn hamstring by enrolling in a yoga class. A weak and loosely strung individual prevents sprained joints by swimming or weight training. Depending on individual needs and progress in dance, sometimes students also need to be counseled to stop or switch cross-training. An aerobics fanatic may need to switch to a stretch class, or a student showing signs of chondromalacia (injury involving the patella) should be counseled to stop jogging. Dancers are often overachievers, so while cross-training can be a healthy addition to dance training, it can also add dangerous psychological pressures. In a study about exercise dependence, Pierce and Daleng found a "high level of exercise addiction among elite dancers." (Pierce and Daleng 2002, 4) A teacher must be observant of both personality and body needs.

Conditioning Practices Within the Class

Because of the limitations of time within a dance class, one or two conditioning principles should be highlighted as needed. By analyzing the needs of each class, the teacher develops limited and attainable conditioning goals. After one day with a group of students, it is common to hear a teacher lamenting to colleagues, "The nine o'clock class is so lethargic; by the time they got done with the first three exercises, they were exhausted." The solution lies in the problem—a heavy dose of cardiovascular endurance would work wonders with this group. If a class demonstrates poor strength, a series of floor exercises with a plan to increase repetitions daily or weekly would help. Conditioning goals should also address muscle groups. A teacher may go on a campaign to increase flexibility, but the next question is where—hip joint, spine, or feet?

Kinesiologists approach conditioning by studying the imbalances between muscle groups. If a student were hyperextended in the lumbar spine (lower back), a kinesiologist would say to strengthen the abdominal muscles and stretch the lumbar spine. This is a helpful approach to many of the alignment issues teachers address, but caution must be paid to its limitations. Conditioning for alignment should always be done in conjunction with neuromuscular reeducation. (See chapter 10)

A large percentage of dance students are *hyper*-hyperextended in the lumbar spine. (The lumbar spine has a natural hyperextended curve, which dynamically balances the thoracic and cervical curves. It is only when the lumbar spine is *too* curved—*hyper hyper*—that there is a problem. This is technically called lumbar lordosis.) As humans adapted to bipedalism, the lumbar spine became the structural weak point of the human design. Our sedentary culture puts even more stress on the lumbar curve. The body conforms to what it does the most, which is to sit. Our hip flexors become short in their resting state, thereby pulling the pelvis forward when we stand. One of the first alignment issues every teacher is drawn to is protruding bellies as the pelvic bowl spills its contents forward. Looking through the eyes of a kinesiologist, the abdominal muscles controlling the spine are weak and the lower back extensor muscles are tight. The hip flexors control-

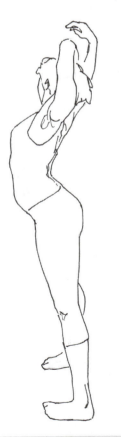

A hyper-hyperextended lumbar spine.

ling the hip joint (the iliopsoas and the rectus femoris) are tight and the hip extensors (hamstrings and gluteus maximus) are weak. Putting this information together, a teacher setting conditioning goals for a beginning class might focus on strengthening the abdominals and hamstrings and stretching the back extensors and the hip flexors. While it won't solve hyperextension entirely, these exercises will increase students' awareness of the problem.

Each athlete is shaped by the demands of their particular sport. One has only to watch the parade of Olympians to see how each sport shapes the body—the bulky and powerful weight lifters, the slight and wiry gymnasts, or the lanky swimmers. This has to do with the principle of specificity. Liederbach explains, "For example, if a dancer wants to become proficient at a particular type of jump, he or she should practice that jump, in a constructive, progressive, and exacting manner, until the ultimate level is achieved." (Liederbach 2000, 58) Delivering specificity means that dance teachers must keep abreast of changes within dance choreography. For example, dancemakers are choreographing with more arm-supported work, and in our equal-gender world, women are lifting bodies as much as men. Women are particularly vulnerable to back and shoulder injuries because they tend to have less body mass in the upper torso. Incorporating arm-supported movement such as push-ups, the yoga position downward dog, or handstands into the daily class strengthens the core musculature of the torso, the extensors and abductors of the shoulder joint, and the upward rotators of the scapula—all muscles necessary to support weight of another body.

A teacher must also analyze the conditioning strengths and weaknesses of the style being taught. Flow-based techniques explore the natural result of gravity or momentum on a falling body. Speed allows momentum or gravity to do the work, so muscles do less. While momentum-based movement is excellent for neuromuscular coordination, it is a mistake to think that muscular strength is being developed. Efficient use of weight and gravity propels the student into the air, but muscle cushions the landing and provides power and control. Long and very slow adagios build strength. A Horton technique class builds strength but assumes a certain amount of flexibility. A Horton teacher might consciously include a static, passive stretch as part of the cool-down. Knowledge about conditioning allows the teacher to tailor design class, responding to the strengths and weaknesses of both style and students. The following is a discussion about the big four of conditioning—strength, flexibility, muscular endurance, and cardiovascular endurance—as they apply to a dance class.

Strengthening the upper body.

STRENGTH

In *Dance Kinesiology*, Sally Fitt says, "Strength is usually defined as the ability to exert tension against resistance." (Fitt 1996, 392) Strength is built by increasing the resistance or weight. It is preferable to start with a level of weight beginners can handle—perhaps basic adagio work begins with holding a leg up with hands, reducing the weight being held by the hip flexor. This eventually progresses to an adagio with extended limbs. Pilates has a series of strength exercises with several steps increasing weight. Students can also be encouraged to work with elastic bands outside of class; the bands create increased resistance, building the strength capacity of each muscle fiber.

But there is more to strength than meets the eye. Fitt elaborates, "Strength is primarily a neurological phenomenon, requiring the firing of more motor units which contribute to the performance of a given motor task." (Fitt 1996, 392) A dancer wants the strength necessary to jump without inhibiting the ease of movement necessary to soar. Strength and ease of movement have an interesting relationship. Let's look at their interdependence, which is rooted in neurology.

Efficiency and the All-or-None Law

Between the brain and the muscles there are incoming and outgoing highways. The motor nerves are the outgoing highway from the brain to the muscles; they tell the muscle what to do (contract or relax). The sensory nerves are the incoming highway. They tell the brain what is happening in the muscles: "It's cold down here; we are tired; we can't stretch any further." The motor nerves travel from the brain, arrive at the muscle, and attach themselves to what is called a motor end plate. Each motor end plate has control over a bunch of fibers within the muscle. Some motor end plates control a large group of fibers; others control very few. The *all-or-none law* states that when a motor end plate is given the message to contract, all the fibers connected to it contract. If motor unit Number One is told to go to work, all the fibers under its command go to work. Experience tells us that it is possible to have graded contractions—the muscle works differently when picking up a feather than when picking up a piano. So how is this possible if all of the fibers contract? It is possible because there are many motor neurons within each muscle. When all the motor units are instructed to work, there is maximum contraction, and the piano is lifted. When a feather is lifted, a limited number of motor units are triggered. Different muscles have a different percentage of motor end units and a different ratio of fibers assigned to each. The muscles of the eye and hand need to make delicate and refined movements. The gluteus maximus is a grunting labor force, focusing on the large jobs of running and jumping. The motor units in the muscles of the eye have fewer fibers assigned to them than the motor units in the gluteus maximus. The eye can make delicate moves and the butt cannot. Each is suited to its inherent role within the body.

Dancers become increasingly effortless as they progress in their training. They are learning to have more neurological control over their motor end units, which is possible as each fiber in the muscle becomes stronger. A muscle is stronger when each of the fibers within a motor unit is strong. Whereas a beginner needs to trigger many motor units to get the job done, an advanced dancer triggers one, because each fiber in the unit is strong and capable. This allows the other motor units to rest, refreshed for the next task.

Watching swimmers doing sprints is an excellent metaphor for this phenomenon. During sprints, swimmers are given a certain amount of time to reach the end of the pool, and then the gun goes off again. The good swimmers are fast and have more time to rest before the next sprint. The less-trained swimmer is slower, has less time to rest, and ends up exhausted. A conditioned dancer has built up reserves in the muscle fibers that can be called into play for accent or power. Refined, subtle actions take the place of brute force—effortlessness and grace are the result. It is useless to ask a beginner to replicate the precision of a professional.

Comments are better spent on gross alignment issues, not on subtleties. It will come together in time.

Isotonic and Isometric

A muscle's strength is particular to *how* it has been strengthened (the specificity principle). Muscle contraction in a static position, working against resistance, is called isometric. Isometric exercises build strength of a particular muscle in whatever position it does the work, but the muscle is weak in any other position or movement. (Weightlifters are not known for their dancing abilities.) When the length of a muscle changes it is called an isotonic contraction. Isotonic exercises build strength over the full range of the muscle. In dance, there is constant interplay between the two: one joint stabilizes while another joint moves. Core muscles, such as the abdominal muscles, the hamstrings, and the back extensors, need a heavy dose of isometric (nonmoving) exercises for stabilization. A ballet barre is excellent for trunk stabilization. But there are few exercises that specifically address isotonic strength of the abdominal muscles in a ballet barre. (Even the port de bras is primarily for the back extensors.) So the core muscles work isometrically, and get strong in a specific range, but a static spine will result if those muscles are not worked isotonically. A ballet teacher would be wise to add an isotonic strength exercise (a sit-up would suffice) prior to or within the daily class. Speaking very generically, modern classes tend to move so much that they don't provide the stillness necessary to practice isometric holding patterns; students lack the core strength to stabilize and so extensions and jumps suffer. A teacher who emphasizes movement would serve the class well by building slow adagio sequences or floor work, isometrically strengthening the core.

Concentric and Eccentric

Any time a muscle moves it is either lengthening or shortening. If it is shortening and doing the work (lifting a leg) it is called a concentric contraction. If it is lengthening and doing the work (letting the leg down) it is called an eccentric contraction. How can a muscle lengthen and still do the work? Imagine hoisting a pail of water up to a third floor with a rope. On the way up, the distance between you and the pail is shortening and you are working to get it up. On the way down, the distance between you and the pail is getting longer and you are still working to break its fall. If you simply let go, the pail would fall to the ground.

Let's look at the spine rolling up. The action is extension. Gravity would make the spine flex, so the extensors of the spine are shortening as they roll the spine upward. The extensors also work as the body rolls downward; they control the fall as they lengthen. This is called an eccentric contraction.

Reaching the Intrinsic Muscles

Dance teachers argue about the role of the butt, otherwise known as the gluteus maximus. Some teachers dictate, "Squeeze the butt; show me the dimple." Other teachers cajole students to "let the butt go, let it all hang out." Which is correct? What is a teacher supposed to do? The answer is both are right, depending on the stage of learning. The body will get support from wherever it needs it, but as

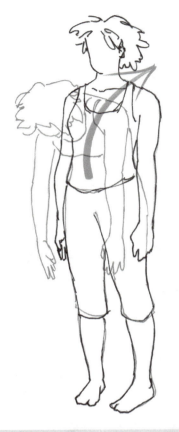

Rolling up—A concentric contraction of the back extensors.

Rolling down—An eccentric contraction of the back extensors.

students develop strength, they no longer need all the muscles to do everything. The muscles become more efficient, thus changing how we look at it.

Let's begin with an analysis of the role of the gluteus maximus on the supporting leg. Much of a dancer's time is spent standing on a straight, turned-out leg. The role of the supporting hip joint is one of maintaining lateral rotation, extension, and abduction. As gravity or resistance acts on the supporting leg, the hip joint tends to medially rotate, flex, and adduct. Therefore the hip is in an isometric contraction of lateral rotation, extension, and abduction. The gluteus maximus is a major player in each one of these actions; its role is to laterally rotate, extend, and abduct. Therefore the conclusion must be to squeeze the butt; it has to work while standing. But wait—there is more to the story.

As one peers into a body in a cadaver lab, its complexity is elegantly apparent. Like phyllo dough in baklava, there are layers upon layers of muscles, a web of backup and support teams. The superficial muscles lie on top. Most familiar to the eye and to the touch, there tends to be more awareness of this outer layer. But who are the quieter backup teams? One backup team is the six deep rotators that lie underneath the gluteus. Closest to the bone, they do their job without a lot of attention. But because their only job is to rotate, they do it efficiently. In terms of extension, once again there is a backup team; the hamstrings also extend the leg. The hamstrings are thought to be weaker players in the action of extension because they also flex the knee, but when dancers stand on a straight leg, they can put all

Layers of muscle.

their attention toward the hip. Finally, lying underneath the gluteus maximus are the gluteus medius and minimus, whose sole job is to abduct the hip. So it is possible to stand on one leg while liberating the butt from its time-honored position of duty. The "let it all hang out" group wins. But wait, there is yet another chapter to the story.

A beginner needs to use everything because no one muscle is strong enough to accomplish the task. So squeezing the butt and pulling in the belly are not all together bad instructions for beginners. It is a way to begin. But as the student progresses, things change. After years of activating the butt, it is now time to see if it is possible to let it go and trust the smaller intrinsic muscles. Knowing when a student is ready for the change is key. If they let go too soon, they will flail and never develop the strength necessary. If they never let go, they will overkill every movement and eventually become injured. The key lies in the breath. When students are breathing deeply, they are probably ready to progress to the next stage. The butt takes a sigh of relief after all those hard years of work.

Another issue being discussed in Pilates is the principle of the neutral spine when lying supine on the floor. With the legs bent and feet resting on the floor, the spine can either honor its lumbar curve (neutral spine), or the lower back can reach for the floor, i.e., the pelvis can tuck under to accomplish a flat lower back. (Note that because there are significant individual differences in spinal structures, neutral spine does not always look the same from person to person). Functionally, neutral spine is preferable for the efficient functioning of the limbs, and students should understand this goal. But as beginners struggle through the rigors of manipulating a leg against gravity, they need to protect the lower back by engaging the abdominal muscles, and for a beginner without the subtle control of an advanced dancer, erring on the side of tucking is preferable. The command to keep the lower back working toward the floor reminds a beginner to use abdominal power. As the students become stronger and more flexible, they will have the subtle control to maintain a neutral spine.

The same is true while standing. Ultimately, when muscles are balanced and the pelvis is hanging in correct alignment, the abdominal muscles can relax in their postural duties and lavish more attention on diaphragmatic breathing. Watch the belly of a professional onstage—it expands and contracts fully with each breath. But this is the privilege of the professional, not the domain of a beginner.

Proprioceptive Neuromuscular Facilitation

Weight-training equipment takes a single-muscle approach; each machine is built to strengthen a specific muscle. Pulling in one direction or plane, the machine promises an enlarged biceps, a bulging deltoid, or six-pack abdominal muscles. Our weight-lifting Adonis looks great but goes out to play touch football and injures himself after an hour of play. Doctors call these jocks "weekend athletes." "Why am I injured?" they complain. "I work out every day." They are injured because muscles do not work as independent agents in a single direction but as cooperative teams that spiral and twist in space. Strengthening or stretching an individual muscle is appropriate for the dancer when there is an injury or a repatterning to be addressed, but in terms of neuromuscular patterning, another approach is particularly useful for dancers. The specificity principle enters once again.

Dr. Herman Kabat, a specialist in neurology, developed Proprioceptive Neuromuscular Facilitation (PNF). While PNF is a complex system physical therapists use for rehabilitation, the most relevant aspect for dancers is its approach to spatial patterning. Based on the belief that the brain does not register individual muscle actions but rather thinks in terms of larger movement patterning, Kabat began to explore spiraling patterns. His ideas are explained in *Proprioceptive Neuromuscular Facilitation: Patterns and Techniques*, "The mass-movement patterns of facilitation are spiral and diagonal in character and closely resemble the movements used in sports and in work activities. The spiral and diagonal character is in keeping with the spiral and rotational characteristics of the skeletal system of bones and joints and the ligamentous structures. This type of motion is also in harmony with the topographical alignment of the muscles from origin to insertion and with the structural characteristics of the individual muscles." (Voss, Ionta, and Myers 1985, 1) Rarely running in straight lines, the muscles attach to the skeleton in a beautiful web of diagonals. PNF patterning utilizes all three planes: flexion/extension (movement of the joints forward and back or in the sagittal plane), adduction/abduction (movement side to side on the lateral plane), and medial/lateral rotation (rotation in the transverse plane). This sounds complex, but PNF simply utilizes diagonal patterns with rotation that can be done in the limbs or the spine.

The diagonal patterns of PNF.

Muscles are best strengthened or stretched when working on all three dimensions of movement. Voss, Ionta, and Myers continue, "The spiral and diagonal patterns of facilitation provide for an optimal contraction of the major muscle components. A pattern of motion that is optimal for a specific 'chain' of muscles allows these muscles to contract from their complete lengthened state to their completely shortened state, when the pattern is performed through the full range of motion." (Voss, Ionta, and Myers 1985, 4) Physical therapists work with their patients in these diagonal patterns, restoring proper functioning of muscle patterning. Diagonal, spiraling patterns are fundamental to movement. Conscious manipulations of diagonal patterns with rotation can facilitate the full range of muscle strength and stretch. Gyrotonics, a weight-training method, strengthens the muscle through three-dimensional space. Rudolf Laban understood this principle; the glorious movement scales performed within the Icosahedron reflect it. Irene Dowd has incorporated many of these ideas into her integrative "Spirals" series. "Spirals" is now available on videotape through The National Ballet School in Toronto, Canada. For more information on PNF, read *Proprioceptive Neuromuscular Facilitation: Patterns and Techniques* by Voss, Ionta, and Myers or *Science of Flexibility* by Michael J. Alter, or watch for news in the *Journal of Dance Medicine & Science*.

FLEXIBILITY

There is currently a lot of research being conducted on the complex subject of flexibility. Much of our current knowledge about this subject is intuitive—we have observed what works. As scientists learn more about this fascinating subject, dancers will greatly benefit.

The authors of "Warm-Up: A Brief Review" describe flexibility for a dancer: "Flexibility can be defined as the ability to move a joint through the required range of motion without undue stress to the involved musculotendinous units." (Volianitis, Koutedakis, and Carson 2001, 77) In dance, the muscle must be able to move through a large range of activities, but as Sally Fitt says, "There is an inverse relationship between mobility and stability. As mobility increases, stability decreases and vice versa." (Fitt 1996, 19) They are indeed interdependent. Balance between strength and flexibility is key to efficient movement patterning in well-trained dancers and is particularly important for the prevention of injuries. A teacher constantly balances the amount of stretches and strength exercises in a dance class. Sometimes these become one, which a further study of flexibility will illuminate. But first, when mobility is the goal, there are two things to consider—alignment and speed.

Alignment in a Stretch

Although we think in terms of lengthening a muscle, a muscle doesn't really get longer. The goal is to build a better rubber band. Elasticity is desired in the muscle, not the joint. So the first and most critical skill developed in flexibility training is alignment. Alignment is crucial when stretching; the joint needs to be securely "fastened" in order to stretch the muscle and keep the joint tissue from being torn. Donna Farhi, a yoga expert, speaks about alignment in *Yoga Mind, Body & Spirit: A Return to Wholeness*. "The first state of alignment is like laying down a railway track, aligning each segment of the track with the next so the train can run in a smooth path. The second step of engaging the alignment involves running force through the body." She goes on to explain, "As force flows along the bones and across the joint spaces positioned through your conscious directional intent, the muscles begin to follow suit, streaming parallel to the bones like the current of wind that follows after a train has run down the tracks." (Farhi 2000, 50) A teacher facilitates good stretching practices by making students critically aware of alignment— the hips level in a second stretch, knees over toes in a lunge—and then watches for the wind. When the alignment is right the energy will move through the structure.

The energy lines of a stretch.

Speed and Flexibility

Training in dance must incorporate methods to acquire speed as well as length. In *Science of Flexibility*, Michael Alter says there are three stretches related to speed: static, ballistic, and dynamic. Static is a stretch with "no emphasis on speed." Ballistic flexibility is usually associated with "bobbing, bouncing, rebounding, and rhythmic motion." Dynamic flexibility is the ability of muscle to perform in slow or fast actions; some call this *functional* flexibility. "Obviously, most athletic events involve dynamic flexibility. Here too, the type of flexibility is specific to the type of movement (i.e., its speed and angle) of a given discipline and thus not necessarily related to just ROM (range of movement)." (Alter 1996, 3) Dance teachers must incorporate all three methods for full integration of flexibility.

Ballistic Flexibility

In the 1960s and 1970s there were contentious debates about bouncing warm-ups. Graham, Cunningham, Erick Hawkins, and Alwin Nikolais all began class with a series of bounces. Certain camps declared these bouncing exercises bad for the body. Understanding principles of kinesiology shed light on this debate. Let's look at the *stretch reflex,* a reflex built into the hard drive of the muscle.

The stretch reflex is really not a stretch at all, but something that inhibits stretch. It protects the muscle from too much stretch. Each muscle has *muscle spindles* — nerve cells in the shape of long coils. Muscle spindles wrap around specific muscle fibers within each muscle. Whenever the muscle gets stretched, the spindle gets pulled and informs the central nervous system that the muscle is being stretched. The central nervous system responds by telling the muscle to contract so that it does not tear. Therefore, whenever a muscle stretches, there is a natural reaction of that muscle to contract. The stretch reflex facilitates a jump. Every time the calf (gastrocnemius) stretches, it has a reflexive reaction to contract. A stretch preceding a contraction creates a more powerful contraction.

Bouncing awakens the natural and powerful coil inherent in the muscles, creating the rebounding and springing actions so necessary in dancing. Nijinsky had a powerful set of stretch reflexes. Bouncing is not bad; it is simply misunderstood. It does not further increase flexibility, but it does assist a coiling action. If increased range is the intention, a slow, weighted stretch is a better choice. But done at moderate tempo, in a small range with gentle force, bouncing is an excellent warm-up for the muscles. It is only damaging when a cold body is forced to bounce hard and fast. Teachers of the Horton technique must make sure the body is warm before attempting the hard and fast ballistic stretches that are characteristic of the style. Graham, Hawkins, Cunningham, and Nikolais can rest in peace.

Static Flexibility: Passive and Active

In order to increase flexibility, the stretch reflex must be tricked. Stretching slowly enough with passive weight gets "under the doorway," so to speak, of the stretch reflex before it fires off. Long, slow stretches bypass the natural instinct of the muscle to contract, and allow the muscle to stretch. The dance teacher should keep the class in a stretch as long as possible and watch the comfort level of the students. Instruct students to listen to their own bodies and exit the stretch at any time. If the goal is long-term changes in the range of motion, the stretch must be engaged for at least 20-30 seconds. This type of stretch should not be performed as part of the beginning warm-up; consider it a deep internal stretch, which should be done after the muscle is warm. Present a long, sustained stretch right after something very energetic. Ballet technique usually incorporates a deep stretch after the barre, when the body is warm. A deep stretch is also a very effective cool-down at the end of class as long as students have the opportunity to gently gather the body back together before exiting class. A static stretch can be done either passively or actively.

A *passive* static stretch is a dance with gravity. Standing on two legs and hanging over from the hip sockets is a passive stretch for the hamstrings, if the hands reach the floor. The weight of the upper body provides traction as gravity pulls the body downward. Yielding to gravity, the muscles let go. An *active* static stretch uses the antagonist muscle to aid the stretch. Let's go back to the same stretch. As the body hangs over, the target muscles to stretch are the flexors of the knee and extensors of the hip (hamstrings and gluteus maximus). The antagonist, or opposite, muscles are the knee extensors and hip flexors (quadriceps, iliopsoas, pectineus). Actively engaging the quadriceps, iliopsoas, and pectineus pulls the hamstring and gluteus maximus to new lengths, far beyond what gravity would do by itself. In yoga, students are instructed to lift the kneecaps, creating an active stretch and stabilizing balance. Both passive and active stretches are good; they serve different needs. Passive stretches help students learn how to yield, breathe, and surrender. Active stretches are helpful when it is time to move to another level of flexibility. Alternating the two is particularly effective. Hanging over, begin with the passive phase and follow it with an active phase. Active, static stretching is based on another scientific principle particularly useful to dance teachers called reciprocal inhibition.

The muscles are organized in pairs called agonist and antagonist. These muscles work as a synergistic team. Whenever a flexor muscle contracts (the muscle responsible for movement is the agonist) its opposite muscle (the antagonist) relaxes and goes into a stretch. This cooperative relationship is called *reciprocal innervation*. Even more curious is the following aspect of their relationship. Explained very simply, whenever a muscle contracts, it sends chemical messages to its antagonist (the opposite muscle) to relax because it does not want the extra burden of fighting its antagonist. The longer and harder the contraction, the more inhibiting the messages. For instance, while the quadriceps (the thigh muscles) are in maximum contraction, a chemical message is being sent to the hamstrings to *relax*. Therefore,

A reciprocal stretch—the contraction phase.

A reciprocal stretch—the stretch phase.

after a hard or long contraction of the quadriceps, it is ideal to stretch the hamstrings because they have collected chemical messages to inhibit a contraction. This is called *reciprocal inhibition*. Taking advantage of the reciprocal inhibition pattern would mean contracting an agonist prior to stretching an antagonist. For instance, an exercise strengthening the abdominal muscles would precede a stretch of the back extensors, or holding an arabesque would precede a stretch for the hip flexors (iliopsoas, rectus femoris, pectineus) or a relevé (contraction of the calf—gastrocnemius) would precede a stretch of the foot (dorsiflexors of the ankle joint).

While recent studies are still looking into the exact benefits of reciprocal inhibition, it has remained an effective tool in flexibility and strength training. The PNF system uses this theory in structuring and organizing strength and flexibility sequences. The Ashtanga yoga series makes sense in this light as well; almost every stretch is set up with a contraction by the agonist, thus making the body instinctively ready for the next exercise. The yogis of yesteryear did not know about reciprocal inhibition, but they listened to their bodies. The founders of the great techniques were above all, brilliant observers of the body. Scientific research confirms many of their wise choices.

> *The founders of the great techniques were above all, brilliant observers. Scientific research confirms many of their wise choices.*

Dynamic (Functional) Flexibility

Dynamic flexibility is the ability of the muscle to function within the tasks to be performed. It is interesting to watch yoga experts take a dance class. While they are at a distinct advantage because of their flexibility, they do not have the necessary speed for a grand battement or grand jeté, nor do they have the power for a jump. Indeed, they will progress much faster than a student with no background, but they will need to practice the skills of dance in order to custom tailor their flexibility. For instance, a great preparation for a grand jeté is a grand battement both forward and back. The fast snap of the leg with rotation prepares the muscle for the speed and the form necessary to perform the grand jeté. Endless hours of stretching the hamstrings in a passive stretch will help develop length, but ultimately the body needs to practice the skill itself. The aesthetic goals of dancing are not counter to the goals of conditioning. Alter speaks about the importance of the aesthetic aspect of flexibility. "It is flexibility that allows the individual to create an appearance of ease, smoothness of movement, graceful coordination, self-control, and total freedom." (Alter 1996, 293)

There are also biomechanical aspects to be considered. Biomechanics is the study of the

A *grand jeté.*

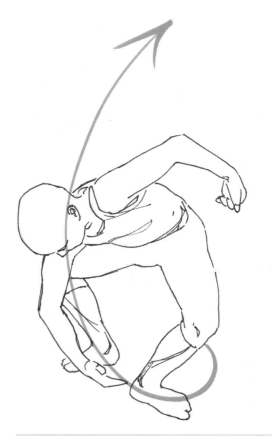

A wind-up plié.

A jump.

forces acting upon the body and the way the body responds to those forces. Alter explains, "For example, in tennis an increased range of motion allows one to apply forces over greater distances and longer periods of time." (Alter 1996, 294)

A wind-up really works. A dancer kinesthetically knows that a grand battement forward is immensely easier and more powerful when the working leg starts in a fourth-position lunge rather than first position. The hip flexors (iliopsoas and rectus femoris) are in a lengthened state, thus providing a more powerful contraction. Timing between the wind-up and the contraction is critical—if too much time lapses, the stored elastic energy turns into heat. A teacher must pay attention not only to form, but rhythm as well. And, of course, there is the point of no return. If a muscle is stretched to its limit, the wind-up fizzles. The splits rarely rebound back into the air.

In summary, a dance teacher must encourage efficient alignment practices and incorporate three forms of flexibility into class:

1. Ballistic stretches should be done in moderate tempi for warm-up and only at more extreme tempi when the body is warm. These stretches activate the powerful elastic coils necessary for movement.

2. Both passive and active static stretches are necessary for developing more range of motion. Deep stretches should be done when the body is thoroughly warm, either during the middle of class or at the end in a cool-down.

3. Dynamic flexibility is developed by practicing the skills of dancing—jumping, falls into the floor, leaping. These should be practiced in a range of speeds and forms.

Incorporating these forms into a sequence of exercises will be discussed further in chapter 7.

MUSCULAR ENDURANCE

Muscular endurance is different than muscular strength. Muscular endurance is the ability of the muscle to work *over time,* whereas muscular strength is its ability to exert tension against resistance. Increased repetitions over a period of time increase muscular endurance. Repetition is crucial to building muscular endurance, but repetition is boring, so dancers tend to stop at the magic number eight. If a muscle stops before it has reached capacity, it does not get stronger. How many repetitions are necessary? Sally Fitt says that listening is crucial. "When a muscle has been contracted over a period of time, it begins to produce a burning sensation. Five repetitions past the onset of the 'burnies' is an effective rule of thumb for increasing muscular endurance." (Fitt 1996, 395) Conversely, if students are asked to repeat far beyond the 'burnies,' the muscle will eventually fatigue and other muscles will take over, distorting alignment. Thus, there is a small window of opportunity. This is particularly difficult in a dance class, where the windows may be slightly different for each student. A teacher can set a median—for instance, two sets of jumps—and allow students to find their range within the class parameters. This is appropriate if students have been trained to recognize their endurance limits.

Muscular endurance is possible to integrate into the ongoing technique class because students are consistently present. In professional or community classes this is nearly impossible. Look at the overall length of time spent with students: maybe three weeks, maybe a year. Too often teachers go into the first day of class giving the same amount of jumps as the last day. During a six-week course, the first week should be limited to eight jumps in place. Then it is possible to increase the number of jumps gradually. By the end of the course, students should be executing three to four times as many jumps. This same principle can be applied to tendus, pliés, or other exercises. If endurance is impossible to attain within the class, advise students to perform a series of repetitive exercises with very light weights or elastic bands outside of class. Dancers should not work with heavy weights since this will build bulk, destroying the delicate mobility/stability ratio.

CARDIORESPIRATORY ENDURANCE

"Cardiorespiratory endurance is the ability to continue aerobic activity over a period of time." (Fitt 1996, 395) In order to condition the heart, the target heart rate must be maintained for at least 20-30 minutes. (Target heart rate charts can be found in *Dance Kinesiology* and on various workout sites on the Internet.) Dancers fare least well in cardiorespiratory endurance. Technique classes and rehearsals are not designed to keep the heart rate up for 20 minutes or more. We stop and analyze, correct and discuss technical issues. Rehearsals are usually spent preparing a work rather than running all the works in the show. Many times, the first run of the entire concert is during tech week. Choreographers and teachers need to be aware that dancers tend to injure themselves around performance time largely because of weak cardiovascular systems. Choreographers can help ensure that the show goes on by running the full repertory at least a month ahead of a concert or instructing their dancers to participate in outside aerobic work.

It is possible to incorporate aerobic work into technique class. African classes do an extraordinary job developing cardiorespiratory endurance. The beat begins and it does not stop. This traditional training builds both muscular and cardiorespiratory endurance. African classes incorporate complexities of dance through internal rhythmic patterning. The legs keep going while a new rhythmic pattern for the arms is added, while another pattern is added for the head. All of this is learned and incorporated into the movement without stopping. Following the model of African classes, teachers can build long patterns that are rehearsed over and over at the end of class without stopping. Or, if the students know a set of warm-up exercises, they can move through the series without stopping. Building muscular and cardiovascular endurance dwells on repetition, which is admittedly boring. But there is another side to boredom—a meditative trance that is centering. Most ancient dance forms were designed to build rejuvenating energy. The nonstop bouncing of aerobics and raves are contemporary ways of returning to the ecstasy of the ancients.

NEW DANCE CURRICULA

Many dance educators are rethinking curricula in dance programs, taking innovative steps to incorporate the best of scientific knowledge. At the University of Utah, kinesiologist Sally Fitt began a conditioning program that includes a physical assessment of new students and tailors conditioning techniques to the dancers. Irene Dowd has been working closely with the National Ballet School in Canada, integrating conditioning practices into the training process.

Dance teachers and dancers need to be informed about anatomy and kinesiology as well. Analytical knowledge coupled with inquisitive observation fosters complete truths, empowering both dancer and teacher to assess, analyze, and create individualized paths toward excellence. As John Wilson, a professor at the University of Arizona, says, ". . . the student advances toward becoming his own textbook, laboratory, and teacher." (Wilson 1999, 162) Dance curricula of the future should include a careful blend of ethnic forms, somatic practices, and conditioning programs as supplements to dance training, along with adequate study in anatomy and kinesiology. Given the limitations of resources and time, imagination will be necessary to accomplish the task, but it can be done. Students will benefit from learning cultural styles and contemporary conditioning practices while learning to address their individual needs. Most important, without the sole burden of conditioning, technique classes will have the freedom to dwell on artistry. The athletes of God will run faster, more elegantly, and further into the future than ever imagined possible.

Investigations

1. In each of the following assignments answer the following questions: Which joint should be targeted? Which muscles? Why? Which exercises would strengthen or stretch the appropriate muscles? At what point in the class would you present these exercises?

   ► You want to build better jumps. How would you prepare the foot, ankle, knee, and spine?

- ► You've observed that students have extreme hyperextension in the lower back.
- ► You want to prepare students for leg extension work: front, side, and back.
- ► You have observed that students have very limited range in their hip sockets. Invent seven different stretches that target all the muscles in the hip.
- ► Students are having trouble moving to and from the floor.
- ► Students are performing in a piece with complex partnering and they are injuring their backs and shoulders.

2. Build an exercise targeting specific muscles for strength. Create a series of exercises that increases the weight or resistance. For instance, if abdominal muscles are selected, lifting one leg is easier than lifting two while lying on the back. Build a progression for beginners to advanced dancers.

3. Build an isometric (static) and isotonic (moving) strength exercise for the flexors of the spine (abdominal muscles) and the extensors of the spine (erector spinae). To be most effective, situate the body so that the chosen muscle has to work against gravity. For instance, the abdominal muscles have to work hardest when you are lying on the back and the extensors of the spine have to work the hardest when you are lying on the belly.

4. Practice analyzing movements, and discern the role of the muscles in concentric and eccentric contractions.

5. Go to a cadaver lab, or work on an anatomical CD-ROM. Remove layers of muscles. Study those closest to the bone.

6. Create three types of stretches and incorporate them into a dance sequence.
- ► Create a ballistic stretch in the spine, legs, and arms that is suitable for warm-up (performed at moderate tempo, with light energy, and in medium range). Encourage the elasticity of the stretch reflex.
- ► Create passive and active static stretches for spine and hip joints. These should be placed in the class when students are thoroughly warm.
- ► Create a logical series of stretches for specific dance movements such as a grand jeté. Start with the end goal and build from there. For instance: If the end goal is a grand jeté, both hip flexors and hip extensors need flexibility. Begin with a gentle ballistic stretch for hamstrings (hang over) and hip flexors (a lunge). When the students are warm, do the same stretches in a passive and active static stretch. Follow with grand battements. At the end of the class, ask students to perform a grand jeté.

7. Perform a series of repetitive movements. How many does it take before your body reaches the "burnies"? Observe how long it is before beginners or advanced students reach the same place.

8. Plan a six-week course and address one area to target for muscular endurance. For instance, for jumps, increase the number each week.

In-Class Investigations

1. Observe and advise each student. In your discussion and analysis consider the following:
- ► Determine conditioning strengths and weaknesses (strength, flexibility, endurance, cardiovascular).

- ► Target specific joints. Are there previous injuries or current pain or discomfort? What joints are locked when the student moves?
- ► What is the student's history of movement training? Are they currently practicing any other movement or sport?
- ► What role does their personality play? Are they an overachiever? Do they tend to do what they are good at? Are they in need of discipline?

2. Look at the balance within the dance curriculum where you teach. Are ethnic forms offered—African, tai chi chuan, classical Indian forms, flamenco? Are conditioning classes offered—yoga, Pilates, Gyrotonics, weight training? Are somatic practices offered—Alexander, Bartenieff Fundamentals, Feldenkrais, Body-Mind Centering? Are anatomy and kinesiology classes offered? If not, start advocating change.

Reflection: SURRENDER

Letting go of clenched jaws, determined eyes and other unnecessary frills is all part of the effort that begets effortlessness.

Erika Dufour, photographer; Suet May Ho, dancer.

I am stuck in a traffic jam returning from Dick's House of Magic when I realize I need to let go of the balloons. Dick is the premier expert on balloons, having engineered the balloon drop for the Republican Convention. He explained every detail of the balloon drop in a four-hour session. "One million balloons are blown up not more than one week ahead of time. See, they lose their air at a compression rate of . . . "

I interrupt him. "Fascinating, but I want to know whether you can create an environmental set for a dance. I want hundreds of balloons covering the stage and rising slowly throughout the piece." (I've always had a deep fear of a blank stage).

"Well, you've come to the right person; I've created all kinds of sets for strippers to burst out of."

I see where he is going. "No, this isn't that type of dance; this is a set for contemporary dance. Are you familiar with contemporary dance?"

He belts out one of those belly laughs filled with sexual innuendo. "Oh yeah, baby—I've seen the dolls gyrate right in front of the camera. I assure you I wasn't born yesterday. You should see what I do with silver Mylar balloons."

Abandoning any attempt to explain contemporary dance, I pursue the image. "I need plain white balloons rising slowly from the floor to the ceiling—about 30 feet—over 30 minutes."

"Oh, so you need a little magic, huh? Well that will cost you, sister. You're gonna need lots of equipment and yours truly will need to be there to orchestrate the whole thing. You got any naked girls in your act?"

The guy in the car behind me is lying on his horn. I fill my lungs from a tank of helium Dick gave me and shout in a high, squeaky voice, "Up yours, partner." I reflect on magic and how quickly it turns to baggage. Balloons were going to be much too heavy. I call Dick on my cell phone and tell him in a low, whispering, sexual voice that he will have to get his glimpse of nude dancers at the local strip club. I am going to be naked enough.

chapter 6

Shaping Phrases

D A N C I N G

*C*ombination dancer the over during turtle a the tripped leap. Our minds immediately begin to unscramble the coded message in this random series of words to discern meaning, even though it begs us to question what the turtle was doing in the studio. A dance phrase is comparable to a sentence in language. In the classic book *Dance: A Creative Art Experience,* Margaret H'Doubler speaks about stringing movement together to create a phrase. "Organization demands a *sequence* of the movements employed—an order in which one movement follows another. It is more than a mere arrangement. A single movement is potentially expressive in itself, but, unless placed in juxtaposition to other movements that form a larger expressive unit or phrase, it is not significantly expressive—just as a single note cannot, by itself, be a melody. It is this contiguity, this necessary closeness, of one movement to another that distinguishes sequence from arrangement." (H'Doubler 1968, 141) Nothing furthers the skills of dancing more than dancing itself, so teachers compose movement phrases for their eager students. But more than an arrangement of movements, these phrases must provide an opportunity for dancers to hone rhythmic skills, spatial intent, and flow of energy. Covered in this chapter is the art of composing movement phrases for technique class—the dance.

BUILDING PHRASES

It may be helpful to begin by defining the difference between a dance phrase and what dancers love to call the *combo,* or movement combination (known as the *routine* in jazz lexicon). While dance phrases are comparable to a sentence, a dance combination is comparable to a paragraph. Longer paragraph-like combinations in dance training build endurance, focus, and concentration, which are critical to performance skills. Concise phrases dominate the warm-up, although run-on sentences do exist in the classroom. Crucial differences exist between composing movement, whether phrases or combinations, for choreographic purposes and for dance training.

Much of the difference lies in the intent of the instructor. A phrase created for class should be designed to teach the skills of dancing, not to fulfill the choreographic ambitions of the creator. Teachers who simultaneously choreograph and teach often compose similar phrases for both class and rehearsal, saving time and energy for the teacher or dancemaker. If the movement is specifically shaped to stimulate learning, an exciting crossover between choreography and technique takes place; but the intention in the classroom must be clear—it is to train dancers. If not, the students merely serve as unpaid servants. Students learn from dancing well-structured, inventive movement material, so learning from the masters can be educational. Ideally this is handled in a repertory class; but if resources don't allow for this type of class, it is possible to integrate repertory into the daily class as long as the focus remains on teaching the student about rhythm, line, form, and intent.

Another crucial difference dominates the classroom. Choreography values imaginative choices, but technique is based on logical organization of movement, particularly in warm-up phrases. Architectural design of the body, spatial intent, use of energy, and rhythmic structures all must be considered when composing phrases, because they provide consistency and order. Does the phrase address every plane of the body? Has every joint been warmed up? Has the warm-up engaged every muscle? Does the phrase segue from the right to the left side? Is it possible to reverse a phrase, such as reversing from en dehors to en dedans? Is the rhythm repeatable? The great master of space and time, Merce Cunningham, designed rigorously logical phrases, which are deeply satisfying to do.

Phrases and combinations should highlight the essence of technique. The frills can be added later in the choreography studio. Toshikatsu Endo, an installation artist from Japan, speaks about the removal of artifices. "From minimal art I learned about removing superfluous elements. The removal of unnecessary elements makes a given form more powerful. The idea of removing everything is also part of Zen thought. Zen Buddhist concepts permeate Japanese culture, and Zen Buddhism has had a significant influence on my ideas. After everything is removed, only the absolute remains. This principle is significant on the level of technique as well as providing a method for refining various concepts." (Fox 1990, 49)

SPATIAL INTENT

We build dance phrases by returning to the movement concept or principle being taught. Spatial concepts might include size, range, directions, floor patterns, level, focus, and internal or external space of the body. If the movement principle is directions, the teacher might build a series of warm-up phrases containing a logical system of direction changes (four diagonals and four cardinal directions), followed by a carefully crafted combination chock full of unusual direction changes. If a teacher selects size as a movement principle, a phrase or combination might incor-

Spatial intent.

porate very big to very small movement. Exquisite shaping of space teaches students the power of space, both as a technical skill and as a potential tool in dancemaking.

Frank Lloyd Wright understood the emotional power of space. In his home and studio in Oak Park, Illinois, he built a small, enclosed hallway leading into a child's playroom. After burrowing through a claustrophobic hallway, one enters a playroom exploding with light and height. Wright wanted the children (and adults) to feel euphoric upon entering. The spaces where class is planned and presented will inevitably shape the spatial design of the movement material.

Studio Space

Rather than become frustrated by the drawbacks of the not-so-ideal studio, teachers can create phrases and combinations that utilize the studio's shortcomings. Long hallway-like studios beg for creative spatial designs because they force everyone into two-dimensional thinking and being. Zigzag patterns that move everyone unevenly through the space break up the space and provide traffic control. Using rectangular floor patterns along the outskirts of the room allows students the satisfaction of performing more than one run-run-leap. A large, square room is ideal for star patterns (dancers moving in and out of the center from each corner) or long diagonal sweeps through the space. A large space enables the teacher to design raw surges through the space; a small space invites intimacy. Phrases designed for postage-stamp studios may highlight delicate and subtle articulations.

Movement Initiation

When creating phrases, a dance teacher must analyze the source of movement initiation. Does it begin with a reach of the hand, a push from the heel, or a contraction at center? In anatomy, two terms convey relationships between the center and the periphery of the body. *Distal* means farther away from the center. *Proximal* means closer to the center. While making any phrase, analyze whether the foot or the hip joint is beginning the movement. Does an arch begin in the center or from a reach of the head? Do the shoulders or the eyes initiate the direction change? This simple quest often leads a teacher to define his roots and personal style. If both the movement and the teacher's directives are clear, students learn to transcend mere mimicry.

ENERGY

Although concepts of space are fairly universal in the dance world, concepts of energy vary greatly, depending on a teacher's roots. Laban defines energy in terms of effort. Under the rubric of energy, teachers stemming from Mary Wigman traditions include qualities of movement such as percussive, sustained, pulsing, or vibratory. Emotional intent is often linked to energy, perhaps because emotions most clearly define a state of energy. Students must learn how to shape energy to be on the beat, to mold a satisfying phrase, or to give movement emotional or dynamic intent.

Because there are such divergent ways of speaking about energy and because it is nearly impossible to address the energy of a movement phrase on a piece of paper, I will turn to a distinguished writer for help. Listen to the energy of this writing by Zora Neale Hurston in her novel *Their Eyes Were Watching God*.

> *The years took all the fight out of Janie's face. For a while she thought it was gone from her soul. No matter what Jody did, she said nothing. She had learned how to talk some and leave some. She was a rut in the road. Plenty of life beneath the surface, but it was kept beaten down by the wheels. Sometimes she stuck out into the future, imagining her life different from what it was. But mostly she lived between her hat and her heels, with her emotional disturbances like shade patterns in the woods—come and gone with the sun. (Hurston 1937, 72)*

This is clearly a sequence, as H'Doubler would say, not a mere arrangement. The short no-nonsense sentences and the lethargy of the words are strung together to elicit the stuck quality of the character.

Now feel the difference in energy in another passage by Hurston:

Raw energy.

> *Another thing, Joe Starks hadn't been dead but nine months and here she goes sashaying off to a picnic in pink linen. Done quit attending church, like she used to. Gone off to Sanford in a car with Tea Cake and her all dressed in blue! It was a shame. Done took to high-heel slippers and a ten-dollar hat! Looking like some young girl, always in blue because Tea Cake told her to wear it. Poor Joe Starks. Bet he turns over in his grave every day. (Hurston 1937, 105)*

The energy of her indignation flies off the page through the use of rhythm and vernacular. Whether built with high or low energy, textural dynamics, or dramatic intent, dance phrases teach dancers how to regulate energy, a skill vital to fulfilling the artistry of choreography. While planning class, vary your own energy. Sometimes it is helpful to compose phrases while listening to the sounds of silence, or while playing a variety of music, thus changing your state of being.

MUSICALITY AND RHYTHM

Awed by a stunning performance, an audience member describes the dancing as exquisitely musical even though there was not one note of music played in the silent performance. So what makes a dancer *musical*? A musical dancer is able to shape a movement phrase, giving it breath, weight, meaning, and expressiveness. Creating compelling logic yet refreshing surprises, the dancer takes the viewer on a journey to unknown territory. A musical dancer contains within silence and movement an ever-aware presence of the passage of time.

> *Rhythm gives order to the chaos of time—while time can move forward and backward in Einstein's subatomic world, time moves forward in our everyday world and rhythm is its marker.*

Rhythm is a crucial element of musicality, ordering time events by setting up the expected and unexpected. Rhythm gives order to the chaos of time—while time can move forward and backward in Einstein's subatomic world, time moves forward in our everyday world and rhythm is its marker. In technique class, dance teachers shape movement and, most of the time, give it a rhythm. Movement patterns are given rhythms for two reasons. The first is functional: to keep everyone in unison, making it much easier to observe and correct movement. The second is to teach rhythmic skills, ultimately building a musical dancer.

The art of selecting movement and its correlating rhythms must honor the content of the movement as well as the body's interaction with gravity.

Gravity's Rhythm

Einstein said that gravity bends light, but it also shapes movement. Rhythm springing out of the weight of the human body as it moves and falls through space could be referred to as *gravity's rhythm*. Gravity's rhythm matches the weight of the falling body to the appropriate beat, subdivision of the beat, and tempo. Imagine a child on a swing. A three-beat measure gives one count each for a suspension, a fall, and a rebound. With the tempo set at the natural rate of speed for the falling body, a gravity rhythm would correlate to the movement and rebound out of it. The body swinging in space is circular, absorbing three beats to fulfill its circularity. A two-beat measure would not match a swing movement because it is angular in its construction. Gravity and movement dictate the choice of rhythms.

A dancer in gravity's rhythm.

All too often an arbitrary rhythm is imposed on the movement, creating static and unyielding phrases, choking the dancer, and prohibiting musicality. Beginning teachers try to stuff a movement phrase into 8 counts whether it belongs there or not. To find gravity's rhythm of movement, let the body move with weight in space. Make up the movement without counting. When the movement is fully in the body, begin singing its sound; it will have its own unique rhythm. Where is the end of the sentence? Where do you take a breath? This determines the phrase length. If the movement dictates a longer phrase, why not build a 9-, 10-, or 11-count phrase? A gravity rhythm teaches students to use their weight in conjunction with gravity. A 3-count swing phrase honors the weight of the falling body, and if falling is sought, the rhythm supports the skill. A gravity rhythm helps coordination skills, because it *feels* right to the mover. A gravity rhythm, if chosen correctly, allows a dancer to experience the inherent rhythm of the body moving in space.

Starting From Music or Language

Turn the tables: Start with rhythm, and then create the movement. Singing the five-phrase from Dave Brubeck's famous "Take Five," allow the body to dive, swoop, and balance, finding the unique qualities of a five-phrase. Consciously choose movement that pulls and pushes in a five. Rhythmic challenges might evolve from technical concerns. Perhaps students are having a hard time shifting weight; if so, design a movement pattern that shifts weight on the first beat of every phrase in a mixed meter. If students are having difficulty with shifting accents, create a phrase that copies the syncopated phrases in works such as *The Rite of Spring* by Igor Stravinsky. Listening to a variety of music before composing phrases builds new skills. Jazz music is rhythmically complex, teaching the body to honor syncopation not inherently natural to gravity. World music expands the movement palette.

Language is at the base of music, so using musical forms from different cultures challenges new body rhythms. Even counting in another language can elicit a different rhythm. The only duple between one and eight in the English language is se-ven. Counting in Spanish bounces: *uno, dos, tres, cuatro, cinco, seis, siete, ocho.* By creating a rhythmic construct to follow, the body has to figure out a response that might surprise, delight, and kick it out of old habits.

Abandoning Counts

Many contemporary dancemakers don't use counts. Should count structures be abandoned in the classroom as well? There are times when counting is appropriate and other times when it is not. Teaching without counts allows students to find internal flow. By listening to their breath, weight, and flow, dancers are able to coordinate movements in a deep, organic fashion. A student breathes buoyancy into her body to shape the phrase; the more the weight is released downward, the more satisfying the rebound. Uncounted phrases build ensemble skills as well. Without the crutch of counts, dancers find unison by listening to the noise of their weight hitting the ground, the rush of their breath expanding and contracting. They must abandon "rightness" for a subtler blending with their classmates. Many teachers in the Cunningham technique yell out "One!" and fly across the room and come back; announce "Two!" accompanied by 15 shapes with arms and legs flying; and by "Three!" a lengthy combination is complete. These patterns set up time markers, keeping the class obtusely together but allowing the body to organically sing the phrase between the beats. Not using counted *rhythms* is a powerful tool in the process of learning, but rhythm is instrumental in teaching other skills and should not be abandoned.

Challenge of Rhythm

Consciously manipulating gravity's rhythms, the teacher uses rhythm to challenge. Beginning dancers need to learn how to manage the natural speed of the body falling in space, and a good teacher can enhance this skill by providing clear gravity rhythms. However, advanced dancers need to play gravity's scales. Space, time, and energy are an equation. The quality of the movement, space, and time shift depending on the choice of beat, beat quality, beat division, and tempo. When selecting a beat and a tempo that is not natural to a leap, the dancer has to reach through space to control his weight or change the quality of the movement to accomplish landing on the correct beat. The student's job is to wrestle with the faster and slower tempi until accuracy is attained. Rhythm is a powerful tool teaching the connections between space and energy. Using a triple instead of a duple requires that the student use more reach to cover space. Heaviness is condemned as students hover in the air one more beat than is really comfortable, delighting in the airborne reach of their new helicopter-like selves. Emile Jaques-Dalcroze used to say that if a student was having trouble being on the beat, the problem was not *time*, it was use of space or energy. Expanding into space or using the right amount of energy might help the dancer to land on the beat. While watching the student struggling to find the beat, dwell less on rhythm and spend more time watching his use of space and energy.

Setting Tempi

Tempo is crucial not only to making a phrase flow but also to injury prevention. Galileo tells us that all bodies, whether a feather or a rock, fall at the same speed. However, the teacher's body has more power and strength than a wispy beginning student's. A skilled dancer powers herself into the air higher and has farther to fall than the beginner. Nijinsky's leap took more time because he flew higher, and therefore had farther to go to land. Beginning students will injure themselves if they try to do a leap at Nijinsky's tempo. When planning class, make adjustments to Nijinsky's gravity rhythms, knowing that students can't yet accomplish his slow flight. Once students begin working with the material, make critical adjustments. Increasing or decreasing the tempo challenges each new step.

Shifting Time

Rhythmic patterning seems to shift from the studio warm-up to the classroom setting. The phrase, which flowed in the planning studio while humming the bouncing rhythm of the theme song to *Mr. Ed*, now hungers for melodious flow of "Blue Moon." The students stand patiently or not so patiently, getting cold, as the teacher tries to figure out a new way to count the phrase. Within the class there develops a certain flow that is tailor made to the day, the temperature of the studio, or the energy of the students. Our bodies unconsciously slide into that rhythm, and the teacher must accommodate it. Locking into a beat just *because* is dangerous. It takes practice to adjust the rhythm quickly while everyone is watching, but it is a skill well worth learning.

Just beyond rhythmic accuracy lies artistry. Great jazz musicians speak about playing *around* the beat. They know how to be dead-on accurate, but they also know how to pull us to the edge, surprising and delighting us. Together the dancer and the phrasemaker ascertain gravity's rhythms and stretch us beyond the earth's pull, arresting one moment only to surprise us just before the expected fall. Teachers must train dancers who are capable of making these weighty and buoyant choices.

DEMONSTRATING

The teacher must not only make up a dance phrase but demonstrate its lilt and flow as well as a great jazz musician. Jennifer Homans writes about the artistry of Suzanne Farrell in delivering a dance phrase.

> *When Suzanne Farrell, one of Balanchine's greatest muses, threw herself into a phrase and wound her way to its end as if it were her kingdom to command, she made the music and dance live. Why? Because we watched her take chances and make choices in rigorously restricted frames of time. To pirouette now or a split second later? To accent a movement or pass through it? Each decision had consequences for the next step, for the other dancers onstage, for the shape of the role. Free will, choice, responsibility, relationship to others: The drama was big, bold, and real. (Homans 2002, 22)*

We can't all be Suzanne Farrell, but the artistry of any phrase is in the performance. Teachers need to remember to be an everyday artist.

A certain unnamed and very gifted teacher would periodically sneak over to a sink in the corner during class and peer studiously down the drain. The students wondered what the lure of that old sink was. Curious, a group them sauntered over to find out its attraction. Lying in the sink were copious notes describing each phrase for class and their order. One of the great skills of a teacher is not only to physically remember each phrase and its corresponding rhythm but also to remember the sequence of activities. Some teachers will forever need the backup of notes sitting in the sink, but it is best if they memorize and embody the movement material. This is a practiced skill, taking time and experience, but it lends authority to the teacher's presence and allows dancers to have more time to practice dancing exquisitely composed phrases and combinations.

Investigations

1. Compose phrases for the following:
   - A systematic warm-up phrase for the spine moving on all possible planes
   - A footwork pattern that segues from right to left and back again
   - An arm pattern that is possible to retrograde

2. Compose phrases and combinations based on the following principles. Analyze the initiation of each movement within the phrase.
   - Spatial concepts such as size, range, direction, floor pattern, level, focus, and internal or external space of the body
   - Energy concepts such as quality, dynamics, and emotional intent

3. Make a movement phrase that utilizes the entire studio. Ask the class to keep the same tempo, but do the phrase in a very small corner of the space. How does that change their energy and dynamics?

4. Teach rhythmic principles.
   - Build a foot exercise differentiating downbeat from upbeat.
   - Build a phrase in mixed meter: five, four, five, two. At the beginning of each measure, create a direction change.
   - Build a pattern safely done in three different speeds: half time, regular time, and double time.
   - Build a warm-up in descending counts: 32-16-8-4-2. Build a cool-down in ascending counts: 2-4-8-16-32.

5. Gravity never takes a lunch break. Using the following movements, craft a phrase using gravity's rhythms. Create a beat, a subdivision of the beat, and measure for the phrase.
   - A body swing
   - A skip-and-leap pattern
   - A pattern that moves in and out of the floor

6. Perform a simple jumping or skipping phrase in a simple beat (duple) and a compound (triple). How does it change the feel of the movement?

7. Select a tempo for a movement that is natural to your body, such as a skip. Select a tempo that is appropriate to the skill level of a beginner. Are they different?

8. Create a phrase that honors the weight of the body falling in space. Sing the sound of your weight and breath. Practice repeating it consistently without the aid of counts.

9. Make up movement while counting in another language. Are the phrases different?

In-Class Investigations

1. Compose a combination using gravity's rhythms. Present this as an uncounted phrase to the class. Ask them to perform it in duets, trios, or groups, blending their energy to find unison.

2. Observe a student who is having trouble being on the beat. Watch her use of space and energy.

Reflection: TRANSITIONS

Viola Farber is presenting a seamlessly connected movement phrase while teaching class. An eager student asks a question about a transitional moment. She says with great disdain, "There is no such thing as a transition."

Erika Dufour, photographer; Kristen Bauza, dancer. Courtesy of Zephyr Dance.

Moving at 6 trillion miles per year, the light enters the window and reflects off the dancers' expectant faces. The teacher blinks, spreading tears that bathe the hard and leathery cornea, which welcomes the light bouncing off the dancers. The sphincter muscle shrinks the pupil, keeping the light from overwhelming the receptors. The rays of light move to the Cheerio-size lens, which produces a sharp visual image. Way in the background the retina—which is fragile as a wet leaf—transfers the light rays to electrical signals. When the image is finally in a form it can decipher, the optic nerve buzzes with excitement. Acting like telephone cable, the optic nerves from both eyes hook together at the base of the brain in the optic chiasm; the Grand Canyon of "Aha!"-ness. There, the funny patterns and colors of light are interpreted as a group of dancers waiting to begin.

The cerebrum decides on a course of action and our evolutionary core, the odd, tubelike brainstem connecting brain to spinal cord, goes to work sending out the message. The hypoglossal nerve dreams up a secret code for the tongue, the spinal part of the accessory nerve organizes enticing rhythms for the head and shoulder, and the trigeminal nerve endings plan to move the jaw toward a slight smile. All these impulses race to deliver their message; but first, there is protocol. The nerves must stand patiently in line as they are processed by the wrinkled cerebellum, which, incidentally, has tripled its size in the last million years or so. The not-so-useless cerebellum will smooth the transitions between smile and speech, between head toss and hip wiggle.

A rhythmic explosion of activity takes place, all perfectly timed and coordinated. The lips move, the tongue pushes, the sternocleidomastoideus contracts and the larynx vibrates.

"Let's begin. Five, six, seven, eight."

chapter 7

Weaving Light
SEQUENCING

E very dancer knows the feeling of a good class: The body is ready for each new exercise in the sequence and a flow develops, warming the body and enabling it to jump higher and breathe deeper. A continuity of reasoning provides a seamless thread, and the class goes on a journey with past, present, and future contained in every moment. Teachers sit in the center of a great three-dimensional loom weaving together time, traditions, and body truths into a web of activity. This chapter covers the sequencing of class material in regard to safe anatomical practices, interlacing goals with the class structure, and planning strategies.

SEQUENCING EXERCISES

The process of placing exercises in a sensible sequence begins by listening to the intuitive wisdom of the body. Listen well and the body will know exactly what it needs next. Do not simply listen to your own body, but seek information by observing a dance class. Watch what students do *between* exercises. After a difficult adagio, students hang over, aching for a hamstring stretch. After a long series of jumps, they wiggle their feet and stretch their gastrocnemius. Following the innate wisdom of the body is a good first step to sequencing exercises effectively. But before paying attention to the details, look at the overall form. What happens at the beginning, middle, and end? (See tables 7.1 and 7.2)

> *A continuity of reasoning provides a seamless thread, and the class goes on a journey with past, present, and future contained in every moment.*

Beginning

The beginning of any endeavor is crucial because it sets the tone for the entire journey. In dance, the first moment of class establishes breath, focus, and concentration. There are many ways to open a class. Some classes begin by honoring the earth. Bowing to four cardinal directions, Akira Kasai's butoh-based class provides connections between the earth and human boundaries. Built on the rhythms of breath, yoga begins with a salutation to the sun. Circle-based meditations provide a sense of community. Pliés in ballet, the back series in Cunningham technique, or Graham contractions provide welcome familiarity. Whatever is chosen, it should be repeatable and consistent, opening the doors to the work ahead.

Warm-Up

Following the opening ritual, the next series of four to six exercises should gently wake up each major muscle group and body part. Following the logic of developmental movement sequences, the first exercise would be homologous (flexion and extension on the sagittal plane), the second exercise homolateral (abduction and adduction on the lateral plane), and the third exercise contralateral (rotation or spiraling movement on the transverse plane). Perhaps these are combined into one exercise. Wake-up exercises should be gentle and moderate in tempo and include movement for every joint in all its planes of motion. This section includes such choices as walking; light jogging; wiggling; stretching; and sustained, flowing, or pulsating movement. Sharp movements and extreme tempi should be avoided during the wake-up period. There are endless possibilities, but by the end of this series the dancer should break a sweat and be breathing deeply. Now it is time to move on to the deeper musculature.

The beginning.

Warm-up.

Deep Work

This section of class is designed to work muscles closest to the bones, visceral organs, and deep connective tissue. The previous sections softened and warmed the large, outer muscles such as the quadriceps, hamstrings, abdominal muscles, extensors, deltoids, and gastrocnemius. Now the body is ready to innervate the small postural muscles lining the spine, the scapula, pelvis, and feet. These intrinsic muscles are difficult to identify and locate because they cannot be seen or touched. The dancer must be thoroughly warm, focused, and attentive to discover these muscles.

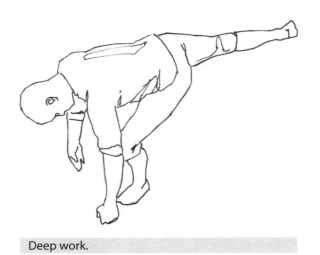

Deep work.

This section of class dwells on deep, long stretches, grand pliés, adagios, and fast foot-work. Extremes of tempo, both slow and fast, are useful, challenging the mind and the body. Extreme complexity and simplicity also have their place. Sections from the major movement pattern can be broken down and rehearsed, giving the body time to integrate stylistic variations. For instance, if the main combination includes a fast leg swing with an unusual arm pattern, a similar coordination pattern might be presented in the adagio. The intricacies of the movement are thereby practiced at a slow speed before attempting the fast sequence later. At the end of this section, dancers should feel warm down to their bones.

Movement Combinations

The whole class dances, but this is where it all comes together. Dance skills such as turning, jumping, running, and leaping are rehearsed and ultimately woven into dance phrases and combinations. This often takes the form of "across the floor" and the "main combination" in modern class. At the beginning of the across-the-floor sequence, reengage the feet with simple prances, runs, or slides. Simple locomotor movements prepare the body for moving through space, and simplicity allows students to integrate the subtle alignment lessons learned earlier. If done at extreme speeds or with quick direction changes, locomotor skills quickly become complex. Tradition says that large leaps and jumps should come at the end of class. But sometimes it can be satisfying to put them before the main movement combination, depending on the flow of the overall class.

Finally, the dance skills so rigorously practiced throughout class culminate in a final combination, a tapestry weaving all the movement threads together. Often, far too much emphasis is put on *the combination*. The final combination is not the point of class. It is one more tool to engage students in learning to dance. The movement combination should flow from the main principle being taught. If the movement principle is elasticity and the strategy is to understand push and pull, then the combination should reflect those. A very good class may never get to the combination. This is OK. Perhaps a breakthrough was happening in pliés, so the class spent time exploring push and pull. Tomorrow is another day.

A dance phrase.   Cooling down.

The end of class traditionally dwells on the hardest skills: jumping and leaping. If the class has been a full experience, students should be sweating and breathing deeply by the end of class.

Cool-Down

Sweating bodies pumping with blood explode into applause at the end of class. A longtime dance tradition, this practice neglects a very important ending ritual, the cool-down. When the muscles are warm, the blood is circulating fast. If the body is not slowed down properly, blood pools in the muscles, causing soreness and cramping the next day. A cool-down can be a variety of activities. A stretch is ideal while the muscles are warm. Gradually decreasing the intensity of the exercise is another method, similar to a horse trotting around the ring at the end of a race. If the class has been breathing hard, the head should remain above the heart for a short time, at least until the heart rate has come back down to normal. If the head is put below the heart while the heart is pumping fast, all the blood will rush to the head. The instant the dancer stands up, the blood rushes the other way, causing a feeling of lightheadedness. Even though hanging over and stretching the hamstrings feels good after class, wait a few moments before putting the head below the heart. Just as saying "amen" closes a prayer, the ending ritual brings closure.

DESIGNING A CLASS TEMPLATE

Keeping in mind the general flow traveling from beginning to warm-up to deep work, now you build a template for the sequence of exercises. In this template the exercises are assigned an order that provides a thorough and safe progression for the body. Day to day, variations occur within each exercise, but the template remains fairly constant over a semester or course. It is useful to build several templates—perhaps one standing and one floor.

To design the template, begin with the wisdom of the body. Center yourself in a studio with a pen and a sample graph at your side. Working just in the columns "The exercise" and "Body part," first explore concepts physically, then write down what you did. At the very beginning, what do you like to do? Roll around on the floor, stretch, jog? Whatever it is, write it down under "Beginning." Upon entering the warm-up phase, follow the logic of your body. Think about what feels right and what parts of the body need attention. Don't worry about composing the rhythm or shape of the exercise in great detail at this point; most important is the flow of sequencing. In the column "The exercise," write down a simple statement describing the exercise—for example, a shoulder/arm pattern or foot rolls. Under "Body part," write down what is emphasized—the spine, shoulders, feet, or head. Perhaps it was an exercise that emphasized everything; if so, write down "whole body." At the end of the warm-up phase your body should break a sweat. As you enter the deep-work section, ask your body what is needed to get down to the bones. Perhaps it is time for a deep stretch or a quick tempo. Where would it be appropriate to include some phrases preparing the body for the main pattern? What feels satisfying to end this section?

Now it is time to analyze your body logic. Fill in the columns "Conditioning" and "Spatial planes." Is there a specific time to address all four conditioning needs? Did you include all planes of every joint? Taking into consideration all these variables, go back and revise the flow of exercises. Perhaps you left out a deep stretch because your body is already too flexible. Perhaps you avoided footwork because you hate it. This revision forces you to transcend your own body's needs, likes, and dislikes and prepare a more universal class welcoming to all types of bodies.

Planning a Specific Class

As you develop a specific class, the generic template expands with detail. Now it is time to interlace the main movement principle and strategies throughout the class. What is the movement principle to be addressed in your class and what is the strategy to get to that principle? In table 7.1, the main movement principle is elasticity, and the strategy is to work on push and pull. In table 7.2, the main movement principle is three-dimensionality and the strategy is to work on curves in space. The core principle will influence how the template shifts each day, just as the light changes gradually throughout a day and night. If the principle is swing, the rhythms might be predominantly triples. If the principle is elasticity, flexibility might be favored over strength. As the principle changes over time, the overall graph will shift.

The focus of the exercise should always refer to the movement principle. Returning to the body, explore pull and push in each exercise. Compose feet, leg, and spine exercises that fulfill the learning objective. Let your body move through the warm-up and deep work once again, adding more details. Write down the fruits of your body labor. In the column "Focus of the exercise," write down the point of the exercise. Later this will become the teaching cue—the focal point when making corrections. Now fill in the rest of the columns.

Analyze the results with balance as the monitor. For instance, if you are teaching swings, perhaps a triple meter is appropriate for the entire class. If it is a performance day, perhaps all the exercises are slow to conserve energy. Consciously driving the class toward extremes is simply another way to find balance. If the class

Table 7.1   Standing Sequence

GOAL: ELASTICITY. STRATEGY: PUSH AND PULL.

	The exercise	Focus of exercise	Body part	Conditioning	Centering	Moving/ stationary	Spatial planes
Beginning	Yoga ritual with breathing	Establish breath	Whole	Flexibility (passive)	Biometric	Stationary	Sagittal
Warm-up (standing)	Circular back exercise	Reach and pull of side stretch	Spine		Geometric	Stationary	Lateral-sagittal/ circumduction
	Arm circles with spirals	Distal-initiated pull	Arms/shoulders/ spine		Biometric	Stationary	Transverse-PNF
	Flat back	Work on hip mechanics	Hip joint	Strength	Geometric	Stationary	All 3 planes
	Foot prances with plié	Build coil in foot for elasticity	Feet/ankles/knees		Geometric	Shifting weight	Lateral/sagittal
	Tendus with plié	Emphasize pushing floor	Feet/knees/hips		Geometric	Shifting weight	All 3 planes
	Movement pattern	Move with push and pull	Whole	Cardiovascular	Biometric	Moving	All 3 planes
Deep work	Long/deep stretch	Build a lengthening reach	Hip/spine	Flexibility (active)	Biometric	Stationary	Sagittal
	Grand pliés with back swing	Push of legs/ pull of arms	Hip/spine/arms	Flexibility (ballistic)	Geometric	Stationary	All 3 planes
	Dégagés with spatial design	Prepare end movement pattern	Whole/feet	Endurance	Geometric	Moving	All 3 planes-PNF
	Leg swings	Elasticity of legs in improvisation	Legs		Biometric	Moving	All 3 planes
	Adagio	Balance and elasticity	Whole	Strength	Biometric	Stationary	Lateral and transverse
Combinations (across floor)	Prances across floor	Wake up feet again	Feet		Geometric	Moving	Sagittal
	Slides with arm pattern	Prepare end movement pattern	Whole		Geometric	Moving	Sagittal/ transverse
	Main movement pattern	Focus of the phrase: elasticity	Whole		Biometric	Moving	All 3 planes
	Large jumps and leaps	Coiling push of the pliés	Whole	Cardiovascular and endurance	Geometric	Moving	All 3 planes
Cool-down	Walking improvisation	Slow down heart rate	Whole		Biometric	Moving	Sagittal
	Stretch	Reinforce elastic pull	Spine and pelvis	Flexibility (passive)	Geometric	Stationary	All 3 planes

From *Harnessing the Wind* by Jan Erkert, 2003, Champaign, IL: Human Kinetics.

GOAL: ELASTICITY. STRATEGY: PUSH AND PULL.

Levels	Slow/fast	Pulse/no pulse	Duple/triple	Phrasing	High/low energy	Improvised/learned	Simple/complex	Old/new
Transitions	Slow	No pulse			Low		Very simple	Repetition
Standing	Slow to moderate		Triple	12	Moderate		Moderately complex	Repetition
Standing	Moderate to fast		Duple	6	High		Complex	New
Standing	Slow		Duple	8	Low		Very simple	Repetition/adding new spirals
Standing	Moderate		Duple	8	High		Simple	Brand new
Standing	Moderate		Triple	5	Moderate		Moderately simple	Repetition/adding back
Standing	Moderate to fast		Triple	12	High		Complex	New
Floor	Very slow	No pulse			Low		Simple	Repetition
Standing	Moderate		Triple	5	Moderate		Moderately complex	Repetition
Standing	Very fast		Duple	12	High		Very complex	Repetition
Transitions	Moderate		Triple	Mixed meter	Moderate		Moderately complex	New
Transitions	Very slow		Duple	16	Moderate		Simple	Repetition
Standing	Moderate		Duple	8	Moderate	Improvised	Simple	Repetition
Standing	Very fast		Triple	12	High		Simple	New
Transitions	Moderate to fast		Triple	Mixed meter	High		Very complex	Repetition with new sections
Air	Moderate		Triple	8	High		Very simple	Repetition
Standing	Slow to moderate		Duple		Moderate		Simple	New
Transitions	Slow	No pulse			Low		Very simple	Repetition

Table 7.2 Floor Sequence *3-D strategy: work-curves*

GOAL: ELASTICITY. STRATEGY: PUSH AND PULL.

The class	The exercise	Focus of exercise	Body part	Conditioning	Centering	Moving/ stationary	Developmental sequences
Beginning	Walking curves in space	Introduce concept of curves	Whole		Biometric	Moving	All three
Warm-up (lying)	Bartenieff heel rocks	Engage flexors/ extensors	Whole		Biometric	Moving on floor	Homologous
	Bartenieff lateral shifts	Engage lateral muscles	Torso		Biometric	Moving on floor	Homolateral
	Bartenieff X-rolls	Engage muscles of rotation	Torso		Biometric	Moving on floor	Contralateral
	Sit-up/push-up	Engage upper/ lower body	Torso/arms	Strength	Biometric	Moving on floor	All three
	Leg swings	Engage leg in spatial curves	Hip joint		Biometric	Stationary	All three
	Rolling movement pattern	Prepare end pattern	Whole	Cardiovascular	Biometric	Moving	All three
Deep work (standing)	Deep lunges	Stretch iliopsoas and hamstrings	Hip/spine	Flexibility	Geometric	Stationary	Homolateral
	Demi-pliés and relevés	Get legs ready for low walks	Ankles/knees/hips		Geometric	Stationary	Homolateral
	Foot prances/move in space	Articulate feet while moving	Whole/feet	Endurance	Biometric	Moving	Contralateral
	Grand pliés and flat backs	Moving 3-dimensionally	Hips/whole	Strength	Geometric	Stationary	All three
	Leg extensions and battements	Release hip sockets	Hips/whole		Geometric	Moving	All three
	Upside-down level changes	Prepare end pattern	Whole	Cardiovascular	Biometric	Moving	All three
Combinations (across floor)	Slides across floor	Wake up feet again	Feet/whole		Geometric	Moving	Homolateral
	Running curves in space	Prepare main concept	Whole		Biometric	Moving	Homologous
	Main movement pattern	Focus of the phrase: curves	Whole		Biometric	Moving	All three
	Large running leaps	Incorporate curves into the air	Whole	Endurance	Biometric	Moving	All three
Cool-down	Partner stretch	Create stretching curves	Spine	Flexibility	Biometric	Stationary	All three

From *Harnessing the Wind* by Jan Erkert, 2003, Champaign, IL: Human Kinetics.

GOAL: ELASTICITY. STRATEGY: PUSH AND PULL.

Levels	Slow/ fast	Pulse/ no pulse	Duple/ triple	Phrasing	High/ low energy	Improvised	Simple/ complex	Old/ new
Standing	Moderate		Duple	4	Low	Improvised	Simple	New
On floor	Moderate	No pulse			Low		Simple	Repetition
On floor	Moderate	No pulse			Low		Simple	Repetition
On floor	Slow	No pulse			Low		Simple	Repetition/ adding new spirals
Transitional	Moderate		Duple	8	Moderate		Moderately complex	Repetition
Sitting	Moderate		Triple	8	Moderate		Simple	Repetition
Transitional	Moderate to fast		Triple	8	High		Complex	New
Transitional	Very slow	No pulse			Low		Simple	Repetition
Standing	Moderate		Triple	6	Moderate		Simple	New
Standing	Fast		Duple	6	High		Complex	Brand new
Standing	Moderate		Triple	5	Moderate		Simple	Repetition
Standing	Moderate		Duple	12	Moderate		Moderately complex	Repetition
Transitional	Moderate to fast		Triple	8	High		Complex	Repetition with new sections
Standing/air	Moderate		Duple	8	Moderate		Simple	Repetition
Standing	Fast		Duple	8	High	Improvised	Simple	New
Transitional	Moderate		Triple	12	High		Complex	New
Air	Moderate		Triple	8	Moderate		Simple	Repetition
On floor	Slow	No pulse			Low		Simple	Repetition

is out of balance it should be an informed choice for a particular purpose. Awareness is key. Observe the dynamic flow of the class by drawing an energy line through the columns "Slow/fast" and "High/low energy." Is there a natural build to the class? There is no right or wrong, only a long continuum of possibilities. This complex weaving will eventually point you where you need to go to develop each exercise in the sequence. While watching each continuum flow, you will begin to see that it directs you to what is needed next—a deep stretch in duple for the hip joint or a shoulder exercise that transitions into the floor, simple and slow.

Planning Forward or Backward

Once a template has been designed, daily planning is a process of responding to the students and their progression in learning. Questions from the day before should guide the process. What did students understand and what are they still struggling with? Where to go next? These questions linger in the mind and body as planning begins. Sometimes movement will come fast and instinctively. Planning backward, you can filter movement from the main combination back into the warm-up by adding a turn to the daily leg swings or an unusual shape to the adagio. It is like having all the laundry done and putting it back in the drawers. Other days it will not be so easy; everything will seem arbitrary. On those days, a ritual warm-up can be grounding while you're meditating on the questions of the day. As the questions guide the mind and body, adding certain variations to the pliés or leg extensions might seem to make sense. By the time the ritual is completed, there is usually enough material to create a class that has been shaped organically by the students' needs. Will it make sense in class? That is another question.

Rigorous planning allows a teacher to be more spontaneous. If nothing else, it prepares the mind to be focused and ready for the coming improvisation. When you're standing on a cliff with a good harness, the thrill is jumping off; anything can happen.

CONTINUUMS

Merce Cunningham believed there must be something fast and slow, easy and complex, old and new, and big and small within each class. When sequencing exercises in technique class, look at opposite forces. Black and white are at opposite ends of a continuum containing varying shades of gray along the way. Spectrums of light gradually change from pale amber to brilliant yellows. Pale amber or bright yellow are neither good nor bad; they are just extremes of an ever-changing continuum. A lighting designer creates a three-dimensional painting with numerous shafts of colored light (continuums). A teacher weaves together continuums of dance elements to create a satisfying whole. There are as many continuums in dance as there are colors of light. Here are a few basic colors to begin the weaving. For the next section refer to tables 7.1 and 7.2.

Body Parts to Whole Body

This continuum runs from details (specific body parts) to whole-body work. Of course, the foot is never pointed without connecting to the whole, but in planning class it helps to emphasize details at one moment, then integrate them into the whole the next moment. After three or four exercises emphasizing details, return to the whole body to integrate the information—a moving pattern, a full-body spiral, a movement combination. Notice how in table 7.1 the beginning exercise establishes breath and internal connections in the whole body. The warm-up targets each body part and returns to the whole in the last exercise. The deep work goes back to details and ends with the whole body. Finally, during movement patterning, whole-body activities are emphasized in culminating material.

Conditioning: Flexibility and Strength

Although all movements have some components of conditioning, every class should have at least one exercise that targets each aspect of conditioning: strength, flexibility, muscular endurance, and cardiovascular endurance. Strength is specifically addressed in the slow flat-back exercise in the warm-up section and the adagio in the deep work section. Endurance is sought during the last jumps and leaps. There is a conscious effort to increase the amount of jumps given, from 8 to 32 or 64 during the course of a semester. Cardiovascular activity is placed at the end of the warm-up section to transition into deep work. It is done again as the first across-the-floor exercise, stimulating blood flow and deep warmth before the main combination is addressed.

Notice that flexibility is a major concern in table 7.1, so it is addressed four times. A cold body needs a gentle stretch, so the first exercise is a *passive static* stretch targeting the major flexors and extensors of the body, which is done at a moderate to slow tempo without metric stimulation. By the end of the warm-up section, bodies have broken a sweat and are breathing deeply from a cardiovascular exercise. This is an ideal time to present an *active reciprocal* stretch. After the active stretch, a *ballistic* stretch accompanies the pliés to integrate the stretch into dancing skills. The cool-down returns to the targeted muscles of the day in a *passive static* stretch.

The balance of attention in conditioning should shift depending on the level of class. For instance, in beginning classes, a strength exercise, such as a leg extension, might precede a release exercise, such as a leg swing. Thereby, the muscle just used relaxes before returning to another strength exercise. In more advanced classes, the number of strength exercises done in a row should be increased. See discussion on flexibility, strength, endurance, and cardiorespiratory endurance in chapter 5.

Spatial: Planes

A good warm-up works each body part on all possible planes of motion and follows a developmental sequence. The first three exercises in table 7.1 encompass spinal work. The yoga exercise begins with homologous movement, the next spinal exercise concentrates on homolateral movement, and the third exercise is built to stimulate contralateral movement. Later, the dégagés and leg swings are performed in the ballet en croix pattern (the shape of a cross) or in diagonal and circular movements such as a rond de jambe, stimulating PNF patterning. See discussion on PNF in chapter 5.

Centering: Geometric and Biometric

In table 7.2, the beginning and warm-up are designed to center the body using the biometric mind-set. Constantly moving the center by walking, rolling, tossing, and turning encourages the navel to lead and the limbs to follow. During the deep work section the geometric mind-set predominates. The biometric mind-set transitions into the movement combination, where both models are integrated in a complex web of spatial demands. See discussion on geometric and biometric centering in chapter 4.

Spatial: Moving and Stationary

Traditionally, the first half of class is stationary and the second half is moving. Nuggets of moving are placed within stationary work or moments of stillness are placed strategically within a moving class. It is also possible to reverse tradition. Create a moving warm-up and a stationary ending to class. What might be the advantages? See discussion on spatial intent in chapter 6.

Up and Down

In table 7.1, movements to and from the floor are inserted primarily in the deep work section. Transitioning to and from the floor is strenuous activity. The body should be deeply warm to guide the body into the floor and to power the body out. In table 7.2, the warm-up is on the floor and the deep work is standing. Within these sections, movements that transfer the weight downward and upward are put in the transitions between sections. Large air moments are generally best near the end of class. See discussion on floor work and standing work in chapter 4.

Slow and Fast

Moderate to slow time feels good in the warm-up. In the deep work section, extreme tempi challenge the musculature. Overall, there should be a carefully choreographed range of speeds gracefully accelerating and decelerating. Regulating acceleration can enhance muscle performance. A very slow activity followed by a very fast activity jars the muscle, so placing a moderately paced exercise in between enables the muscles to spurt with vigor. See discussion on pacing in chapter 8.

Pulse or No Pulse

Does everything need to have a pulse, to be in meter? Unpulsed time creates new dynamics. Maybe once or twice in the class, allow sensed time to break the pulse, the meter, and the clock. It will feel like floating. See the discussion on abandoning counts in chapter 6.

Duple and Triple

Rhythm is made up of duples and triples. This continuum will be greatly affected by the main principle being addressed in each class. If the class focus is swings, triples

will rule. Duples will command attention in a pulse-based class. Conscious awareness of this continuum will evoke adulation from both the accompanists and
students. See the discussion on gravity's rhythm in chapter 6.

Sound or No Sound

Is it crucial that the accompanist play for every moment? Pick at least one moment
in each class for silence. See the discussion on silence and stillness in chapter 11.

Phrasing

Judiciously play with the lengths of phrases and mix them up for variety. A long
sentence demands more breath, more flow. Two-word sentences command punch
and accent. Shorter sentences, all the same length, are easier for beginners to grasp.
The long, tricky phrases should be concentrated near the end of class. See discussion on musicality and rhythm in chapter 6.

High and Low Energy

Extremes of energy create a wavelike effect in class. Just when students are so
exhausted they think they are going to drop, a calm, deep stretch is thrown in to
revive their energy. Just as they begin to enter the zone-out stage, a high-
energy percussive combination is presented. See discussion on energy in
chapter 6.

Spontaneous or Learned

In a technique class, a student learns through mimicry; every sense is engaged in
observing and replicating movement. Switching the focus by decreasing the stimuli
through an improvisational assignment can be a great relief. See discussion on
improvisation in chapter 2.

Simple and Complex

A playful juggling between simple and complex elicits intense concentration
and focus. Complex movement patterns force the cerebrum to go into double
time and jettison students from their glassy-eyed state. In simple exercises, the
cerebrum takes a rest, allowing the integrating cerebellum to take over. In
addition, complex patterns take time; simple patterns do not; if the class is
behind and needs to move quickly, a series of simple exercises moves it along.
See discussion on the continuums of simple and complex and old and new in
chapter 8.

Old and New

When do students need an old, well-worn blanket and when do they need a shiny
new toy? Relying on neurological principles is key to knowing when to repeat and
when to offer something new. See the discussion of repetition in chapter 4.

Investigations

1. Observe a dance class and write down what students do between exercises. How do students relieve the tension and stress of the previous exercise?

2. Go into the studio and give yourself your own class. What does your body intuitively want or need after each exercise? Make a list of the sequence of exercises that feels good to your body. Pay attention to the order. Write a sentence after each exercise explaining why it felt right at each moment. Reasons can be multiple and varied, such as needing to focus during the beginning breathing exercise or feeling a need to relate to the space during a back exercise.

3. Build a class template. Physically work through each exercise in the template. Prepare a written graph for the beginning, warm-up, and deep work sections. Analyze aspects of conditioning and spatial planes. Revise the graph and give yourself a class based on the new template. How does it feel?

4. Build a specific class. At the bottom of the graph, write the main movement principle and learning strategies for the class. Weave all the continuums. Take your own class. How does it feel?

In-Class Investigations

1. Spend an hour in a studio before class. Meditate on the questions raised in the previous class. Spend the time by yourself and plan the next class. Plan it forward or backward.

2. After careful planning, wing it. Jump off the diving board and see what happens.

Reflection: CENTERING

Everywhere Studio

Four white walls. Flat. Narrow and confined, like a strip mall without parking privileges. Flat. A black marley floor, wrinkled. Flat. Nasty blue lights give no texture to the flatness. Steel bars are riveted to the wall. Mirrors suck my image into a two-dimensional illusion. I cannot find my lungs; they are too round.

Erika Dufour, photographer; Tiffany Van Cleaf, dancer. Courtesy of Chicago Moving Company.

State Dance School, Managua, Nicaragua

There are large gaps between each splintering floorboard. In air thick with dust, I maneuver between the slats that provide no rebound. Jumping is not a good idea, sliding is not possible, and turning is precarious. My pampered body does not like this space. The students enter with palpable excitement in their eyes.

The Erlanger House, Champaign-Urbana, Illinois

The inside is the outside and the outside lives indoors. Gardens fold into a studio with sprung cherry wood floors. A sunken living room and a sumptuous, sculptural fireplace hug the dance floor. A grand piano sits in the corner, quiet. Strangely, I want to lie in the center and go to sleep.

MoMing Dance & Arts Center, Chicago, Illinois

A church-turned-dance-performance-space is now a condominium. Decades of performances, rehearsals, sweat, frustration, exhilaration, ecstasy, and disappointment seep into the brick and mortar. I walk through the fancy Euro kitchens, with high ceilings and stripped brick walls. Shiny metal pipes carry cool, clean air. Is nothing left of all our efforts?

Athenea's Studio, Ignacio Saragosa, Ocotopec, Mexico

Textured white walls and warm wood floors spill into the garden filled with bougainvillea, calla lilies, and roses. The smell of flowers takes me on a magical trip with my ancient ancestors. I wonder what they are doing in Mexico.

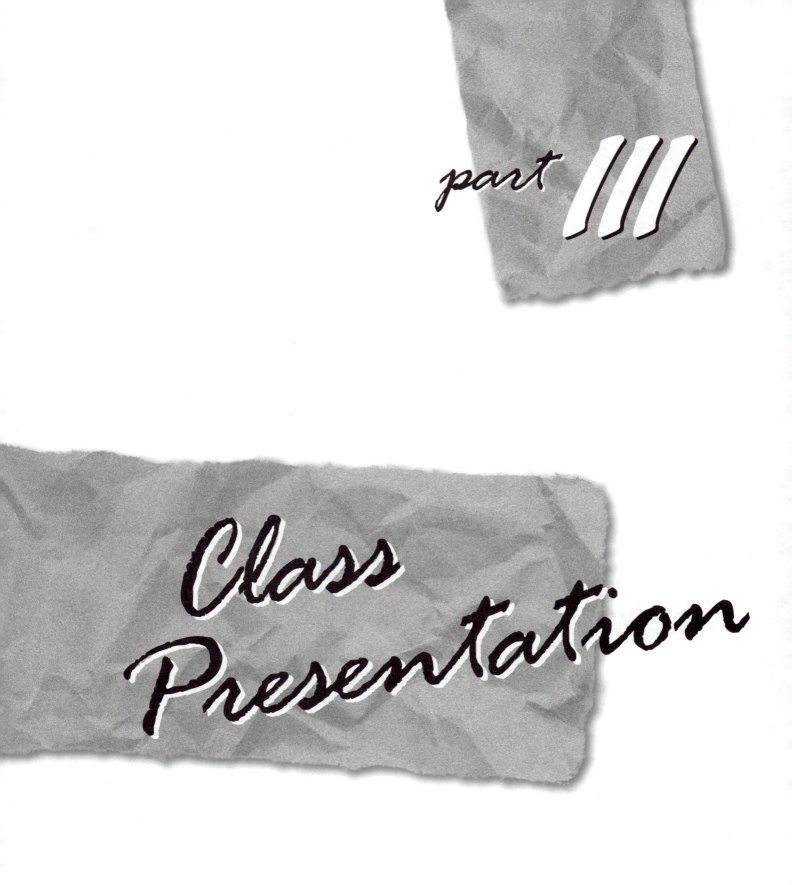

part ////

Class Presentation

William Frederking, photographer; Frank Fishella, dancer.

Time Flowing
PACING

The teacher enters the studio and class begins. Like a good alchemist, the teacher reads all the signs and makes spontaneous decisions, creating a flow of energy. Each class is unique as the teacher responds to the students' energy, the class' personality and history, the day, month, and season, and special circumstances such as performances, weather, and national disasters. Without wasting a moment of precious time, the teacher carefully measures out the mix of ingredients for the day. Some days need a potent catalyst; other days will be better served by nonreactive ingredients. This chapter covers the delicate art of pacing.

READING TEA LEAVES

The unknown sits in the air at the beginning of class. As much as one prepares, the class itself is always an improvisation. At the root of teaching is the ability to both plan and throw out the plan. Where are the students today? The lake winds have blown right into their bones and the studio is bitter cold, so the planned yoga breathing exercise will not work. Switch gears quickly and ask students to rub muscles and take a soft jog around the space while they tell each other the ordeal they went through to get to the studio that day. Now the plan is off, so winging it is the only choice. But if it is working, students will be engaged and ready to focus.

Choices to spontaneously create new material or stick with the plan are made by being aware of all elements swirling through the studio. The teacher gathers information as if reading tea leaves, asking, "How are you? How are your bodies today?" Right before a holiday, students might be feisty; this is a great time to deliver a rigorous running and jumping class. After traumatizing world events occur, a class that challenges students to channel the emotional weight of the world might be in order; after all, connecting body to soul and soul to emotions is the art of a performer. If the lethargy hanging in the room is due to a tough, late-night dress rehearsal, a stretch class might be appropriate. Sometimes sticking with the plan is a better choice; students can easily lead the teacher on a tangent, and they may need to be brought back to the rigor of the original plan: "No, we can't go out to the beach today." Sometimes responding to lackluster energy with a slow class can be deadly. Base choices not on what students want, but on what they need. Honor where they are while moving forward.

By reading the telltale signs, a teacher designs the class to suit the students' needs. Such adaptability demands that the teacher spontaneously follow an idea without losing the pace of the class. It's a sophisticated skill that develops after years of teaching. To begin building these skills, practice making phrases quickly in private. As your confidence grows, do this with others present, perhaps a few close friends who are patient. When ready to go public, leave several sections of the class open or deliberately throw out the plan, even though doing so sends shivers up your spine. Once you've built up enough confidence, walk into the room and wing the whole class. The experience is liberating.

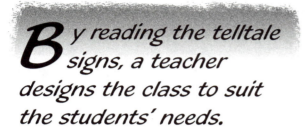

By reading the telltale signs, a teacher designs the class to suit the students' needs.

FLOW

The dance class is a ritual that at its best achieves a state of flow. Flow occurs when the body and mind synchronize to become a fluent whole and the dancer experiences complete engagement. In his book *Finding Flow: The Psychology of Engagement With Everyday Life,* Mihaly Csikszentmihalyi explains the term *flow.* "The metaphor of 'flow' is one that many people have used to describe the sense of effortless actions they feel in moments that stand out as the best in their lives. Athletes refer to it as 'being in the zone,' religious mystics as being in 'ecstasy,' artists and musicians as aesthetic rapture."(Csikszentmihalyi 1997, 29)

In dance, flow is best achieved when the body moves without interruptions. When movement flows, the cerebrum (the part of the brain that analyzes) is quieted and the cerebellum (the lower, more instinctive brain) takes over, commanding movement coordination. When left to its own devices the cerebellum coordinates movement in the most efficient manner possible. The state of flow teaches lessons that are more profound than any words or images a teacher might conjure up. The body makes deep connections as it listens to its own wisdom. Interruptions and talking get in the way of flow. Words entice the cerebrum to be too active, destroying the harmony between mind and body.

Flow should be sculpted to create waves. Aerobic exercise equipment comes equipped with fancy display panels showing waves of activity, which get progressively larger as the workout continues. Creating increasingly high and low waves challenges both the physical and mental capacity of the dancer.

Flow.

Flow in Other Disciplines

Many eastern art forms, such as yoga and tai chi chuan are taught to achieve flow. Without interruptions, the learner has to see and react. There is no time for the mind to confuse the body. In yoga, the deep, consistent breathing creates the essence of the practice. The teacher does not dare interrupt the ongoing ritual that develops *pranayama,* the flowing breath. Yoga students study philosophy by reading or taking special workshops separate from class. In Eastern traditions, the teacher repeats a movement over and over again without ever saying a word. Each time the eye is forced to see more and the mind arrives at a heightened sense of concentration. Silently, the movers go about their work.

Analysis and Flow

Ballet, jazz, and modern dance classes are traditionally taught in a stop-and-go fashion. The teacher presents new patterns, gives insight, corrects alignment, or shares philosophy between bits of movement. Why has the Western world ended up with this fragmented approach? Cerebral analysis has been favored in our school systems. Learning is accomplished through lecture, discussion, and analysis. In all fairness, the body needs analysis in order to expand movement choices, which yogis don't deny; they just address it outside of the class. Also, the complexity of dance movement patterning requires more than a show-and-do approach. Uninterrupted flow is easier to maintain when there are not fifteen direction changes in syncopated rhythms. But if left to analysis alone, the body never has the chance to sort things out. A dance teacher needs to find ways to balance analysis and flow.

Over days, weeks, and months, alternating between analysis and flow will heighten engagement in the work. Without questions and corrections, a class moves in silence. "Flow" days, when phrases blend seamlessly together without stopping, are balanced by days of analysis, examination, and philosophy. Giving students a chance to discuss their learning opens up a floodgate of questions and awakens their intellectual curiosity, bringing them to new levels of awareness.

ART OF PACING

Pacing class is an art of great delicacy. A teacher's intuition is a finely tuned antenna, reading when a class is ready to learn from flow and when analysis will help break up unwanted static. Pacing is practiced not only moment to moment, but week to week and month to month. Several simple techniques will help the teacher with this tricky skill.

Demonstrations

The students' frustration builds when the teacher spends too much time trying to figure out what comes next. Careful planning enhances flow. But there is another step: the way a pattern is demonstrated. When showing a pattern, keep focused on student learning. First, students need to see the whole picture. If you break it down, give cue points, and start over five times, it will be harder for students to learn the pattern. Picking up steps is an important technical skill; a clear demonstration enhances the students' ability to see. Multitasking aids the demonstration if done in a subtle form—the voice carries hints about the qualitative energy, the hands point different directions providing spatial clues, and the body demonstrates correct alignment. Students read your subtle messages and pick up faster, allowing more time to be spent dancing.

Students will learn much faster if you face the same direction as them when you are teaching fancy patterns with multiple direction changes. But when teaching simple one-directional exercises, it is helpful to become a mirror—turn around and face the students, using the opposite leg or arm. Pacing is quickened when the teacher can observe student progress and problems simultaneously. But beginning teachers may fumble when they try to start on the left after a lifetime of starting on the right. Havoc breaks out in the classroom as everyone looks around to see which foot to start with. A beginning teacher is served well by assisting an experienced teacher, if for nothing more than practicing facing the class and beginning everything on the left side. The apprentice teacher will know she has arrived at professional status when she begins to confuse the right from left just like her mentor.

Making Corrections

Teachers can be overwhelmed by the myriad of nasty problems that show up in class; it is tempting to blather, "Shoulders down, use your heel, the weight is on four, connect your arms, and why aren't you breathing?" It is a difficult task to choose one thing to comment on; it means that so many issues will be left behind. But a class not bogged down by multiple agendas yields better results. Corrections are important, but they can create a stagnant pond. A helpful rule: Demonstrate an exercise; watch the students perform it; give one comment and one comment only; repeat part of the exercise so the students can integrate it; move on. Pacing is enhanced when hands-on or verbal corrections are made while the music is playing and the dancers are dancing. The student has to hear, process, and change without stopping.

Economy of Words

The focus of a technique class is the physical accomplishment of skills. If the students do not move, they will not accomplish physical skills. As much as many teachers like to expound, technique class is not the place for it. A technique teacher should speak like a poet, not a novelist. Verbose language gets in the way of the critical pace of a technique class. If three words communicate an idea, there is more time for the student to move. Economy of words creates greater potency, much like reducing a sauce in cooking. A potent, poetic image links mind and body. Studying great poets enhances a dance teacher's skills.

A technique teacher should speak like a poet, not a novelist.

Questions

Questions from students interrupt the flow. But questions are crucial to understanding, and the teacher must balance the need for information with flow. There is always one student with a constant hand up who simply likes the attention gained by asking questions. It is helpful to take these students aside and ask them to use their skills of observation before they ask the question. If flow has turned to stagnation and the class goes into a zombie-like stare, questions *from* the teacher can stimulate curiosity again. Deliberately limiting or opening the class to questions can be useful. "Today, no questions," confirms a day of body-focused wisdom. "Today, ask any question you have been dying to ask," allows everyone to slip to a different state of mind.

Continuums of Simple and Complex, Old and New

Balancing simple and complex patterning allows the teacher to control flow. Complex patterning requires more talk, more stop-and-go, more time. If every exercise is complex, the class spends all its time learning instead of dancing. Simple patterning can be done in the "follow me" mode. Weaving simple with complex patterns is an easy way to manage the flow of the class. Relying on old material also builds momentum; repeating a phrase from the day before takes less time than teaching a new pattern. A teacher should always have a little treasure chest of old material that can be thrown out at any moment to speed the class along.

Speed

Speed is another aspect of pacing. There are slow days and there are fast days. Each creates a challenge to the students. It is exhilarating to teach at a breakneck speed, watching dancers' concentration grow as they keep pace with the speed of delivery. But if locked into speed, students will become fast with little depth of understanding. In some somatic techniques a whole day is spent just rolling the spine up and down. In technique class, the spine rolls up and down, side to side, and spirals five ways, all in eight counts. How much of this is useful every day? The body integrates information differently without a clock. Sanity is restored. Breath returns.

THE CLOCK

A ballet class is structured around time. In a 90-minute class, barre and center are each about 45 minutes long. Breaking it down even further, halfway through the barre, the class should be past dégagés. Within 20 minutes of the end of class, jumping should begin. A practical gauge keeps the teacher on track. Modern technique is too idiosyncratic to pin down, but there are some helpful hints. The halfway point is a good time to change gears. If the students have been standing in one place for over 50 percent of class, it is time to move. There is nothing worse than looking at a class and realizing there are only 10 minutes left to move. By establishing guideposts, you can stay on track and arrive on time. Ideally, the warm-up should be 25 to 30 percent of the class, the deep work 25 to 30 percent, and movement combinations and cool-down about 40 to 50 percent.

The class structure varies considerably depending on the length of class. Traditionally, dance class is 90 minutes. It is a great luxury to teach 2-hour classes and incredibly painful to deliver a 40-minute class. Time limitations demand choices in both delivery and planning. If key exercises are consistently left out due to lack of time, it is imperative to rethink the plan. Teachers often leave out what they like least. Perhaps adagio exercises are dreaded, but if skipped too often, when evaluation time arrives students will look pitiful when asked to balance. When making a class plan, it is helpful to make a note each day before class of what can be sacrificed and what cannot.

LENGTH OF CLASS

As somatic practices have permeated dance technique, an interesting development has taken place. If a class is to warm up properly and get to dancing, an hour-and-a-half class does not allow for the luxury of time somatic practices require. Teachers are faced with a dilemma if they want to include the juicy information from Bartenieff or Feldenkrais—either take the time to move slowly and never get to the dancing, or dance and never get to the slow, careful work of the somatic practices. Different schools are solving this in different ways. Some are moving to two-hour classes so that teachers have time to explore both worlds; others are offering separate classes in somatics, allowing the dance class to dance. Whatever the solution, the teacher must carefully manage class time so that dancing and learning do not suffer.

In *Zen Mind, Beginner's Mind*, Shunryu Suzuki says, "I often see many stars early in the morning. The stars are nothing but the light which has traveled at great speed many miles from the heavenly bodies. But for me the stars are not speedy beings, but calm, steady, and peaceful beings." (Suzuki 1970, 104) The teacher's job is to manage speed with a calmness of a star.

Investigations

1. Practice making up patterns quickly in private. When you feel confident, practice in front of friends.
2. Observe a class.
   - ► Read the signs of the day. What do your instincts say about pacing for the day?
   - ► Clock the time spent moving and the time spent talking. What are the percentages?
   - ► After each exercise, choose *one* comment. Did the teacher stick to one comment?
3. Practice demonstrating phrases. While moving through them clearly and precisely, use your voice to communicate quality and your hands to demonstrate spatial intent.
4. Study a work of poetry and a short work of prose. What is the difference?
5. Make clock guideposts corresponding to your class structure. Target several exercises to delete if you run out of time.

In-Class Investigations

1. On entering the studio, read the signs. Ask the students, "How are you? How are your bodies today?"
2. Present a "flow" day through nonstop movement or no talking. Present a day targeted for questions, corrections, and discussions.
3. If you are a student teacher, assist a professional. Practice mirroring the class on simple exercises (starting with the left) and flip to the same direction as students on complicated spatial patterns. When you become skilled at this task, begin to observe students while performing the pattern.
4. Say only three words when making a comment. Use them wisely.
5. Present a very fast or very slow class. Notice the students' reactions.
6. After teaching class several times, are you always behind? Go back and adjust the plan. If you always are left with more time, bravo! Use it well.

Reflection: STILLNESS

Rod Murphy, photographer; Erica Wilson Perkins, dancer. Courtesy of CounterGroove Dance Company.

With an artist's grant to travel to Mexico, I was in search of a project. I began the journey by traveling on first-class, fancy buses all over Mexico. Up above the world, I scanned the scenery from the comfortable, air-cooled cubicle and practiced language skills by watching John Wayne Westerns dubbed in Spanish. Finally, I settled in a little town called Tpotzlan, a village tucked inside a cupped mountain range, like the bottom of a bowl.

From Tpotzlan I began taking the *express* bus to Cuernavaca, a town about 15 minutes away by car, about 45 minutes by bus. I listened to conversations in Spanish; major topics were the deaths of dogs, a protest against a golf course, and Maria's tryst with the butcher. People hauled chickens, flowers, beans, cacti, corn, fruit, dolls, jewelry—anything and everything about to be sold at the market. Invariably, someone would cradle a dusty guitar and sing an old love song about his *corazon*.

Soon the express bus was not slow enough so I sought out the local buses— actually someone's rusty minivan—to towns with an abundance of Xs and Zs. One day the "bus" couldn't make it up the hill—just plain stopped in the middle of the road 10 miles from town. Everyone took the bad news silently, got off the bus, and started walking. Butterflies swarmed overhead and the stink of dead goats mingled with the sweet mountain air. Discarded beer bottles littered the roadside crosses, elaborately memorializing travelers killed on the highway. I sat down on a rock, stilled my body, and listened to the wind rustle my hair. This was my project. I knew why I had come.

chapter 9

Body Listening

C O R R E C T I O N S

*I*n his book *The Fifth Discipline: The Art and Practice of the Learning Organization*, the founder and director of the now defunct Center for Organizational Learning at MIT's Sloan School of Management, Peter Senge, writes about "systems thinking," a new way of addressing organizations: "A cloud masses, the sky darkens, leaves twist upward, and we know that it will rain. We also know that after the storm, the runoff will feed into groundwater miles away and the sky will grow clear by tomorrow. All these events are distant in time and space, and yet they are all connected within the same pattern. Each has an influence on the rest, an influence that is usually hidden from view. You can only understand the system of a rainstorm by contemplating the whole, not any individual part of the pattern." (Senge 1990, 6)

The body is a complex system of neurological patterning, physical realities, hereditary gifts, emotional scars, memories, and stories. Because they are distant in time and space, many of the causes of or influences on these patterns are hidden from view, or at least are not floating obviously to the surface. It is critical for the dance teacher to *listen* to the language of the dancers before entering their complex webs. This chapter concentrates on the skills of listening. Listening to the body is the art of seeing, sensing, doing, undoing, feeling, and touching—making connections between the whole and all its parts.

> *L*istening to the body is the art of seeing, sensing, doing, undoing, feeling, and touching—making connections between the whole and all its parts.

SEEING AND SENSING

There is an old Sufi tale about a rug merchant who tries to flatten out a bump in the center of his carpet. He jumps on it, and to his satisfaction the bump disappears, but moments later it reappears in the far corner. He keeps jumping and kicking, ironically destroying the carpet as the bump keeps magically moving. Finally, to his amazement, a snake crawls out from under the carpet. When making corrections, if a teacher steps in too soon to fix the problem without properly observing the habit, the snake will simply slip to a new place.

Developing an Eye

When I first began teaching, I corrected everyone as much as possible, trying to make my mark as a good teacher. None of my corrections really worked, but no matter; the job was being accomplished. Fortunately for my students, I injured my foot, which forced me to sit down. Sitting invited stillness, and in stillness, I began the practice of seeing. At first my razor-sharp eyes would zero in on the apparent problem; but if the lens of the camera were opened and I looked again, the subtler problem underlying the obvious ones emerged. By keeping quiet and observing further, the same pattern would play itself out in other movements, such as jumping and running. If the pattern were corrected too soon, I would disturb a chain of reactions, destroying my opportunity to see the whole.

"She has a good eye," we say of a teacher who makes good corrections. This teacher has practiced seeing, operating her eyes as a good photographer operates a camera. Changing the lens on the camera allows the teacher to create a lively interplay between very specific details and the whole picture. A wide-angle lens gives a holistic view, a reference point to return to. A telescopic lens gives specifics. By narrowing the focus to just the feet, the teacher makes particular and potentially insightful observations. If she narrows the focus even further to a big toe, she finds the missing DNA. But if the lens stays focused on details without consistently returning to the wide angle, the details are not incorporated into the whole. The best photographs of an immense space, such as the Grand Canyon, often focus on a small detail. A flower is highlighted in reference to the vastness of the red cliffs.

Filtering the Information

Paradoxically, sometimes it is necessary to close the eyes or at least put a filter on the camera. Seeing the shoulders up by the ears, the faces tight with grimaces, and the eyes bulging with anticipation overwhelms even the most expert teacher. Without the filter, the tendency is to bark our multiple commands in one breath: "Shouldersdownbellyupdropthepelviskneesovertoesrelaxyourjawlifttheankles and —don't forget to breathe!"

One thing at a time will yield more results. Careful observation brings a thousand corrections to mind. Nothing is accomplished when too many suggestions exist, so rivet the attention toward one comment. Simplify everything at that moment. If rolling through the foot is the focus, strip away as much as possible—the rhythm, the arm carriage, or the movement pattern. Ask students to articulate every joint of the foot with awareness and conscious control, and then put the layers back together. Can they roll the foot in rhythm while standing on one leg, lifting the arms, and spouting poetry?

This layering back and forth from simplicity to complexity weaves the class together. The "Aha!" moment of discovery is electric when a student suddenly experiences the application of the foot roll in a more complex jump. This weaving moves forward or backward in time. At the end of class, you might observe that everyone juts their chins out while leaping. On closer investigation, you observe that the knee rolls in and the pelvis tucks just before the chin goes out. Make a mental note to do a plié tendu action early in the next class, and carefully observe the interaction of the knee, pelvis, and neck.

Pay attention to weight-bearing joints first because they are more prone to injury.

Pay attention to weight-bearing joints first because they are more prone to injury. Protection is a priority. Knee and ankle alignment deserve attention before worrying about shoulder and arm placement. All are connected, but the journey must start somewhere. One fine day when the weight-bearing joints are sliding toward alignment, a joke will turn the grimaces to smiles and the shoulders will drop down effortlessly. Composer Mary Ellen Childs titled one of her works "The Capacity of Calm Endurance," and she explains this title as the "definition of patience."

Observing From All Angles

A dentist takes X-rays of the teeth from all angles to access complete information. Moving either yourself or the students around allows you to see a three-dimensional image of the body. Roaming the class or facing it in different directions gives different information than holding court from the front. Observation from all angles holds true with individual bodies as well. When stumped by a particularly difficult alignment issue, ask the student to do a headstand. An upside-down body yields different information. The clue to unlocking the door may be masked in the normal standing position. If a student is struggling to do a turn, have her do a facsimile of the turn horizontally, as a roll on the floor. You just might find the missing key.

Catching the Moment

A photojournalist is trained to seek the action, the important moment. Where are you looking at any given moment? It takes effort to look at a student who is awkward and struggling; the eye tends to gravitate to the dancer who is floating and soaring. The teacher–student relationship is a human one, full of inadequacies. However, teaching is different from friendships; you can pick your friends. Students come in all shapes, sizes, and voices, and some are easier to like than others; but that should not determine the amount of time spent observing them.

The camera continues to search for the right picture. Are you focusing on the rhythmic patterning when the problem really lies in shifting weight? Are you obsessing about the shoulders when a potentially dangerous twist of the ankle is occurring down below? Sometimes we have a one-track mind. Three-year-old children are famous for this behavior. A child was so obsessed with seeing the penguins at the zoo that he completely skipped everything else. "I want to see the penguins," he kept saying. When he got to the penguins, they were gone. So what's the use of that? Being present and open to what is swirling through the space is crucial to the art of teaching. One day a fortuitous accident will occur and you will see just the right thing at just the right time; you will be the photographer who clicked the shutter as a soldier kissed a woman on V-E Day.

KNOWING ONESELF

To understand the system of another body, a teacher must be able to see beyond the scope of his own. Scan body proportions on the street or inspect physical idiosyncrasies in the grocery line. Ideally, lie on a nude beach in some exotic locale, thoroughly researching the subject matter. Each body is unique for thousands of reasons; size, color, proportions, structure, energy, and personality are just the beginning. Observe how differently bodies are put together: long torsos and short legs, big breasts and no butt, long feet and tiny head. Why is this important? Each individual's proportions determine the center of gravity. The center of gravity is derived literally from the intersection of the three primary body planes (sagittal, lateral, and transverse), separating the body in half equally by weight. If a person has a heavy upper body and a slight lower body, he has a relatively high center of gravity. If a person carries her weight in the bottom half, she has a lower center of gravity. A right-handed tennis player has more weight in his musculature on the right side, creating a physical center slightly to the right. Dolly Parton's endowed chest moves her center of gravity forward, whereas an endowed bottom moves the center toward the back of the body. Each person's center of gravity is distinct, and as a teacher approaches each unique body, awareness of the differences is crucial.

A teacher with short legs and a massive upper body is effortlessly demonstrating a pattern that plunges into the floor and soars back up again in a second. He instructs the class to "use your center," pointing to a place high in the rib cage. Many bodies in the class (especially female) are built in the reverse: slight upper body and a strong, long, lower body. They drop easily but soaring back up again is another matter. The students try over and over to contract where he is pointing, but it only creates more effort and frustration. He is imposing his center without taking into account the variations in the students' body proportions.

Breathe by imagining the lungs are filling from the bottom to the top or from the top to the bottom. One way will feel familiar, another will feel strange, a road less traveled. A teacher can easily jump to the conclusion that because one way feels better, it must be the right way to breathe. But is it? Perhaps there are many ways to breathe. Slip into unknown territory and experiment. Build awareness as the guide and students will find their own applications.

A dance teacher must learn to observe not only visually but also kinesthetically. Walk behind people on the street and practice incorporating their movement language. How do they initiate their legs for the walk? How do they stop the body's momentum? This game of subtlety and deception (never let yourself be caught) teaches kinesthetic listening. As a movement chameleon, observe a particular student and slip into his skin. What choices is the student making? Slipping into the students' physical psyches provides new insights.

REFLEXES

Before diving into the complex subject of correcting alignment, let's take a side trip to look at reflexes, a web of triggering devices that influence each individual movement choice. When I first took a Body-Mind Centering class, we were working with the rooting reflex. The rooting reflex is one of the first to be set up in our hardwiring. If a baby is stroked on the cheek close to the mouth, he will turn his lips toward the stroke. Mothers learn this trick to attract the baby to the nipple. This is fundamental to being fed. Lying on the floor during the workshop, our partners stroked our cheeks. I became frustrated very fast. "I'm a trained dancer; I can turn my head any direction I want." I was told to have patience, so I let go of my resistance and simply enjoyed the sensation. The stroking had continued for some time when suddenly the smell of baby powder permeated the air. I never did turn my head, but the experience grounded my understanding of the power of reflexes buried within the body.

Building Blocks

Reflexes control the first commands to the body: Find food, push to see, and coil for comfort. Reflexes are the front line of survival. But as the infant learns about the world, reflexes become deeply embedded in the body; they disappear underneath the surface, so to speak. We begin to have choices about whether or not to turn our heads, whether fight or flight best suits the situation. However, if we listen deeply, the web of triggers can still be called on to help.

Bonnie Bainbridge Cohen has done extensive work on reflexes. In *Sensing, Feeling, and Action: The Experiential Anatomy of Body-Mind Centering,* Cohen explains in detail how these fundamental building blocks underlie all integrated and effortless movement. A thorough reading of these articles is a must for any dance teacher. Let's take a brief look at this alphabet and its influence on movement training.

Cohen distinguishes three categories of automatic patterning underlying movement: primitive reflexes, righting reactions, and equilibrium responses. She sees these in a hierarchy; each underlies the next in a sequence of increasing complexity. Primitive reflexes, managed by the spine and the brain stem, establish basic gross movement patterning. "Righting reflexes are more advanced patterns of movement that are controlled primarily by the mid-brain." They control the head in relation to gravity and the torso. "Equilibrium responses are automatic patterns of response for maintaining balance as a result of the shifting of one's center of gravity and/or base of support through space, from lying to standing to flying." (Cohen 1993, 124) Equilibrium responses are found in our outstretched arms as we trip over a rug or in a contact improviser's ability to effortlessly maneuver the body to the floor during a fall.

Primitive Reflexes

Teachers are often heard saying, "Get out of your head." Literally, this means get out of the cerebral cortex, the analyzing part of the mind, and into the low brain, or cerebellum. Performing the job quietly and effectively, the cerebellum finds the most efficient pathway in movement. Take for example the flexor withdrawal reflex, which withdraws the arms and legs. In African dance forms, the legs often withdraw in a jump. In ballet the legs tend to extend in jumps. Watching a trained ballet dancer execute a withdrawing jump in African dance, it is clear that the dancer's overtrained body needs to go back to the most basic reflex, a withdrawal similar to a child tucking its foot up after being tickled. This pattern underlies the first attempts at walking, when the thrust into the floor is followed by a retraction and lift. A teacher helps the student by providing retraction images that stimulate the knowledge hidden under all the layers of learned movement behavior.

Sometimes a reflex triggers a powerful response that is not particularly useful to the dancer. The extensor thrust reflex is triggered when an infant's foot or hand is stimulated and the baby pushes away. When powerful extensor muscles, such as the hamstrings and gluteus maximus, are stimulated, all the other extensor muscles rush in to join the fun. This explains the classic cheerleading jump and the tendency of students to arch backwards when jumping. A teacher needs to bring awareness to the flexors of the trunk (abdominal muscles) in order to balance the affects of the reflex, allowing choices beyond the cheerleading classic.

Righting Reflexes

The righting reflexes convey where we are in relation to gravity. Any time the body is tossed upside down, righting reflexes act to upright it. Watch dancers' heads pop up in a tilt or handstand, trying to find some semblance of vertical. As champions of falling, rolling, and inverting, modern dance teachers need to understand what is at play here. Cohen explains it this way, "I feel that what happens when you just let your head go heavy is that you're actually going below the righting reaction, you are tapping into even lower responses. So in a certain way you're more primitive and have even less choices because you don't have any response except for the yielding

Flexor withdrawal.

Upside down movement.

The head as a limb.

to gravity [Tonic Lab] which is controlled by the low brain." (Cohen 1993, 133) This listening to the lowest rung of the ladder in the reflex chain is a great beginning—it gives the dancer full-bodied weight. A dancer learns about gravity's pull much as an infant does fresh from the womb. The primitive reflexes teach the body the basics.

Equilibrium Responses

Operating out of the mid-brain, the righting reflexes are responsible for creating a partnership between head and torso; they are essential guides to finding a plumb line—alignment. As righting reflexes are incorporated into the more complex equilibrium responses, the body communicates with higher centers in the brain. According to Cohen, "If you want to go above the RRs (Righting Reflexes) to the ERs (Equilibrium Responses), then the head becomes an extremity in its own right, so that it can move into space the same way that the arms and legs do. I would also say that the tail becomes a limb. With the equilibrium responses you go to the forebrain control, in which case everything is possible. Using the head as another limb allows more possibilities; it opens up cortical imagination." (Cohen 1993, 133) Guiding students to efficient alignment stimulates not only better mechanical functioning but creativity as well.

ALIGNMENT AND POSTURE

Much of a dance teacher's time is spent addressing alignment. But one more side trip is necessary before entering the rubric of correcting alignment. First we need to understand what alignment is and why it is so important in dance training. Efficiency of movement is key to ease in dancing. If the muscles are overworking to keep the structure from falling, too much effort is being expended. If the bones are aligned, the structure can withstand the forces acting on it. Weight should be poured through the bones—if Tinkertoys are not stacked properly, they will fall over; if the bones in the body are not aligned, the muscles will take over. In the early article, "The Balancing of Forces in the Human Being: Its Application to Postural Patterns," Mabel Elsworth Todd illustrates the concept: "The bones, as the weight-bearing members of the body, should be so adjusted that the muscles will be free to perform their function, that of movement; they should not be obliged to hold in place unbalanced weights. As the body moves, the weights shift at the joints and these shifts should be made with as little strain as possible. Therefore, a position should be found which insures such a balance of parts as would favor the best mechanical advantage in movement." (Todd 1929, 56)

Dynamic Alignment

If alignment is the efficient stacking of bones, what is dynamic alignment? In an interview with Joan Skinner, founder of Skinner Releasing Technique, Stephanie

Skura learned, "When we're dealing with alignment in these classes, we're dealing with multidirectional balancing—not holding the balance in any part of the body, but relating to multigravitational fields. When this alignment is harmonious with the larger energy systems, it releases the individual. Distortions of alignment constrict the individual. These distortions are constrictive because they are warps of the energy patterns, which flow through us and around us and out of us and into us. A Releasing alignment is not a fixed alignment; it's always in flux. Everything is relative to everything else. So I see it as harmonious or not harmonious. When it's harmonious, then something is unleashed; then power and energy are released and that becomes Releasing dance." (Skura 1990, 13)

The dance teacher is searching for efficient, dynamic alignment of the bones. An engineer is trained to see the results of the forces of gravity: weight, compression, tension, torsion, and sheer. But there are other forces for the human being. Psychological and emotional forces also play a role.

Postural Patterns

In *BodyStories: A Guide to Experiential Anatomy,* Andrea Olsen says, "Posture is the way we live in our structure—the energy and attitudes which moment by moment shape our bodies." (Olsen 1991, 9) Posture is an accumulation of physical and psychological forces acting on a structure, as a riverbed that has been shaped by the river that runs through it. If a child is yelled at most of her life, her chest deflates, her

Dynamic alignment.

Posture.

eyes withdraw, and her structure collapses. Like posture, *body attitude* is a distinct term, specific to Bartenieff Movement Fundamentals. Rudolf Laban first introduced the idea of body attitude by observing the expressions of the body in terms of expansion and contraction. Psychoanalyst Judith Kestenberg says that body attitude "indicates the qualities of movement which, through frequent use, have left their imprint upon the body" (Bartenoff and Lewis 1980, 111).

Social forces and moral attitudes add to the complexity. Todd says, "Too often have the positions of our bodies been the result of response to some preconceived idea of the 'proper' (morally perfect) instead of the balanced (mechanically perfect) position." (Todd 1929, 12) The forces of life create character in the body. The proprioceptors (sensors of position and movement) become used to whatever position one has lived in. Asking for a mere opening of the chest or a softening of the sternum causes shock waves—both physical and emotional—throughout the body. The teacher enters the Grand Canyon riding the rapids.

FIXING OR GUIDING

With a hunger to *fix* things, a teacher moves in. *Fix* is a paradoxical word; as much as it means change, it also means permanence, as in fixed star (a star whose position in relation to other stars appears not to change). *Fixity* is a state of permanence. But fixing is a one-way street. A two-way street offers possibilities, providing the tools for the student to go on a journey. Sometimes that means putting up roadblocks to old behaviors and sometimes that means providing a new map. Rachel Naomi Remen speaks about the falsity of fixing in *Kitchen Table Wisdom*. "Much in the concept of diagnosis and cure is about fixing, and a narrow-bore focus on fixing people's problems can lead to denial of the power of their process. Years ago, I took full credit when people became well; their recovery was testimony to my skill and knowledge as a physician. I never recognized that without their biological, emotional, and spiritual process, which could respond to my interventions, nothing could have changed at all. All the time I thought I was repairing, I was collaborating." (Remen 1996, 224)

The founder of the Alexander Technique, Frederich Mathus Alexander, was a champion of collaboration between the student and teacher. He believed that in order to change habitual responses and attitudes, it is necessary to give up the old response habit. According to Alexander's philosophy, changing a habit involves three components: awareness of the habit, inhibition of the habit, and mental directions for a new pathway. The teacher addresses the first component through careful observation and communication with the student: Sally is made aware that she raises her hip every time she performs a grand battement. The second component is inhibition, or what Alexander liked to call *conscious inhibition*. Because saying no to the old takes time, this step is largely foreign in the dance world. Technique moves too fast. But stillness is important because it provides time for the brain to unhook the sequence embedded in the computer hard drive. Once the hardware is unhooked, all kinds of new information can enter. To *not do* is terribly uncomfortable for a dancer, since they pride themselves on the *doing*. But with enough coaching to undo, the student finally takes a breath and lets go. Now the body is available for new choices. The third step is to provide mental directions so that new pathways are encouraged. This is done through imagery and touch. Imagery is discussed in chapter 10. But how does a teacher effect change through touch?

TOUCHING

Touch is the teacher's most effective tool because it is so immediate. One research project found that a waitress who casually touched her clients received greater tips. The teacher lifts an arm to correct form, touches a neck to relax tension, or pulls a leg to stimulate length. Touching each person in class at least once every day is a rule to live by. With large classes of 40 or more, it is a challenge, but it communicates that you are there, and it is the fastest way to reach each person. One pass around the class and you can soothe one person's neck, shake a hand, or stretch a foot, acknowledging each soul's presence in the journey of change.

Safe Touches

Remembering that stories lurk below the surface, begin with *safe* touches. Limit your contact to areas that are more accustomed to being touched, such as the back, neck, and arms. Put an antenna out for those people who are tense when you come near. Go slowly, always sensitive to the body's unwritten language. As the class gets used to touch, expand the possibilities. Dance teachers are notorious for grabbing a crotch because they so passionately want the student to find the subtlety of the adductor muscles. But to outsiders this behavior can be easily misconstrued to be a different kind of passion. Male teachers are particularly suspect and should proceed with caution.

Pressure

Touch can overwhelm the sensory neurons. A teacher grabs a leg and squeezes with all her might. "Do you feel it?" she yells. Of course you feel it. You feel her hands, the pressure, and the pain. Did you feel turnout? Not in the least; the pressure of her hands overwhelmed the sensory neurons. The touch should match the need. Sometimes a pull or yank does the trick, but a gentle touch is generally most useful. It allows the student to listen to the underlying message of his own proprioceptors.

A teacher also needs to be completely aware of the way her touch enters and exits the student's body. It is helpful to think of moving through layers. First establish a skin touch – lightly communicating with the heat of the student's body. Next, if the correction warrants more force, press deeper to feel a muscular energy. It will feel elastic and juicy. Finally, if a deep sensation is necessary, allow your weight to shift to the structure of the bones. When exiting the body, especially in deeper touches, take the time to move slowly, recognizing each layer.

In yoga there are classes based on a style of teaching in Mysore, India. During these Mysore classes the student practices the asanas, or postures, under the careful eye of the teacher. While in a posture, the teacher pulls, prods, or sits on the student to encourage the body to stretch to new levels. In the hands of a bad teacher, this can be a very frightening experience. Pouring all her weight into the student's body, which is already stretched to its limit, the teacher's ego glows when she pushes the student beyond the edge. Smart students learn to retreat 10 to 15 degrees in the posture before the teacher comes near; the teacher's ego is satisfied and limbs are not in danger of separating from the body. Extreme pressure can sometimes bring the student across a new threshold. But check your ego at the door. Take time going in and going out, respond to the resistance in the student's body, and listen to the breath patterns.

Spatial Intent

Spatial information is communicated through touch. Rubbing a student with one hand while tapping and punching with the other hand gives too many spatial messages. Think about one clear direction when touching a student. Imagine the flow of energy you want to encourage and let your hands create clear and direct messages. Float the hands out from the center of the sacrum to create pelvic width or trail your fingers down the neck to encourage the release of the upper trapezius. Correct only with touch. If students follow effortlessly with no verbal direction, your touch is speaking loud and clear.

Touching techniques should foster student awareness. Instead of pushing a limb where you want it to go, lightly tap the limb, encouraging the student to move toward the touch. This empowers the student for it engages the muscles that need to work allowing the teacher to carry a lighter load for the day.

Awareness Within the Teacher's Body

Pay particular attention to your own body while making a correction. How is your body aligned? What is the energy flow in your body? Some schools of thought encourage the practitioner to create mental images within the body while touching a student. For instance, if a student's energy flow is stuck in the neck area, put your hands on the student's neck and imagine your own neck softening. Imaging sends subtle messages through the body and reminds the teacher to be receptive and listening. Caution must prevail while using this technique, for it may lead to self-injury if a teacher is too sensitive. The harmful energy of a student may enter the teacher's body. Be judicious in deciding what works for you.

Most of all a teacher must have the right mental energy. Dowd calls this "…a state of lucid 'neutrality': mechanically balanced, emotionally calm, mentally open, and without any urgency to succeed. Otherwise, my own internal activities function as a kind of 'white noise' that interferes with my ability to perceive the person I am touching." (Dowd 1995, 78) Attaining a state of openness with a complete lack of expectations is a difficult task. Dowd provides a helpful image, "I use my hands as much as I use my eyes when teaching movement to another person. It takes, therefore, only a small step to conjoin the activities of touching and seeing into the same metaphoric vehicle. However, any step is movement into the unknown. In striding out, the landscape around me will surely change into one that is strange and mysterious. The metaphor I carry with me may serve as a beam of light into this new land, but all else will be shadow. New metaphors will have to follow if the whole environment is to be illuminated." (Dowd 1995, 77) A teacher enters a mysterious land with each new touch.

Collaboration Between Student and Teacher

The most obvious place isn't always the best place to touch. The pelvis seems to be the most obvious place to correct, as it is the center of physical weight; change the center and everything else will follow. However, pushing the pelvis in one direction often allows the snake to sneak to another part of the body. Teachers of the Alexander Technique gently guide the body toward new patterning by touching the head. With a gentle touch on the occipital ridge (the back of the head) and the smallest suggestion upwards, the head guides ribs and pelvis into a more efficient alignment true to each individual body. Stimulating the righting reflexes in the head and neck region allows the complex structure to find its own way through the maze. Collaboration takes place between student and teacher. With one hand guiding the head upward, the other hand seeks out the holding patterns; for example, if it is in the sternum, placing the second hand there produces a message of weight and release.

When a person has spent a lifetime moving a certain way, the patterns become comfortable even though they might not be mechanically efficient. Interfering with this comfort is tricky. As the teacher moves in to soften a chest, the weight moves forward and the student will invariably say, "But it feels like I'm falling forward." It indeed feels forward, because the proprioceptors (body sensors) have become familiar with a backward thrust; they are comfortable with the pattern even though it means muscles are overengaged to maintain the balance. In addition, when the weight shifts, the student will often feel a new sense of self, perhaps more confident or assertive. With both alignment and posture shifting, how does the teacher perceive the "right" place? What should the teacher listen for?

The Still Point

Ask the student to move slowly from an exaggerated old pattern to the new pattern being learned. Using hands-on technique, guide the student slowly toward a more balanced alignment. You will know the optimal place because it will be a *still point* full of nothing and everything. Listen for a hum of energy, a calm flow, or a sigh. Let the student remain in the still point for at least 10 seconds, listening to the new sensations. The proprioceptors need time to get used to a different logic. Now ask the student to repeat this several times, gradually relying less on outside stimuli. This journey from old to new provides the nervous system time to integrate new rhythms and paths. It also strengthens and lengthens the appropriate musculature, preparing the body to move through new and unfamiliar pathways. In the end, how do you know a student has arrived at the still point? Go back to seeing and listening. Both the teacher and student observe whether breathing is easier, the spine is longer, and jumping is higher.

EMPOWERING STUDENT OBSERVATION

In order to empower students' choices in movement reeducation, a teacher needs to bring historical and personal context into the classroom, ask the right questions, and develop independence in the student learner. This takes work in and out of the classroom.

Presenting Historical Context

Martha Graham made very different choices about movement than a release-based teacher would. A teacher needs to be aware of the stylistic and historical choices that frame personal choices and communicate this to students, giving context to what students are learning. For instance, Graham technique moves from the center and radiates outward. A release-based technique may initiate movement from a distal point, but thread it back towards center. Imagine Graham performing a released movement and the teacher saying, "That's totally *wrong, Martha!*" Right and wrong have a historical, social, and philosophical context. Proponents of arts education have embraced a movement called discipline-based arts education, which has a goal "to develop students' abilities to understand and appreciate art. This involves knowledge of the theories and contexts of art and abilities to respond to as well as create art." (Clark, Day, and Greer 1987, 130-193) Teachers bring context to the classroom, so the correction from one teacher to drop the weight and another to lift the weight can be understood in terms of the larger picture.

Asking the Right Questions

Students teach the teacher to listen; their powerful perceptions lead the teacher to the moment of truth the students are ready to hear. If a group of students is particularly bad at getting movement sequences, targeted questions reveal what they don't understand. "What don't you understand—spatial directions, rhythmic patterns, shifting weight, sequencing of movement?" Students answer back, "Sequencing of movement and spatial patterns." So with every turn of direction the teacher asks, "What's next?" They began to map the movement in terms of "what's next" points. One student starts naming them: "Turn right at buffalo, slide on groundhog, and jump at crazy horse," The images give them something to latch onto. By guiding the teacher, they shape their own learning.

Developing Students' Independence

Ultimately, a dancer becomes his own teacher. The teacher's job is to wean the puppies off the teat. Although it is satisfying to the ego to come up with wise answers to all their precious questions, at some point, the teacher should turn the questions back to students. This can be frustrating for both parties, but ultimately the teacher's job is to develop the students' personal responsibility toward learning. After exercises ask, "What worked? What was your experience?" Invite students to access their inner teacher, and the weaning process begins. In the Buddhist tradition, teachers provide the students with koans, seemingly impossible questions. Their intention is to provoke, not necessarily to answer.

Bonnie Bainbridge Cohen speaks about leaving doors open for students to discover on their own in *Sensing, Feeling, and Action: The Experiential Anatomy of Body-Mind Centering.* "I try to slip in under the consciousness, while still giving people enough of the conscious experience so they can recreate it in some way, or be able to keep that doorway open until the information comes through by itself, through a personal experience." (Cohen 1993, 13)

Students As Teachers

Students benefit from watching other students. Seeing a problem objectively gives context to their struggle. Teaming students in pairs during hands-on corrections allows every student to receive physical attention and trains the critical eye. In a big class where the teacher is pulled in a thousand directions, this is a very effective tool. The *toucher* learns to see with an objective eye (building teaching skills). The *touchee* receives valuable kinesthetic lessons. Both students become engaged in the act of teaching and learning. In order for this to work, the teacher needs to focus attention on the toucher. When the teacher demonstrates exactly where the touch is, how much pressure to use, and the spatial direction, the toucher learns the skills of observation and touch. The teacher should rove the class to assure that the touchers are working correctly. Is this possible to do with beginning students? Beginners are not ready to correct a classmate's subtle hip placement, but simple activities with defined rules are possible. Perhaps a student places hands on a partner's neck, giving weight and creating calm, while the *touchee* does a simple plié.

Trying Too Hard

Then there is the old saying "you can lead a horse to water…." Once the correction is given and no progress is being made, how should it be reinforced? Sometimes it is best to let it go for the time being and come back to it later, respecting the body's own time clock. In *The Art of Teaching Dance Technique,* West Coast teacher Gloria Newman advises, "I have found that many times the dancer's difficulty in making a correction is based on trying too hard, which creates too much tension in the body. This inhibits the ability to really see and experience the movement and commonly leads to frustration. The need then is to redirect the focus, energy, and/or attitude." (Schlaich and DuPont 1993, 62)

Sometimes an intervention in a problem creates undue strain, and a teacher must recognize when it is time to back off. In systems thinking this is called *compensating feedback:* ". . . Well-intentioned interventions call forth responses from the system that offset the benefits of the intervention. We all know how it feels to be facing compensating feedback—the harder you push, the harder the system pushes back; the more effort you expend trying to improve matters, the more effort seems to be required." (Senge 1990, 58)

Private Discussions

It is helpful to take every student aside sometime during her course of study. Private time provides an opportunity to discuss issues that need slow and careful attention, such as alignment or personal goals. Outside of class, formality is forgone and deeper discussions result. Valuable information surfaces, enhancing understanding of the struggles the student is facing, such as past injuries, a death in the family, or psychological fear. Private time provides a space to address delicate issues that could possibly be humiliating to the student if presented publicly. For instance, a student may be asking questions to seek attention. If curtailed publicly, the whole class receives the message that questions are bad, and the student feels humiliated. In a private discussion, issues of attention-seeking can be addressed, guiding the student toward a path of visual learning. Private time is also an excellent place to discuss personal goals. Are the individual's goals in line with the class goals? If not, how can they be realigned? All the parts that make up a person are distant in time and space, and yet everything is connected. It is the teacher's role to comprehend the whole picture.

Anne Michaels writes in *Fugitive Pieces*, "We think of weather as transient, change-able and above all ephemeral; but everywhere nature remembers. Trees, for ex-ample, carry the memory of rainfall." (Michaels 1996, 211) While a teacher's touch may be ephemeral and students transient, the rain seeps in.

Investigations

1. Study bodies:
   - ► Take a series of photographs of bodies on the street, or ideally, on a nude beach. Take pictures from every angle. Include wide shots and close-ups. Spreading out the photographs in front of you, look for a variety of infor-mation. Where is the center of gravity for each person? What alignment patterns do you notice? How does posture influence alignment?
   - ► Take pictures at a sports event. Try to capture *the moment*— the athlete in the air with the ball, the elation in the face of a victor, a fall, a goal, or an injury. What do you notice about your sense of presence while photo-graphing? Where are you looking?
   - ► Practice the art of a movement chameleon. Walk behind people on the street (without getting caught). Slip into their skin. Notice the way they initiate a walk, the carriage of the spine, and how you feel.
2. Observe a class:
   - ► Pick one student to observe. Watch his body structure, his energy, his spatial intent, and his rhythmic abilities. Where does he initiate movement? What is his favorite part of class? Where or when does his concentration fade?
   - ► Watch the student who is struggling in the back of the class. How does this observation change your perception of what is being learned in the class as a whole?
   - ► Watch a movement exercise in class and narrow your focus to just the feet. What do you see? Open your lens and observe the whole, then go back to the feet. How does one inform the other?
   - ► What corrections does the teacher give after an exercise? Do the com-ments effect change?
   - ► Observe a class from the front, side, and back. What is the difference in your observations?
   - ► Observe the flexor withdrawal reflex in a baby nursing. Observe the extensor thrust reflex when a baby jumps on someone's knees. Observe the righting reflexes when the baby is turned off her vertical axis. Observe the same patterns in a dance class.
3. Exaggerate a faulty alignment pattern. Move slowly to the *still point*. What do you observe in your body?
4. Write a biography about the teachers who most influenced your movement and your philosophy. Why did you gravitate to these particular teachers? Write a fictional story about a student who encounters you for his first dance class.

In-Class Investigations

Note: A student can do these as a teaching assistant.

1. Teach a class and do not make one comment. Simply watch, listen, and observe.

2. After watching a movement exercise, make only *one* comment.

3. Build an entire class around an observation you made the day before.

4. Touch every person at least once every day.

5. Correct only through touch. Observe a student carefully, then put your hands on her tension spot. Pay attention to the location, direction, and use of force. Pay attention to your own body.

6. Spend a day sharing your history of training and philosophical point of view with the students.

7. Learn something new. Be a beginner at basket weaving, diving, painting, golf. How does it feel to be corrected? What makes you laugh at yourself? What remains a mystery?

Reflection: CONNECTIVITY

The following are journal entries from Authentic Movement sessions. Authentic Movement is a somatic dance-movement process begun by Mary Starks Whitehouse and continued by Janet Adler. In Authentic Movement one person moves with their eyes closed while another witnesses the journey. Afterwards both the mover and the witness write about their experiences. Stories lurk beneath the skin.

Erika Dufour, photographer; Paul Cipponeri and Kimberly Nelson, dancers.

September 21, 2000—*I am a witness.*

She begins by talking with a hollow breath. I imagine a story in which she is talking to her ancestors—jumping, blowing, clearing, and cleansing out the empty space. She moves to the corner, and like an autistic child, she makes strange noises. She pushes her head against the wall. Precariously balanced, she is in danger, but I feel it is useless to tell her to stop. She falls with a crashing boom. She tries to wrap herself around the wall. I want to give her hooks to climb on. Finally I have had enough as she simply leans against the wall. With the weight of the wall supporting her, I am at peace.

A major decision is pending for this mover.

November 5, 2000—*I am the mover.*

Eyes closed, I plunge downward, my witness providing a tether to the world above. A large horizontal expanse appears above and I poke my head through the hole in the sky. I can see vast empty space, light and airy. I return to the place underneath the sky going under, under, under until I'm on my back, spread out as an eagle pinned to the ground. The insides of me open; my viscera are exposed. Great carrion birds fly in to eat my carcass. Compressing my head, I feel separate from my heavy body. Suddenly, I need to stand. Skimming the surface of the soft air, I'm dancing on top of my grave. A shaft of light hits my body and I play the shaft of air as if playing a flute.

After burying my mother, I have been worried about her body being cold in the ground.

April 7, 2001—*I am a witness.*

She lies on the floor, on her back, quiet. At first glance she seems to be doing nothing. As I look closer, her breath consumes me. Lying on a cloud, she is immensely light, floating above the earth. She takes one long breath, then she sinks down to the earth. She begins twitching and the intervals between inhale and exhale lengthen. Breathing stops. Her core shakes, nostrils flare, and pelvic floor rumbles. Like a magnet, her arms float up delicately, drawing energy to a single line bisecting her body. I don't want any of the threads to fly away.

This person is recovering from cancer.

chapter 10

Space Moving
IMAGES

When the right image is offered at the right moment, the space moves, the ground trembles and the class takes one flying leap toward understanding. Why did the image work? An image for movement is held in the space of the mind. The nervous system then selects the most efficient path for that image to be carried out by signaling the muscles and bones involved in the master plan. A complex computer is at work in every move we make. If the teacher tries to micromanage and dictate which muscle to use when, the body will rebel and become confused. Given just the right image, the body will choose the most efficient path, thus honoring the innate wisdom of each unique person. Images create the bridge between the brain and movement. This chapter explores how to use the power of images.

POWER OF IMAGES AND METAPHORS

An image is the reliving of a sensation in the absence of the original stimulus: a representation, a symbol or emblem, a type of embodiment. An image is a method of communicating what the body is to embody. The nervous system comprehends movement by creating visual, auditory, or kinesthetic pictures. The clearer the picture, the better it functions.

Metaphors are useful images. A metaphor is a word or phrase that ordinarily means one thing and is applied to another to suggest a likeness or a concrete representation of an abstract idea or concept. In *Taking Root to Fly: Articles on Functional Anatomy,* Irene Dowd explains the usefulness of metaphors in teaching movement.

Metaphor can be the fist that breaks through the dark glass between what is already known and what is still mystery.

Through the vehicle of metaphor, we can participate in that movement from what is to what can be.

Once in the new land on the other side of the dark glass, we can use the metaphor as a landmark from which to foray into the new world.

Eventually the metaphor dissipates in explosion outward from its core into the space of new landscape. Finally, another metaphor coils around the landscape, coalescing into a new vehicle in which we continue the journey. (Dowd 1995, 69)

Gerald Zaltman, a member of the Mind/Brain/Behavior Initiative at Harvard, has created a new approach to marketing research called ZMET, the Zaltman Metaphor Elicitation Technique. This approach is based on studies of neuroscience as well as Jungian psychology. Zaltman says, "Because we represent the outcome of thoughts verbally, it's easy to think that thought occurs in the form of words. That's just not the case." *New York Times* reporter Emily Eakin elaborates, "Mr. Zaltman argues that consumers can't tell you what they think because they just don't know. Their deepest thoughts, the ones that account for their behavior in the marketplace, are unconscious. Not only that, he insists, those thoughts are primarily visual as well." (Eakin 2002, A17)

In Howard Gardner's groundbreaking book *Frames of Mind: The Theory of Multiple Intelligences,* he describes six types of intelligence: linguistic, musical, logical-mathematical, spatial, bodily-kinesthetic, and personal. Spatial intelligence is the ability to imagine, enabling thought to take place across the domains, connecting musical and bodily intelligence or logical and personal intelligence. He explains, "Indeed, underlying many scientific theories are 'images' of wide scope: Darwin's vision of the 'tree of life,' Freud's notion of the unconscious as submerged like an iceberg, John Dalton's view of the atom as a tiny solar system are the productive figures that give rise to, and help to embody, key scientific conceptions. It is possible that such mental models or images also play a role in more mundane forms of problem solving." (Gardner 1983, 177)

Images in Somatic Training

In this century, the use of imagery in movement training has exploded, particularly in somatic practices such as Ideokinesis, Alexander, Body-Mind Centering, and Feldenkrais. Although different in their approach, each explores the connections between mind and body, between nerves and muscles. Dancers have been eager participants in these practices, and people such as Joan Skinner (founder of Skinner Releasing), Irene Dowd (who works with dancers in neuromuscular training), or Bonnie Bainbridge Cohen, have integrated body and mind connections into their practices. Explore the books mentioned in this chapter, since limitations of space prohibit a full discussion. Ideokinesis has developed information and images that are particularly useful to technique teachers, so a brief history follows.

Short History of Ideokinesis

As a movement teacher at Columbia University Teachers College in the early 1900s, Mabel Ellsworth Todd explored how the body responded to the will of the mind. She experimented with her students using a holistic approach honoring the emotional, mental, and physical capacities of the human structure and the body's relationship to gravity and force. Rebelling against the rote practices of physical education and military training, she revolutionized the field of movement education. Originally published in 1937, her book *The Thinking Body* is an elegant treatise about the construction of the body and the power of the mind.

Lulu Sweigard was a student of Todd's who further developed her ideas into a practice called Ideokinesis. Identifying nine lines of movement, she developed a palette of powerful images for neuromuscular repatterning. Her process began by stilling the body, allowing the mind time to stimulate the nervous system through images; she was confident that the nervous system would make the wisest choice for each individual body. "When a person imagines movement, putting forth no voluntary muscular effort to aid its execution, the coordinated action of muscles which produces the imagined movement will be patterned subcortically. Imagining the movement is a thought process only; it involves no muscular effort by the subject, because muscular effort interferes with the skeletal changes which the imagined movement is designed to produce." (Sweigard 1974, 222)

Other teachers and practitioners carry on the work of Todd and Sweigard, such as Barbara Clark, Andre Bernard, Irene Dowd, and Eric Franklin. Dowd, Sweigard's assistant at the Juilliard School, wrote the gem *Taking Root to Fly: Articles on Functional Anatomy* and maintains a private practice in neuromuscular training. Eric Franklin's books, *Dance Imagery for Technique and Performance* and *Dynamic Alignment Through Imagery*, provide technique teachers with a wealth of useful imagery.

DEVELOPING A BAG OF TRICKS

Every teacher needs a big bag of tricks when it comes to images. While training, the dancer adds the first few toys. During the long hours of sweat, images from former teachers implant themselves in the muscles. But practicing professionals must develop their own distinct repertory unique to their training, history, and personality. Here are some guides to develop a successful bag of tricks.

Direct and Indirect Images

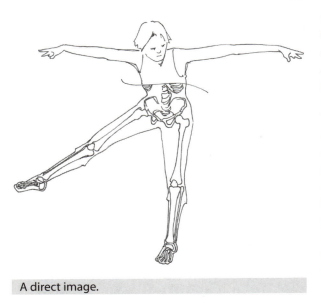

A direct image.

Direct or indirect images trigger responses. Overby (1990), who has written about the use of imagery in dance, describes direct images as something that you are doing physically, such as visualizing the head lengthening upward. Indirect imagery is "metaphorical": You create a picture in your mind that is not real but that enhances the movement coordination, such as imagining a balloon floating out the top of the skull. A guest teacher once declared that she didn't use images, didn't believe in them; then she pulled out a skeleton and proceeded to teach class with one of nature's most elegant images. The skeleton is a visual replication of our inner landscape. Using the skeleton provides a direct image, a physical truth to be embodied. The direct concrete image of a bone quickly transcends to another world when given a broader context. Consider this passage from the exquisite book *Bones: The Unity of Form and Function*. "*Tibia* was the Latin name for the shin bone, but it also meant flute, and the Latin word *fibula* meant pin. European archaeologists have found many Roman and later flutes made from tibias of sheep and of birds such as cranes or geese. They have also found plenty of pins from the Early Christian and Viking periods, carved from fibulas of pigs." (Alexander 1994, 14) "Play the bones like a flute" might be a useful indirect metaphor some day. Both direct or indirect images do the job; whichever method is used will depend on the way one sees the world.

Imaging the dance.

Inner and Outer Imagery

Franklin distinguishes between inner and outer imagery. He describes inner images: "These are images that improve alignment, such as visualizing the central axis inside your body." Outer images are "images that control the external environment." (Franklin 1996, 52) Athletes use outer images to imagine winning a race, beating the world-record high jump, or getting to the top of a mountain. Olympic divers are trained to see the dive before they take off; if their mind sees a perfect execution before takeoff, their body will follow. Listening to their stillness before the dive, one can almost guess which dive is about to be performed. Dancers need to spend silent time visualizing the perfect turn, the fluid phrase, the centered performance; too much time is wasted doing without thinking.

Potent Images

The more precise and concrete the image, the more potent the medicine. A writer makes us visualize, hear, and smell the details. "Pull up," "Use your center," and "Turn out" are overused, bland images that have lost their potency. They don't give a detailed picture and are therefore difficult for the mind to process. While executing a relevé, the image "pull up" begs for where, what, and when. Instead of thinking about pulling up, imagine squeezing a tube of toothpaste from the bottom, allowing the paste to move upward and out the top (an indirect image). If the toothpaste tube has holes, the toothpaste will squirt out in all directions. Better to channel the energy upward. Providing a direct image such as floating the occipital ridge upward would also work. Both communicate clear information about where the initiation of the movement comes from and the spatial intent of the energy.

The more precise and concrete the image, the more potent the medicine.

Cultural and Geographical Relevance

The image must not only match the movement in visual, spatial, and kinetic terms but it must be familiar to students culturally and geographically. Teaching in other countries and cultures creates unique challenges to the teacher. What makes sense to one group of students will completely fall flat with others. On arriving in Chicago from Utah, I took a class with Nana Shineflug, a very edgy and fierce teacher from the city with big shoulders. In Utah the image for a piqué was alighting onto a branch like a bird. Nana commanded us to "kill cockroaches" with each piqué. Each culture has a different relationship to images as well. In China, the written language is based on symbols. Images are layered one on top of another to create another image. Growing up with an imagistic language, Chinese dancers have an advantage in perceiving poetic imagery.

A *piqué*.

Ineffective Images

If an image does not work, it is pointless to keep using it. To facilitate the action of the foot in a jump I ask students to imagine squeezing a coil with their heels. One student seemed to understand the image when performing slow warm-ups with the foot, but when he jumped, his heels popped off the floor. (Often this is a structural issue—in this case it was not). Trying to understand the root of this problem, I looked at a videotape of his jump. When I watched in slow motion, I could see that he *was* getting his heels down; it was just at the wrong time. His heels hit before the body reached the bottom of the jump; then at the bottom of the jump, the heels lifted off. This was only partially about squeezing the coil. The real issue was the timing between the hip, knee, and ankle joint. Squeezing the coil was useful up to a certain point, but now he needed a new image that would facilitate the timing between the joints.

Anatomical Correctness

Sometimes images are useful but not anatomically correct. *Float the leg up from underneath* is a good example of an image that makes sense when performing a développé, but insisting that the hamstrings float the leg upward is not anatomically correct. Suspending a 20- to 40-pound weight 90 degrees in the air is hard work, and the image of water floating underneath the leg to buoy it upward is useful. But the image is an image—not the "kinesiological truth." The hip flexors (iliopsoas, rectus femoris) contract to flex the hip. The knee extensors (quadriceps) contract to extend the knee. If the *underneath* muscles, the hip extensors and knee flexors (gluteus maximus and hamstrings), contracted, they would throw the leg back down to the ground. Images can either support kinesiological truths or oppose them. Teachers must know the difference.

Floating the leg in a *développé*.

Developing the Danceartist

Encouraging students to develop their own set of images is crucial to empowering learning. Images are personal. What works for one student does not always work for another. In South America everyone drinks a tea called *mate*. But *mate* is not sold in a restaurant or in public places because it is personal. Everyone has their own cup, their own private straw and thermos. Images are unique to a person's history, culture, and environment, individually tailored to suit each situation. Students should be encouraged to search for their own cup, straw, and thermos. When a student suddenly "gets it," it is important to ask him to not only remember the image but also share it with the class, thus building the bag of tricks for everyone.

Teachers must never lose sight of their job to train dance*artists,* and it is the ability to reach inside and unleash internal images that distinguishes the most riveting performers. Butoh artist Min Tanaka speaks about the power of images stemming from his dancers in performance. "I don't lead. I believe in their images. If the images are deep enough, or wide enough, the dancers can pick up a lot more on the way of their dancing." (Vermeersch 2002, 28)

During intensive dance training immense change occurs in the body, stimulating further psychological and emotional growth. Images potent with messages enter the mind and body through dreams. Keeping a journal of dreams provides insight and guidance and encourages a lifetime of listening to the internal messages of the body; it is a powerful preparation for performing.

THE SENSES

Images come by way of the senses. A deeper listening occurs when senses are isolated; most people close their eyes during a kiss to heighten the sensation of the lips and tongue. The language of the body is foreign and remote when too many senses are crying for attention. Try dancing in an unfamiliar studio where the windows are open to loud street noise, a pounding band plays overhead, and smells of food cooking drift from a nearby kitchen. Somatic practices encourage lying on the floor with eyes closed to stimulate internal listening. Dance classes need moments of the same.

Each person has a particular sense or group of senses that are dominant. As teachers, we must actively develop senses that are not dominant in our own repertory. This is a delicious task, because it opens the body to new experiences and sensations. Visual learners should spend a day blindfolded listening to sounds.

Kinesthetic learners should walk through a summer garden exploding with color. Our preferences are hereditary but also cultural; a trip to a new neighborhood or culture wakens new senses and stimulates new possibilities.

Franklin describes sensory imagery: "If you imagine yourself standing under a waterfall, you may have the sensory experiences of seeing and feeling the water pouring down your body, hearing it thundering all around you, smelling its fresh scent as well as tasting it in your mouth. By using many senses you begin to enrich the image, which makes it more effective." (Franklin 1996, 49)

The senses that we respond to are vision, kinesthesia, sound, smell, and taste.

Vision

The eye is the most dominant sense organ in Western culture. Min Tanaka laments, "The power of the eyes is a sign of European culture and we followed it very much. Eye as first opinions before others—ear, nose, sense, or mouth, by face or styles, whatever, eye chooses the power first." (Vermeersch 2002, 32)

The world provides daily visual images. A teacher has thousands of images to choose from on the daily trek to class: the lightness of the cirrus clouds, a car stuck in mud, the soft pink light reflected off a mountain or a skyscraper, the worn-out clothes of a street person. These images bring the world into the studio, keeping students in touch with life. Paintings, sculptures, and photographs all suggest something to the visually based student.

The teacher's demonstration provides a very powerful key to students' visual imaginations. Rigorous attention with the eyes is necessary to coordinate movement. As the teacher demonstrates, students move around in a flurry of activity, without really seeing. Stilling their motion forces them to see what is there, not what they think is there. Aging is a humble process for the teacher because one loses the power to demonstrate. The ability to create a moving picture in the mind's eye while sitting increases as we age.

Dancers learn by watching other dancers. When students see a professional articulate a movement well, they incorporate it into their movement knowledge. If there is no access to professional dancers, ask the students to work with partners, observing each other. Watch videos of great dancers. By observing a variety of dancing bodies, students see images that communicate the variety of choices they might make. We dance to fully become ourselves, not our teachers. Students copy the teacher's tensions or bad habits as well. It is alarming to suddenly see everyone standing with their arms too far back, pronated feet, or any other charming little idiosyncrasies. Students unconsciously will mimic more than the teacher cares to share; a humbling experience, it renews the importance of the teacher constantly learning.

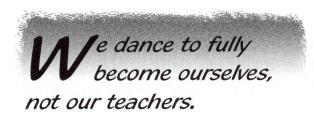

We dance to fully become ourselves, not our teachers.

The space or studio can also be a very powerful visual image. Many teachers work in converted stage spaces: big, black boxes that double up for class and stage. When traveling companies come in and transform the space with a new white floor or an orange wall, the perception of space and energy changes.

Sound

Sound instantaneously engages muscles. The squeaking of chalk on a blackboard, a releasing sigh, or a threatening yell all travel quickly to the emotional centers of the brain. These speedy reactions are useful to the dance teacher; jump-start a dragging class with a booming voice or hover dancers in the air a moment longer with a lilting breath.

The teacher's voice provides powerful emotional imagery, whether it is aggressive or enthusiastic, soothing or confrontational. A teacher was having difficulty with her class and asked me to observe. The class was structurally very sound, so what was the problem? After an hour of watching her teach, my body was tense from the sound of her voice. Nobody was able to relax and move in the presence of her grating and horribly high-pitched voice. Voice lessons improved her ability to teach.

Making sound resonates the organs and internal tissues, thus creating a much deeper experience of movement. Karate screams encourage aggressiveness in movement. Singing long, open vowels while arching invites the body to stay connected, not cutting off the head and throat. Days without an accompanist or without taped music encourage students to listen differently. They are forced to activate their own sound-making and listen to surrounding sounds, such as the hum of the water cooler, the breath of a classmate, the thump of footsteps, or the rain on the rooftop. In *A Natural History of the Senses,* Diane Ackerman speaks about the sounds of our body: "Our cells vibrate; there is music in them, even if we don't hear it. Different animals hear some frequencies better than we do. Perhaps a mite, lost in the canyon of a crease of skin, hears our cells ringing like a mountain of wind chimes every time we move." (Ackerman 1990, 224)

Kinesthetic

Kinesthetic is a word dancers like to throw around. What does it really mean? Sally Fitt (1996) says, "The kinesthetic sense is literally the perception of motion and position." The sculptor Henry Moore had a deep sense of kinesthetic memory as he molded clay with his hands. "He thinks of it, whatever its size, as if he were holding it completely enclosed in the hollow of his hand; he mentally visualizes a complex form from all round itself; he knows while he looks at one side what the other side is like; he identifies himself with its center of gravity, its mass, its weight; he realizes its volume, as the space that the shape displaces in the air." (Read 1961, ix)

A kinesthetic image is the embodiment of the sensation of moving, such as water trickling down the spine, a buzz circulating through the body, or wind caressing the skin. As there is rarely water in the studio to trickle down the spine, a combination of kinesthetic and visual images stimulates responses.

Toys spatially and kinetically replicate movement. Mimicking play elicits giggles, and giggling is useful when learning technique. Here are a few favorites.

- Everyone has probably seen the frog that has rubber legs. There is a tube connected to his butt that runs into a little hand pump. Air pumped into the tube goes from his butt to his rubber legs. The frog jumps, and the heel-to-tail connection is clear as day. An added bonus: If you hold one leg down, the frog pops up into an arabesque.

⚙ Tops demonstrate the principles of centrifugal and centripetal force.

⚙ There is a toy that has a suction cup attached to a coil. Over the top of the coil is a monster head or a clown or some silly animal. Press the monster head down so that the coil compresses and the suction cup holds it to the ground. The students will hover over it, curious to see what will happen. Suddenly, it pops four feet in the air. With no gas, food, or fuel, the toy jumps solely by the power of the coil, demonstrating the potential energy stored in the coil of the plié.

⚙ Muybridge began the film revolution through a series of moving photographs. The more photographs, the smoother the moving picture; the fewer the images, the jerkier the film. With their pages moving so fast that movement looks slow, flip-books elicit flow.

Smell and Taste

It is no mistake that dancers and choreographers are usually good cooks. The sensuality of cooking and eating are similar to the sensual experience of dancing. Eating and dancing are often done together in societies, evoking the immense pleasures of life. The sensation of the tongue, whether it is licking an ice cream cone or relishing the texture of freshly baked bread, is available to everyone. This imagery evokes textures and dynamics from academically dry students. Strangely enough, the thought of food inspires dancers better than actually smelling the food. Smells of popping corn wafting into the dance space have destroyed concentration as hungry stomachs begin to speak. Through imagery, the dance teacher inspires both movement reeducation and artistry.

Investigations

1. Practice using direct and indirect imagery. Study a skeleton. Use anatomical terms to describe a movement sequence. Describe the same movement sequence using an image from a dream.

2. Practice using inner and outer imagery. Describe the flow of energy inside the body when performing a relevé. Describe the flow of energy in a waterfall.

3. Make a list of verbal images stored in your muscles from past teachers. Which ones work? Which ones don't make any sense? How else might you articulate "Pull up," "Turn out," and "Find your center"?

4. Build a bag of tricks. Make a list of the images that stimulated movement learning. Some of my favorites: "Breathe like a whale," "Listen with your feet," "Spherical spine." Share and borrow new ones.

5. Go to anatomy and kinesiology books and check out your images. Are they anatomically sound? Does the image counter physical reality?

6. If you are lucky enough to have the airfare, travel to a foreign country; if not, go somewhere new: the country, the city, or a new neighborhood. Write down all the images you see, hear, or smell. Use these images to describe a dance movement.

In-Class Investigations

1. Encourage students to develop their own images. After a student has made a major breakthrough ask, "What were you thinking?"

2. Create a movement phrase based on a visual, auditory, or kinesthetic image. Bring the object, writing, or sound into class. Have the class study it before doing the movement.

3. Experiment with imagery and learning. Use an abundance of auditory images in one class and kinesthetic images in another class. Which images work better when? Do you notice that certain students respond better to certain images?

Reflection: BALANCE

Brand-new students straggle into the first day of their first dance class. They don't know the drift yet. One woman wears underpants under her sheer tights and leotard. Every detail is revealed—white cotton panties with little red hearts and lace trim. The men are uncomfortable in their second-skin tights, so they alternate between strutting and hiding. Several students sport belly piercings, and surely there are other piercings not presently revealed, all of which will downright hurt when they slide into the floor. The hair ranges from cheerleader ponytails to untamed dreadlocks to strange and vibrant colors like fuchsia, Day-Glo orange, and electric blue. Several baseball caps are turned backward, guaranteed to fall off within the first eight counts. Smells of hair spray and deodorant mingle with perspiration of nervousness, but the students' excitement is palpable. They are a motley crew ready to venture into the unexplored territory of the body dancing.

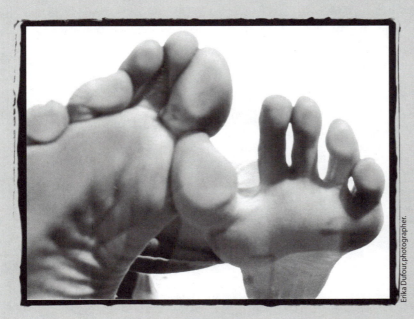

Erika Dufour, photographer.

The beat begins and hats fly off, piercings stretch, and hair flies. They are surprised by the silliness of their awkwardness. Laughter rolls out as they try to coordinate a simple turn.

A teacher explains a relevé, a rise onto the balls of the feet, the fundamental movement germane to balancing: "Imagine a balloon rising and a great weight descending downward." Intently focused on the image, the motley crew balances for some time without strain or struggle. Balance accomplished, they look around and wonder what is next. By tomorrow they will know not to wear hats or jewelry and that wearing underpants under sheer tights is considered slightly risqué, but it will take a lifetime of relevés to figure out just what made balance so very easy on the very first day.

William Frederking, photographer; Jeannie Hill and Billy Siegenfeld, dancers. Courtesy of Jump Rhythm Jazz Project.

chapter 11

Silence Sounding
A C C O M P A N I S T S

Chuck Davis, a big, ebullient teacher of African dance, begins dance class with a chant between teacher, students, and drummers. He sings, *"Ago,"* meaning listen—not only to the teacher but to the drums. Students shout out a response, *"Ame,"* meaning "We are listening." He explains, "In most other societies around the world, you're taught both . . . music and movement are one, and one is brought about as a result of the other." (Teck 1990, 88) The sounds of dancing and the movement of music intersect in the dance studio. This chapter covers the relationship between movement and music, the art of collaborating with a musician, and the *ago* and *ame* of listening.

RELATIONSHIP BETWEEN MUSIC AND DANCE

Music and dance—sound and movement—travel through space and time. Many ancient cultures fail to separate music and dance and space and time as distinct entities. In the article "Ma: Space-Time in Japan," Arata Isozaki speaks about the relationship between space and time. "In Japan, space and time were never fully separated but were conceived as correlative and omnipresent. In a chaotic, mixed condition, space could not be perceived independent of the element of time. Likewise, time was not abstracted as a regulated homogeneous flow, but rather was believed to exist only in relation to movements or spaces." (Isozaki) This fused notion of space and time is called *ma,* defined by Iwanami's *Dictionary of Ancient Terms* as "the natural pause or interval between two or more phenomena occurring continuously." *Ma* is the space between two stepping-stones, representing both the time and space between two moments.

Bruce Chatwin describes in *The Songlines* how the Aborigines create songs that transcribe space into time. "So, if the Lizard Man were dragging his heels across the salt-pans of Lake Eyre, you could expect a succession of long flats, like Chopin's 'Funeral March'. If he were skipping up and down the MacDonnell escarpments, you'd have a series of arpeggios and glissandos, like Liszt's *Hungarian Rhapsodies*." (Chatwin 1987, 108) Music and dance are taught as one because space and time are fused.

Euclid and Aristotle encouraged the Western world to split time and space into two very distinct elements. Like space and time, music and dance became increasingly distant partners. By the twentieth century, just as Einstein was delivering new information about space and time, music and dance reached a pinnacle of separation. Dancers fought for independence from music, which had played a dominant role in the relationship not only onstage but in the classroom as well. The rebellious moderns ripped dance from its age-old partner, discarding sounds laden with the emotional baggage of previous centuries. German expressionist Mary Wigman introduced drums to the dance classroom, allowing movement to find its pure, honest tone. Murray Louis and Alwin Nikolais, descendants of Wigman, taught class without a musician; the teacher played a simple hand drum to provide the necessary essence of a beat. Movement, not music, was to speak. To this day, preference for pure rhythmic sound by percussionists permeates modern classrooms.

If musicians were there at all, they were encouraged to experiment with improvisation, opening the door to a much broader definition of music. Dance gained further independence from music as Cunningham and Cage and a host of others who followed experimented with untangling the threads. Teachers of the Cunningham technique created phrases with no discernible pulse; numbers served only as markers of duration. Release-based technique classes, intentionally given in silence, allowed dancers to listen to the sounds of the body and breath moving. During the twentieth century dance developed its own unique rhythms, structures, and emotional tonality.

When Einstein announced in his special Theory of Relativity that space and time were indeed plastic and inseparable, the Western world began to rethink its tendency to compartmentalize. In the twenty-first century the concept of *spacetime* begs us to seek out once again the essence of the attraction between music and dance.

MOVEMENT AND MUSIC

Cellist Richard Sennett writes, "For musicians, the sense of touch defines our physical experience of art: lips applied to reed, fingers pushing down keys or strings." (Sennett 2001, 31) Movement is the essential link between music and dance. To make any sound, something in the body must move—the vocal cords vibrate, a hand strikes the drum or hits a switch, and an arm draws a bow. Whether it is in large motor muscles or the small intrinsic muscles of the hand, dancers and musicians share kinesthetic sensation. Musician and former dancer Claudia Howard Queen says an accompanist "creates a carpet of sound on which the dancer can glide and fly. The music should be kinesthetic and inspiring, permeating the muscles and filling the room with energy." Movement is the *ma*, the time and space between music and dance. Let us look at the traditional elements of music with movement in mind.

Time

Music and dance move forward through time, and a series of markers defines moments of time progressing. Increasingly bigger packages define the beat, meter, phrase, motifs, sections, and symphony; increasingly smaller packages define the beat and its subdivisions. Tempo speeds the whole thing up or slows it down. In this, there is no inherent difference between music and dance. But dancers are executing large movements through space; therefore, there is another important partner for dancers: gravity. Gravity changes how time is sensed. Emile Jaques-Dalcroze understood this fundamental principle when he developed Eurhythmics, a system of training the basics of music. He asked musicians to experience gravity by moving and falling through space, which in turn made them more accurate and dynamic musicians. John Colman, a pianist for Kurt Jooss and George Balanchine, talks about his training in Eurhythmics:

> *While listening to the improvisation of the Eurhythmics teacher, the students make their own weight-bearing movements match or relate to the various durations heard, traversing physical space as they do so. In this way, they experience musical rhythm by imbuing it with a vivid 'reality' that is otherwise unattainable. If they played these durations on an instrument, or even sang them, they would not have a comparable experience because the deployment of total body weight, which is the learning agent of Eurhythmics, plays little or no part in actual musical performance. (Teck 1990, 27)*

Small Spacetime

Unencumbered by a large mass moving through space being pulled by gravity, musicians occupy a smaller spacetime. Much of a musician's rhythmic life occurs between the beats, in the infinitesimal subdivisions of the beat. But it is the larger world—the combination of beat, meter, and phrase—that creates rhythmic excitement for the dancer. (Exceptions to this are rhythmic stomping forms such as tap, Indian kathak dancing, flamenco, and Irish step dancing.) It is at the intersection of the beat that dancers and musicians find common ground. Musicians and dancers need only know that these two worlds enhance each other; one travels the smaller road while the other sails on the larger highway. Chopin instinctively knew that less activity between the beats and carefully placed accents suspend waltzing dancers upward; a stronger downbeat and more activity between the beats return the dancer to the earth. Flow in the dancer's body is created by more subdivisions, not less. In these ways, the musician uses the small subdivisions and accents to create an overall arc of time, the arc the dancer needs in order to respond to his other partner, gravity.

Organization of Time

Louis Horst taught dancers to respect traditions of music by paying attention to the organization of larger units of time. Forms and structures such as A-B-A, fugue, and rondo use repetition, variation, development, and transformation. While these may no longer be the only rules of contemporary dancemaking, they are certainly in evidence in the classroom. Repetition builds neuromuscular habits, variation builds neuromuscular plasticity, and the transition between one idea and another is the art of dancing. A musician can give shape to the class by repeating themes and developing motifs, just as a teacher develops class material into a final phrase or combination. This conscious weaving of time in both music and dance ultimately provides a satisfying class experience—perhaps even a symphony.

Timbre Space

In *The Songlines,* an Aborigine says, "Music is a memory bank for finding one's way about the world." (Chatwin 1987, 108) The quality of tone, or timbre, finds its way to the inside space of the body. In Body-Mind Centering, Bonnie Bainbridge Cohen speaks about the vibrational tone of different body systems: skeletal, muscular, organ, skin, and fluids. Each body system resonates at a different speed and has a different quality. The muscles have a vibrating, blood-pulsing, elastic tone; the skin has a softer, more amorphous, airy quality; the organs hold rich, weighty emotional language. The dancer changes the quality of movement by changing systems—by initiating the movement in the muscles, skin, organs, or bones. Different timbres wake up different "tones" within the body. A flute elicits the soft and porous nature of the skin, drums vibrate the organs, horns shout at the muscles, strings unleash a flow of fluids, and the human voice enters the body as a partner, perhaps because it is itself a muscle vibrating. A multidimensional musician subconsciously activates the various systems of the body, inviting rich textural performances from dancers.

A group of young children visited a dance class and were duly impressed not only by the dancing but the African rhythms and colorful tones filling the space. Hidden from view, they were unable to see where the voice, percussion, piano, harmonica, and bells were coming from. At the end of class they gasped when one lonely musician took his bow.

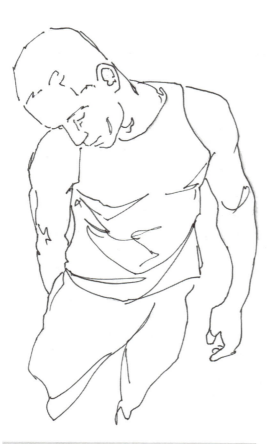

Stories of the heart.

Pitch Timespace

Pitch, melody, and harmony are the violins of music. Musical tones resonate in the body and stimulate the viscera, the soul of emotional life. They tug at the heartstrings, providing a direct physical link to passion, joy, love, and hate. In her book *A Natural History of the Senses,* Diane

Ackerman describes music as "the perfume of hearing." An elixir to the body, the perfume of sound can entice even the most mechanically inclined dancer. Ackerman goes on to explain, "Like pure emotions, music surges and sighs, rampages or grows quiet, and, in that sense, it behaves so much like our emotions that it seems often to symbolize them, to mirror them, to communicate them to others, and thus frees us from the elaborate nuisance and inaccuracy of words." (Ackerman 1990, 206) A twang of a guitar or the gut-wrenching cry of a bow across a cello elicits something beyond the mere mechanical, perfunctory accomplishment of a task. The dancer listens and dances the stories of the heart.

Dynamic Space

Musicians and dancers have the ability to control volume. Musicians play the scales of loud and soft, and dancers play the scales of energy—a lot to very little. Imagine an opera singer singing full voice for an entire opera. The overwhelming sound would eventually overpower the ears, and the audience would run screaming from the concert hall. Volume may create energy in a lethargic class, but constant loud music does not invite or encourage the dancer to find dynamic range in movement. The beauty of a great opera singer is her ability to ride up and down a dynamic range, moving us forward in our seats to hear the subtleties of a whisper and surprising us with a jolt of power that comes wailing from the belly. Often dancers are under the false impression that the more sweat produced, the better the dancing. This devaluing of small, gentle energy creates one-dimensional dancers who only scream. Great teachers of small children captivate their charges with small whispers as well as large, resounding belly laughter.

TEACHERS AND ACCOMPANISTS

The confluence of live music with dance in the classroom is a rich tradition. One need only enter a traditional African class to be reminded of the simple beauty of music and dance acting together in a blossoming collaborative spirit. Behaving as one, drummers dance and the dancers drum. Movement and sound spring from the heartbeat, the center of time. In an African dance class, the drums are the teachers. The drummers play a crucial role: instructing dancers and orchestrating the changes between movement patterns. Dancers learn to dance by dancing, playing, and listening to the drums. At the end of class, dancers face the drummers and pound the floor in respect, and each dancer thanks the drummers as he leaves the studio.

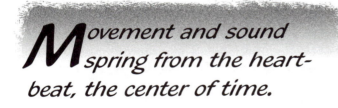

Movement and sound spring from the heartbeat, the center of time.

All too often the immense possibilities between music and dance are not taken advantage of in the modern dance class. Just consider this scene. A talented musician walks into a studio to play her first dance class. Carefully setting up her cherished instruments, she is confident in her ability, having built substantial musical skills. The teacher enters the classroom and presents a whirlwind of movement as the students watch intently. Not even acknowledging the presence of the musician, the teacher yells out, "And!" Without adequate information such as a time signature, style, tone, or even a smile, the musician takes a plunge into the unknown and tries to follow the strange, flailing movement. Pandemonium breaks out in the room as the dancers lose all semblance of unison and flow. The teacher glares over at the musician and politely asks her to stop playing. Working with musicians is a collaboration that takes time, effort, and skill. All teachers would prefer to work with great accompanists, but great accompanists don't just appear; they evolve out of collaborative partnerships with teachers. This process begins with searching for the right musician.

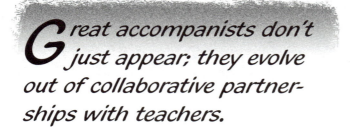

Great accompanists don't just appear; they evolve out of collaborative partnerships with teachers.

Finding and Training a Dance-Musician

Some of the best dance accompanists are dancers, so begin looking for one who is eager to cross over to the other side. If that doesn't produce the right candidate, scout in seedy bars, jazz clubs, and music departments for a musician who is willing to be vulnerable; after all, they will be making their mistakes publicly. Improvisational skills (or at least the willingness to improvise) are essential. Next, look for someone who possesses a physical or visceral sense of sound. A musician who embraces sound with the entire body will understand the glue between music and dance.

A musician who embraces sound with the entire body will understand the glue between music and dance.

There are a few schools that offer dance accompanist programs, for example, Shenanhoah University and Ball State University, but a *sink or swim* mentality is still the predominant method of training. Depending on resources, the best training for a musician for the dance class is assisting a seasoned accompanist. If this is not an option, the teacher takes on the task. Listening is a good way to begin, for there is much to learn for both sides. But first agree to rules of etiquette between teachers and musicians.

Rules of Etiquette

There are some established rules, an abundance of body language, and just plain common courtesy when it comes to working together. Key to a successful collaboration is communication.

Conductor Signals

Musicians are used to responding to conductors' signals. If you don't know these signals, ask a musician to teach you the common signals for *go, stop, slow down, speed up, louder, and softer*. These agreed-on signals keep the pacing flowing and are crucial to avoiding fistfights sometime down the road. Some teachers like musicians to play while they give movement material, other teachers need silence while they explain and tinker with the tempo. Using agreed-on signals allows the teacher to work spontaneously, responding to the immediate needs of the class.

Musicians' Instruments

Learn about the musicians' instruments, the various styles of music they play, and the musical ideas that inspire them. Introduce the musicians to your students and give them time to share this information with the class. Students will listen better if they know what they are listening to. On a daily basis, allow the musician to share when and where they are playing outside of class. There is nothing more satisfying for a musician than developing a core of fans from the dance class.

Pre-Class Communication

Take the time to inform the musician about the goals for the class during a pre-class check-in ritual. This communication gives the musician time to develop concepts that may be helpful to the students throughout the class. Later, it provides a point of reference between musician and teacher, avoiding a public conflict. The teacher is able to say, "The heavy downbeat supports the physical weight; the wind instruments do not." The musician is often improvising, so preparation time is appreciated. Throw out the beat, meter, and tempo at the beginning of an exercise rather than at the end so the musician has a moment to digest it and try some possibilities.

Rhythmic Cues

Most teachers have some kind of rap rhythm going on, like *ya da dee dooh dah*, or *wapa doppa yaaa*, or *she cha, she cha da dee da*. Teachers are not rap wannabees. These mutterings gush forward because the body moves slower than the fingers. Fingers fly, legs only run. For every beat a dancer moves, the musician's fingers tackle two to five smaller beats. Musicians need to know the subdivision of the beat the teacher is feeling. By signaling *one-and, two-and,* the teacher gives the message of a duple beat. *One-e-and-dah, two-e-and-dah* signals a subdivision of the beat into four. *One-and-ah, two-and-ah* is the standard signal for a triple subdivision. Student teachers need to practice this ad nauseum, until it is second nature. Further development of this skill will create a repertory of rapping garble that gives spice and color to the feel of the beat. By signaling the subdivision of the beat, the teacher provides common ground between the musician and the students and orchestrates everyone to begin. Many teachers do fancy little movements of the hips, fingers, or head to signal the flavor of the beat. The more dancers and musicians know about the feel of the beat, the better everyone will synchronize their energy.

The meter should be clear as the movement phrase or combination is presented. When counting off for the class and musician, count off the last three to five beats of whatever meter is being used (the faster the tempo, the more beats necessary). A standard eight count-off is *five, six, seven, eight*. A seven would be *five, six, seven*. If it is a mixed meter phrase, count off the last meter in the sequence. For instance, in a six-three-five-one-five phrase, the proper count off would be *one, two, three, four, five*.

Gwendolyn Watson, a West Coast musician and composer says, "It is not uncommon for teachers in schools and private studios to engage musicians and—with little or no movement demonstration—expect them to produce instantly music that is both perfectly proportioned and inspiring. This type of intensely pressured situation, which I refer to as the *'and'* syndrome, shows a lack of understanding by the dancer regarding what he or she is asking of the musician. It's like asking a dancer to jump out of her bed and without further preparation execute some fancy run-run-leaps." (Teck 1990, 129)

In the African tradition the musicians play a *break*—a clear interruption of the rhythmic pattern signaling a change. Students must listen intently to know when to change a movement pattern. Relying on the musicians to signal change is very useful, especially when students are traveling across the floor—a break pattern signals a return across the floor. This empowers the musician, forces the students to listen to rhythmic patterning, and saves wear and tear on the teacher's voice.

Tempo and Beat Wars

A metronome is cheap, and it might be a better buy than paying a musician who can't hold a consistent tempo. There is nothing worse than a teacher screaming one beat while the musician is slowing down like a train coming into the station. Students are caught in the middle, feeling like the children of quarreling parents. Most musicians get better at this skill over time. Rather than counting louder than the musician or fighting in the classroom, ask the musician to stop. Stand next to him and let him hear your voice as you sing the rhythms for the dancers. Allow him to play softly, accompanying your voice. With a little patience, he will get it; if not, it's time to part ways.

Dance teachers drive musicians crazy as well. The teacher's worst habit is counting out loud when he or she has no idea where the beat is. The teacher calls out seven, the musician is on eight, and everybody is confused. A delightful accompanist once said, "Please be quiet; I'll do my job better." It was a great lesson. Not only was it more pleasant in the room, but students took more responsibility for finding the beat.

Risk Taking

Encourage an atmosphere of risk taking. Musicians are responding in a few seconds to the pulse, meter, phrasing, and color of a movement phrase. Spontaneously creating, they bring immediacy to the classroom. Sometimes these quick choices work, sometimes they don't. Support the good choices with positive feedback and give lots of room for mistakes. If musicians know outlandish choices are valued, they will imaginatively seek out riskier territory. Sometimes the most unusual choice works. One day a musician played an intense rock-and-roll tune with raw passionate rhythms for an adagio, which surprisingly captured the density necessary to sustain the slow movement. Laughter works with poor choices.

Musician As Co-Teacher

The musician is a powerful co-teacher whether invited or not. Percussive sounds pull accents from the air and long lyrical tones create flow in the dancer. A musician orchestrates sound to encourage the dancers' understanding of accent, dynamics, and rhythmic complexities, unlocking the doors to musicality and phrasing. Understanding the visceral feel of movement, a good accompanist plucks just the right rhythm out of the air to "hold" the dancer in the air. They know when a swing needs three beats, not two, and they will tell you so. Suspending the beat just a little longer, they force dancers to elongate their spines and to pounce with confidence.

Sharing time and space, both art forms work with the space between the beats. The musician informs the class about how to make transitions work through the sounds chosen and if invited to, he can share the problems of transitions on his instruments. These words of wisdom from the accompanist provide valuable lessons to dancers, resonating with a much broader truth. In teaching a concept such as rebounding jump, students need only listen to the difference between a percussionist hitting the drum with a rebounding hand, and hitting with a downward slap. The first strike rebounds outward. The second sound is caught down under. Sound teaches movement.

Musicians are sensitive artists with a bird's-eye view of the class. They are intimately knowledgeable about the class, but because they are not directly responsible for it, they are more objective than the teacher. Utilize their vantage point and ask questions. The silent sound-maker in the corner may have some valuable information to share if asked.

STUDENTS AND MUSICIANS

Dance is a complex art that takes years of training. At first just standing on one leg is monumental, but eventually breathing, replicating forms and rhythms, and finally, listening to the musician are added to the overall mix. So, delighted by the stimulating sound of live musicians, beginners listen with ease. They lose this skill while they struggle with tendus and hip placement and all the other chatter that fills up brains during the intermediate stages. It is not until they are extremely advanced that they are able to listen again with the same kind of ease. However, there are some techniques that encourage the art of listening along the way, and musicians are instrumental to the process. For instance, simply inviting the musician to roam through the space singing or playing a handheld drum breaks the spatial barriers and cajoles students to open their ears to glorious live sound.

Progression of Skills

Skills in music and dance parallel each other—both share the act of learning movement. A musician needs only to think back on her very first lessons to understand

The lilt of the phrase.

what a beginning dancer needs. Watson explains, "When students are more advanced, then I'm free to become a more active partner, not just a support system in a secondary position." (Teck 1990, 127-28)

Ultimately, dancers become an active member of the band, creating counterpoint rhythms to the colorful, syncopated rhythms of the musician. If the musician is given the liberty to suspend the relentless beat (known as rubato), the students have to spontaneously react, pause, and stretch to match the musician. The beauty in a Chopin waltz is not metronomic precision, but the plasticity of the beat. The momentary expansion of time gives lilt and beauty to a phrase of music or dance. In the beautiful story *The Last Report on the Miracles at Little No Horse,* Louise Erdrich describes a nun playing music in a convent. "Her playing was of the utmost sincerity. And Chopin, played simply, devastates the heart. Sometimes a pause between the piercing sorrows of minor notes made a sister scrubbing the floor weep into the bucket where she dipped her rag so that the convent's boards, washed in tears, seemed to creak now in a human tongue. The air of the house thickened with sighs." (Erdrich 2001, 14) When dancers and musicians listen and play as an ensemble, reading each others' tones and weight, a true collaboration takes place and art hovers.

Silence and Stillness

It is said that John Cage exited a soundproof room declaring that there was no such thing as silence. The same could be said of stillness; a dancer who has arrested

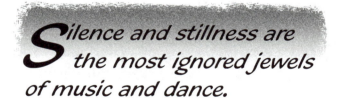

Silence and stillness are the most ignored jewels of music and dance.

movement is never still. Silence and stillness are the most ignored jewels of music and dance. The absence of sound from an accompanist allows a different kind of music to be heard. Without the distraction of external sound, dancers are forced to listen to the internal sounds of the body; the whoosh of breath reverberating in the lungs, the thud of weight falling through space, the pumping of blood and the "ba-bum" of the heartbeat. To alternate between sound and silence, movement and stillness, ask musicians to drop out every once in a while for one or two bars of music. Often, the minute the musician drops out, the dancers do too. It takes time for everyone to become a responsible member of the band. As stillness is invited into movement phrases, dancers and musicians must both accept responsibility for the clarity of their rhythmic intent. A conversation begins as dancers and musicians hear the sound of silence.

Crossing Boundaries

Teachers warm up fast because they are counting, talking, and singing. This deep internal massage of sound warms the body from the inside out. Vibrating sound within the spaces of the body also invites alignment. A dancer cannot belt out a loud note when executing an upper-back arch if the neck is dropped and imploded downward. A long, full note can't be held if there are holding patterns in the breath. Making sound makes movement real and honest—it is hard to be physically wimpy when yelling a karate scream. The vibrational tones in the muscles encourage real attack and real conviction. Sounds and songs elicit full, weighty dancing. As choreographic trends move toward multidimensional productions with both singing and dancing, perhaps the classroom will return to a place where dance and music are one. As Africans have always known, singing and dancing together create a wholeness of spirit. The dancer/musician finds the *ma*, a place where there is no distinction between space and time, sound and movement.

Workshops for Dancers and Musicians

Workshops for dancers and musicians are crucial in building a collaborative spirit. Here are some suggestions for play.

- ☉ Experiment with time and gravity. What accents and subdivisions of the beat support suspension, weight, and flow of movement?
- ☉ Play games with volume control. Dancers experiment with energy scales. Perform a movement combination at an energy level of 1 to 10. Invite the musicians to vary the volume control.
- ☉ Ask musicians to teach dancers the conducting signals for *stop, go, speed up, slow down, louder,* and *softer*.
- ☉ Create a phrase of music and a phrase of dance. Play games with stillness and movement, silence and sound.
- ☉ Have the dancers perform a phrase in silence and ask the musician to critique it for rhythmic accuracy. While the musicians play, ask the dancers to observe and comment on the movement of the musicians.
- ☉ Switch roles. Ask dancers to make sound, musicians to dance. Chant, move, sing, and dance together.
- ☉ Enter each other's space. Allow the musicians to travel through the dance space while playing. Let dancers enter the musicians' space.

Investigations

1. Visit jazz clubs, music bars, and music schools, and watch for a musician who moves. Invite musicians to take dance classes.

2. Interview two accompanists. Ask about their instruments, training, and style.

3. Practice the standard *one-and-ah, two-and-ah* for triple subdivision and *one-e-and-dah, two-e-and-dah* for a duple/quadruple subdivision. Switch quickly from a duple beat to a triple beat. Add flavor by developing a rapping song, such as *one-ya-ha da-da, two-dee ya-hah, three-a-ya ha, four-dipity doo* in the shower. Practice counting off for fives, sevens, and nines. Practice sliding *ready-and-a, go-and-a* (triple beat) into the beginning of a phrase, then jump right back to *one-ya-da, two-ya-da*. Practice this in another language.

Reflection: OPENNESS

Musician 1

A crusty old jazz musician saunters into the dance studio followed by a cloud of cigarette smoke and alcohol fumes. Sitting down at the seen-its-better-days upright piano, he stares blandly

Erika Dufour, photographer; Zoe Harlow Hadley, dancer.

ahead, sipping on stale, gas-station coffee. The count begins and syncopated jazz riffs fly from his gnarled fingers. Not particularly fond of jazz, I stare at him and ask politely, "Could you play something else?" His look of disgust is palpable as he offers a dry rendition of "Mary Had a Little Lamb." Unable to help himself, he turns the song into a complex web of colorful tones and stop-and-go rhythms. Little by little, I begin to syncopate, retrograde, accent, and be-bop my movement. I thank him for paying no attention whatso-ever to my request.

Musician 2

Holding a six-month-old screaming baby, I am desperate for a distraction. Standing on a veranda in the vineyards of Spain, I see nothing but grapes, and my grandson is not interested in wine. Suddenly he reaches out to explore the texture of metal surfaces hanging above us. His pudgy little fingers grab at the shiny object and suddenly there is sound. By wiggling his hand, he realizes he can control when the sound happens. If he pulses his fist, he can make a satisfying sequence of sounds. He reacts with a big smile, a wise toothless conductor at the center of a great orchestra.

part *IV*

Professional Concerns

William Frederking, photographer; Jeffery Hancock and Mari Jo Iribe, dancer

chapter 12

Energy Talking
C O M M U N I C A T I O N

Bonnie Bainbridge Cohen captures the essence of mind and body communication with the simple statement, "The mind is like the wind and the body is like the sand. If you want to know how the wind is blowing, look at the sand." (Allison 1999, 213)

In the deeply embedded traditions of a dance class, communication between teacher and student seems like a one-way conversation—the teacher speaks, demonstrates, and corrects; except for the occasional question, the students remain quiet and listening. However, anything but a one-way conversation is actually occurring. Energy hangs in the room as the dance teacher—the expert in body language—walks into the studio; several dancers stand front and center, clearly vying for attention; one is sulking in the back of class; another with hands on hips and defiant eyes is just waiting for the first correction. All eyes turn to the dance teacher as class begins. Hoisting the sails, the dance teacher tries to figure out which way the wind is blowing. This chapter covers communication between body and mind, between student and teacher.

BODYMIND

The body never lies; flesh and blood carry the truth of our minds. Dancers have always known that *bodymind* should be one word. In 1940 Margaret H'Doubler wrote in *Dance: A Creative Art Experience*, ". . . a desire stimulates a thought, and the thought embodies itself in an act." (H'Doubler 1968, 89) As with space and time and music and dance, research and attention is currently focused on the threads that connect body and mind rather than the differences that define them.

Neurosurgeons and psychologists are pioneering body–mind research, discovering that the brain travels throughout the immune system. In other words, the mind is appearing in the body. Candice Pert, a researcher with the Center for Molecular

*T*he body never lies; flesh and blood carry the truth of our minds.

and Behavioral Neuroscience at Rutgers University, speaks of the turn her research took as she tried to understand the mind.

In the beginning, like many other neuroscientists I was secretly interested in consciousness, and thought that by studying the brain I would learn about the mind and consciousness. And so for most of my early research I concentrated from the neck up. But the astounding revelation is that these endorphins and other chemicals like them are found not just in the brain but also in the immune system, the endocrine system, and throughout the body. These molecules are involved in a psychosomatic communication network. Information is flowing. These molecules are being released from one place, they're diffusing all over the body, and they're tickling the receptors that are on the surface of every cell in your body. . . . We've actually found the material manifestation of emotions in these peptides and their receptors. (Moyers 1993, 177-193)

Emotional intelligence, or EQ, is currently under research in the business world. Robert Cooper defines EQ in his groundbreaking book, *Executive EQ: Emotional Intelligence in Leadership and Organizations:* "Emotional intelligence is the ability to sense, understand, and effectively apply the power and acumen of emotions as a source of human energy, information, connection, and influence." Research supports the notion that a high EQ is far more important than a high IQ (intellectual intelligence) in successful leaders. Cooper goes on, "The word *emotion* may be simply defined as applying 'movement,' either metaphorically or literally, to core feelings. It is emotional intelligence that motivates us to pursue our unique potential and purpose and activates our innermost values and aspirations, transforming them from things we *think about* to what we *live.*" (Cooper and Sawaf 1997, xiii) Corporate America is finally breaking down walls built from statistics and analysis and becoming aware of the whole person—the body–mind. Perhaps in the future presidents of countries and CEOs of major corporations will be required to take a dance class.

The connecting threads of body and mind.

RESISTANCE AND FEAR

Looking at the sand, teachers read the wind. Sometimes the sand is laden with water, shaped into immovable mud piles. Resistance is not uncommon in the dance classroom. Rigid bodyminds with ingrained and unconscious habits stifle the flow of movement. What is resistance but plain and simple fear? Fear of letting go, fear of new, fear of change, fear of self. When the teacher lets her own fear get in the way—fear of not being accepted as authority, fear of not being liked, fear of not making a difference—the situation reaches an impasse, but when teachers move outside their fears, learning occurs. A strong enough wind moves even the heaviest mud pile.

Resistance appears when students hold onto old beliefs without searching for the complex nature of truths. Students will refuse to embrace modern training because "inner consciousness" is antithetical to their previous aesthetic to "sell it, pop it, deliver it." A modern student resists the rigidity perceived to be in ballet technique. The fear says, "If I shed old clothes in order to try on new clothes, the old clothes will be lost forever." Of course, body memory does not work that way; experience is additive. Internal consciousness enhances the ability to pop and sell. Whether one wants to keep the old clothes is a choice made later. Sometimes the mind part of bodymind needs more coaxing than the body.

Students want to please, but it is very hard to please when they lack understanding of what is expected, appreciated, or valued. Administrators and politicians use the word *transparency* to speak about a style of managing that builds a collaborative spirit. If all the cards are on the table, workers might at least understand decisions by management. This openness enhances learning as well. Assumptions are dangerous. After teaching for 40 years, it may be painfully obvious to you why releasing weight is important. But the glowering eyes in the corner need an explanation, a reason, and a philosophical point of reference.

AUTHORITIES OF BODYMIND

Some teachers are shy and soft-spoken, and others foam at the mouth. Some teachers create an atmosphere of learning through drama and tears; others encourage learning through their calm presence. Ultimately, style is irrelevant. What is important is whether the style is true to the inner voice. Parker Palmer links the word authority and author, "Authority is granted to people who are perceived as *authoring* their own words, their own actions, their own lives, rather than playing a scripted role at great remove from their own hearts. When teachers depend on the coercive powers of law or technique, they have no authority at all." (Palmer 1998, 33)

Though it is easy to rely on coercive power—discipline, power, and grades—to create a false sense of authority, true authority lies in the years of knowledge gained while "authoring" the body. The struggles and the lessons learned in the last 5,891 dance classes give power to the words spoken, because this authority took the long, hard journey. The irony is that those who struggled to learn the skills of dancing become some of the best teachers because they had to make choices, ask questions, spit tears, and cry into pillows late into the night. It is through this journey that insight is gained.

The willingness to share these insights creates an infectious sense of learning in the classroom. "What's the trick to balance? What's the secret to keeping the shoulders down?" Some teachers are exquisite dancers, and students learn phenomenal lessons by watching. But there are dangers in being too good; whipping off fancy turns and leaps inspires, but an honest heart should dwell in the classroom. Showing off to gain admiration does not further the student.

Although authority doesn't rest on discipline and power, these are part of the tools of teaching. Discipline is linked to the word *disciple*, which implies to follow. A disciple follows the master. The master sets up rules to share meaning. "The rule: You cannot take class if you are late. The reason: The beginning exercise focuses the mind and prepares the body for physical rigor, and without proper beginnings, there is risk of injury." Discipline is also defined as a penalty for wrongdoing; the first day a student comes late, the consequences should be clear.

Teachers in private dance studios don't have to wrestle with grades. In education courses, teachers have to objectively assess, which is a very subjective process. Fair grading begins at the beginning with clear guidelines for attendance, tardies, and grades. Students need to know exactly what is expected of them. Skill and effort are key components of any grade; however, the balance of these two is very subjective. Should the talented student who never works get an A and the not-so-talented student with tremendous drive and energy get a C, or vice versa? Balancing skill and effort takes an ability to weigh the situation fairly for each student. (See appendix A)

LOVE AND CHALLENGE

Spacetime meets bodymind as the teacher creates an emotional tone in the dance space. The body cannot pattern movement effectively if students are scared and intimidated; shoulders rise up, knees lock, and minds stop. Supporting effort and accepting failures enhances efficient neurological patterning. The student engages deeply in the work. The renowned educator Marva Collins says the most important aspect of teaching is *love*. Love puts the focus on student progress, not on the teacher's prowess. While creating a safe classroom is important, wanting or needing to *be liked* cannot be the underlying need. Examining these needs is crucial to challenging students, and being challenging does not always make the teacher likable.

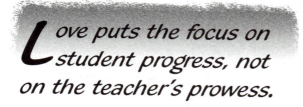

Love puts the focus on student progress, not on the teacher's prowess.

Three students recently talked to teachers at a faculty development meeting: a valedictorian, a renowned artist returning to school, and a self-confessed troublemaker with attention deficit disorder. They pleaded with the faculty for challenge.

Challenge begins with clearly defined goals (see chapter 3). But goals are only the map—the journey is carried out in the classroom. Students learn from each other's strengths. If a peer can do something well, it seems more possible. Emphasizing individual strengths enhances healthy competition in the classroom. Challenging students to race across the floor evokes childhood memories, and they stretch beyond their perceived limits. If students fall apart every time the teacher leaves the role as demonstrator, it is obvious that they have become too reliant on him. It is possible to make the choice to come back and help, but an equally powerful choice is leaving them to flounder. They quickly realize it is their responsibility to remember the pattern.

Challenge and demand are dance partners. If students are challenged to cover more space in a leap pattern, repetition is imperative until the challenge is met. If the goal is not accomplished, ask questions. Is the expectation beyond their technical skill level at this time or are the students just plain lazy? Do they lack proper strength? Are they resisting because they fear the freedom they may attain in the process? The search for the answers plans the next day's class.

Exuding the happiness of a child.

Coming up to a challenge and actually succeeding is what makes learning exciting. Nothing gets past Elana Anderson, a powerful Horton teacher with a drill sergeant's voice. She yells, screams, and barks orders right into the students' faces. But the moment someone truly succeeds, she exudes the happiness of a child.

COUNSELING

Mark Twain remarked that "life would be infinitely happier if we could only be born at the age of 80 and gradually approach 18." Advice winds backward when it comes to dance students. The young naturally seek advice from professionals. Their haunting, piercing eyes ask, "Do I have what it takes to be a dancer?" There are three answers to this question: "Yes,""No," or "Don't ask." The prudent course of action is to answer with the third. The professional world is filled with stories of successful dancers and choreographers who were told to hang up their bare feet by well-meaning teachers. Will and determination win over any skill.

However, teachers do have a responsibility to guide students in terms of assessment. A realistic self-assessment is the critical first step in making courageous choices, and courageous choices build artists along with well-lived lives. In our society, self-assessment is inextricably linked to self-worth. In a February 2002 *New York Times* article, "The Trouble With Self-Esteem," Lauren Slater asks if it is possible to separate self and worth. "Why as a culture, have we so conflated the two quite separate notions, a) self and b) worth?" Rather than relying on the word self-esteem, she advocates self-appraisal and self-control. "I can see. And in the seeing, assess, edit, praise, and prune. This is self-appraisal, which precedes self-control, for we must first know both where we flail and stumble, and where we are truly strong, before we can make disciplined alterations." (Slater 2002, 46-47)

Self-assessment is certainly bonded to self-worth. Susie thinks the world of herself but has no clue that she is immensely uncoordinated. Tony has a powerful reservoir of will and determination but has tremendous structural problems. Molly loves her hair and body and is rigidly holding onto all the bad habits she learned while cheerleading. Dwane is extremely talented yet self-doubt is written on his face. By identifying the strengths and obstacles without judging the self-worth attached to it, a teacher guides students toward realistic self-assessment. Calling attention to the obstacle may or may not tamper with self-esteem, but knowing the obstacles provides opportunities. Students will have the information necessary for soul-searching. Some students will turn their disappointment into ambition and resolve, other students will better match their goals with strengths, and still others will continue living a life of unfulfilled dreams. These are their choices; the teacher's role has been fulfilled.

Investigations

1. Write about the bodymind of respect, authority, power, and discipline.
2. Write about a time you resisted learning. What prevented you from seeking something new?
3. Make a list of rules of classroom etiquette. Explain the reasoning behind each rule.
4. Describe two teachers with different personalities. How does personality intersect with teaching movement?
5. Observe the class environment in a variety of dance classes. Is it a safe classroom? Observe the emotional and physical responses of students. What enhances efficient motor learning?

In-Class Investigations

1. Meditate for five minutes before class.
2. Walk into the dance studio and read the energy of the space. Make a note of who is standing in front and who is standing in back. Move the class around and move yourself around. What is different about your observations?
3. Spend time sharing information about the history and philosophy of the style of dance you teach.
4. Create a healthy environment of competition. Showcase students who have mastered a movement; applaud their growth and let them become the teachers. Create a race across the floor.
5. If students don't meet expectations, ask why and plan the next day's class.

Reflection: PATIENCE

Erika Dufour, photographer; Jan Erkert, dancer.

One day during an improvisational exercise, a teacher was suggesting movement cues while a student was dancing. She encouraged this particularly rigid student to release his weight and be more physically daring. A flood of anger rose up in him and he began screaming obscenities at her. While the stream of anger poured out of his body, he began to make movement breakthroughs. His spine released and his weight dropped downward; the anger seemed necessary to push through the fear. All eyes turned toward the teacher to see how she would react. She screamed obscenities back (not without awareness of a possible lawsuit). "You *!&@#^, keep going!" He did. They screamed back and forth as his exterior surface melted and inner fluidity emerged. Anger turned to tears as he stormed out of the room. The teacher let out a long sigh as her eyes followed him out of the room. Later the following poem was tacked onto the teacher's door. I wonder who posted it, the teacher or the student.

"With great difficulty, advancing by millimeters each year, I carve a road out of the rock. For millenniums my teeth have wasted and my nails broken to get there, to the other side, to the light and the open air. And now that my hands bleed and my teeth tremble, unsure, in a cavity cracked by thirst and dust, I pause and contemplate my work: I have spent the second part of my life breaking the stones, drilling the walls, smashing the doors, removing the obstacles I placed between the light and myself in the first part of my life."

Octavio Paz - Translated by Eliot Weinberger, from EAGLE OR SUN?, copyright ©1976 by Octavio Paz and Eliot Weinberger. Reprinted by permission of New Directions Publishing Corp.

chapter *13*

Excellence Training
HEALTH

Excellence is the prize and the carrot, the end of the road; the dancer aspires to excellence. As a physical activity, dance places great demands on the body, requiring risk-taking, daredevil behavior. Evel Knievel took extreme risks, but he didn't jump off cliffs without doing a little preparation. To promote excellence, the dance teacher has to set the bar high without injuring the precious cargo.

When athletes are in training they follow a very strict regimen encompassing every aspect of lifestyle; their whole lives come under scrutiny. In the 1960s dance teachers had cigarettes hanging out of their mouths while correcting tendus. In the book *Not Just Any Body: Advancing Health, Well-Being, and Excellence in Dance and Dancers,* Deborah Jowitt reviews a conference on dance training in Toronto and The Hague in 1999. "We hope to ascertain without a doubt—and spread the word—that sane and humane practices in the classroom, rehearsal hall, and the day-to-day functioning of dance companies are not antithetical to artistic excellence, but in fact promote it." (Jowitt 2001) We must begin to view dance training as a holistic enterprise encompassing every aspect of lifestyle. This chapter covers stresses relating to a performing career and the dangerous obsessions and injuries that might result if a healthy lifestyle is not intimately woven into dance training.

STRESS

Dance training and performing are rigorous activities, potentially creating a state of fatigue. When fatigue is coupled with the highly volatile, emotional issues associated with dance training, such as performance anxiety, perfectionism, and body image, the dancer becomes vulnerable to dangerous coping strategies. Let's begin by looking at some of the causes of stress.

Fatigue

Dancers are often overachievers, and thus fatigue becomes an inevitable part of the game. When someone is fatigued, there is both a perception that it is becoming harder to perform a task (a leap needs increasingly more effort) and an actual inability to perform the task (the leap fizzles). The "overtraining syndrome" describes a dancer who has reached fatigue level. Evidence shows a significant relationship between exposure to dance for more than five hours per day and increased injury rates among dancers. In an article about fatigue-related injuries, researchers Liederbach and Compagno say, " The overtraining syndrome also known as 'staleness,' 'burnout,' or 'unexpected under-performance syndrome,' is associated with central fatigue. It is defined as an unexpected drop in performance that cannot be attributed to illness or injury. It may occur when performance or training loads are not matched by adequate rest periods." (Liederback and Campagno 2001, 117) They advise teachers to avoid the overtraining syndrome in their students by varying teaching methods to avoid monotony, finding adequate rest periods within the cycle of training, and paying attention to cardiovascular conditioning, hydration, and healthy eating.

Performance Anxiety

Performance involves the exposure of the body and self—often in less-than-scanty clothes—to the scrutiny of hundreds and possibly thousands of voyeurs. No wonder anxiety is attached to performing. Fear of exposure and inadequacy comingle with a mixture of supreme confidence and humility. Liederbach and Compagno write, "As a cognitive event, performance anxiety is typically accompanied by somatic responses, including elevated cardiovascular and neuroendocrine activity." This means that a teacher will see ". . . heightened physical arousal, loss of focus, and worrying." (Liederbach and Compagno 2001, 116) Lack of concentration is a precursor to injuries pre-performance, thus letting the student off the hook for the feared trial by fire. How does a teacher prepare the student for performing?

As a preparatory tool, the classroom should never divorce itself from performance. Small performances within class prepare for bigger performances. Students begin by sharing a phrase one-on-one with a classmate. Next, a group performs in front of another group. At the end of a semester or workshop a class performs a phrase for another class. Stepping-stones are crucial for building healthy attitudes toward performance. Choreographers must join dance teachers in advocating preparatory stages to performing. The final performance is not seen as an isolated event if friends and colleagues are invited consistently to the rehearsal process.

A teacher must also be aware of the fears floating in the studio pre-performance. If a previously focused student loses concentration, seems remote, or becomes injury prone, it might be time for a conversation about fears and attitudes toward performance. Discussion fosters openness about a fear many would rather keep secret.

Perfectionism

Never quite attainable, perfection looms in the distance. How many routines did thousands of gymnasts perform in the Olympics before Nadia Comaneci became the first gymnast to be awarded the perfect 10? Perfection is a rare bird and in the process of striving for it we lose sight of the joy of flight itself. Fortunately, dancers are not competing for medals. Thankfully, one study showed that modern dancers are less concerned over mistakes than gymnasts, but artistry demands its own perfection, and dancers can get entangled in a loop of self-fulfilled failure. Rather than celebrating only perfection, teachers should honor failure as part of the cycle of learning, because it often signals a student's willingness to take risks. A dancer needs permission to fall, fail, or flail to truly arrive at a confident state of balance. If perfectionism is the only goal, the danger zone will never be visited. Mistakes are to be relished.

Body Image

A reflection of self is reported to the dancer daily by the studio mirror. This two-dimensional version of self gives scanty information about the living three-dimensional person. Most people cannot even conjure up an image of their back, because their only reference to self is through the mirror. The mirror reports a skewed version of every pound and every flaw, and dancers adapt faulty visions of their body. Daily staring at self in the mirror can lead to narcissistic tendencies and a troublesome body image. It also tends to mask the kinesthetic feel of movement. While a mirror is a useful visual tool, it should be used sparingly. The mirror, however, is merely a small part of a much larger societal picture.

A flat reflection.

Inundated by the perfect body in movies, magazines, and billboards the size of buses, dancers compete with unrealistic images. Weight, body image, beauty, and performance are tied together in a messy knot. The aesthetic of body fat in the dance world is related to history, culture, philosophy, and style of dance. Degas' dancers would be considered chunky today. An African dancer is praised for a round ample bottom; a ballet dancer is not. Attitudes by choreographers and audiences are changing in the new millennium; many contemporary choreographers are using odd-shaped bodies, preferring diversity and consciously challenging notions of beauty. Despite changing views, the pressure is on for young dancers to fit the mold. Dance teachers have a responsibility to keep their eyes open for students who slip into danger zones of coping with the stresses.

DANGEROUS OBSESSIONS

There is a slippery line between healthy dance training and dangerous addictions. Obsessions run high for the serious dancer—after all, dance is a career where perfectionism, pleasing others, setting high goals, and suffering to reach those goals are rewarded with applause and praise. Sex, illegal drugs, nicotine, alcohol, and food all provide tantalizing and important opportunities for experimentation, but each carries dangers for obsessive personalities. Whichever the obsession of choice, the body leaves telltale signs and dance teachers read the messages. (While all obsessions are worthy of discussion, in this book only nutrition will be addressed.)

Nutrition

Nutrition is as important as proper technique. "You are what you eat" is a mantra dancers need to learn as they embrace foods that are satisfying to the real needs of the body. Peak performance is related to nutrition because food is the body's fuel. Excellent performance is partially a result of excellent eating. Good foods should be cherished, not banished. It is helpful to invite nutritionists and professional dancers to speak with students, not necessarily about dieting but about the role food plays in better performance. One guest artist presented an informative lecture to students about the magic of food in healing her injuries. These perspectives from practicing professionals make a real impact on students' understanding of the role nutrition plays in dance training.

Eating Disorders

Too often dancers think of nutrition as a diet. Losing weight becomes the focus, and suddenly healthy training slips into a dangerous obsession. According to The National Eating Disorders Association, 5-10 million girls and women and 1 million boys and men suffer from eating disorders in the United States. This is probably a low number because secrecy and shame let many cases go unreported. Over one person's lifetime, 50,000 people will die as a direct result of eating disorders. Athletes in fields stressing low body weight, such as dance, are at extreme risk.

Dance teachers should become familiar with the signs of eating disorders. However, they are not always obvious. While extreme body weight, either too high or too low, and extreme fluctuations of weight are outward signs, many dancers with eating disorders live within *normal* weight. A teacher can screen for problems by observing energy; if a student consistently displays extremely high, low, or fluctuating energy, it may be related to some type of obsessive behavior. Unrealistic self-assessment of weight is another sign. If a featherweight student is talking about her fat thighs, it is time for intervention. Excessive exercise is tied into the web of eating disorders, so while teachers may applaud the student who is in class eight hours a day, it is not always the healthiest agenda.

Intervention

In the dark ages, schools and dance companies held weekly or daily weigh-ins, which only served to increase eating disorders. Thankfully, weigh-ins are disappearing, but in the effort to fix the problem, discussions about weight are simply avoided. Open discussions about weight, beauty, and body image must be encouraged in the hallways, studios, and dressing rooms. Posting information about nutrition and eating disorders in dance spaces fosters awareness and allows troubled students to obtain information without exposing themselves unnecessarily.

Determining whether an intervention should take place should always begin with health. If the student is outside the *healthy* range of weight (many charts are available from health organizations), an intervention is necessary. The strength-to-mass ratio is what should be considered at this time. If too thin, the dancer will lack the strength necessary to move without risk of injury. If the body is too large, the dancer may not have the strength to move the mass. Injuries will result. Second, the student's goals should enter the picture. There are different weight norms for a performer, teacher, an arts administrator, or a ballet, African, tap, or modern dancer. By understanding students' goals a teacher has a better sense of what *normal* body weight means relative to career.

If an intervention is necessary, start by asking how the student is feeling. Speak about signs you have observed—high or low energy or emotional withdrawal. Also ask about dance goals. Don't focus on weight alone. Listen carefully. The student will provide valuable information about how to proceed if given space and time. Last, provide information. Have pamphlets, phone numbers, and Web sites for help groups immediately available.

Native Americans have a saying that it takes seven generations to heal. How many generations will it take to create a positive environment surrounding nutrition in the dance field? Looking inward begins the process of healing, exploring our own attitudes toward weight, beauty, and body image. Too often teachers are heard making ridiculing comments about fat dancers. Students are praised for losing weight, even when the warning signs are present. These subtle and not-so-subtle messages create an environment of distress and confusion for our students. Students need teachers to begin the cycle of healing. The National Eating Disorder Association makes the following recommendation: "Be a model of healthy self-esteem and body image. Recognize that others pay attention and learn from the way you talk about yourself and your body. Choose to talk about yourself with respect and appreciation."

Genius is often associated with obsessions; look at the inspiring but difficult lives of Vaslav Nijinsky, Martha Graham, or Isadora Duncan. But teaching students to admire or glorify the cult of craziness does not serve the art or the development of artists. Greater possibilities only become a reality if there is healthy self-care and self-control. As Lauren Slater says, "Ultimately, self-control need not be seen as a constriction; restored to its original meaning, it might be experienced as the kind of practiced prowess an athlete or an artist demonstrates, muscles not tamed but trained, so that the leaps are powerful, the spine supple, and the energy harnessed and shaped." (Slater 2002, 47)

INJURIES

A dancer lands from a jump, yelps a scream, and falls onto the floor writhing in pain. It is the nightmare of every dance teacher. While most of a teacher's life is spent preventing injuries through proper training procedures, life is not perfect and injuries happen. Researcher Liederbach reports, "Injuries are common in dance. Between 50 percent and 80 percent of dancers report overuse syndromes sometime in their professional careers, and up to 46 percent of amenorrheic dancers experience stress fractures. Sixty-five percent of all injuries in dance result from overuse, and the other 35 percent from trauma." (Liederbach 2000, 54)

When a student is injured, health practitioners should and will enter the picture, but the teacher plays an immensely important role, advising on first aid and quelling the hysteria and fear surrounding the injury. If she is knowledgeable about symptoms and health practitioners, the teacher can also counsel the student about the appropriate health practitioner to treat the injury. And last, the teacher can be an invaluable support system for a student as she goes through the heartbreaking and soul-expanding process of rehabilitation and healing.

Be Prepared

There are several ways to be ready for the injury that looms close to the dance studio. The first order of business is to prepare a first-aid kit that is immediately accessible. Rules and regulations get lost in the chaos of an injury, so it is handy to have the institution's injury procedures nearby, right next to the first-aid kit. If your school or studio does not have an injury-procedure guideline, advocate creating one.

First-Aid Kit

- Breakable ice pack. If a freezer is nearby, make sure ice and plastic bags are always stocked. A great cold trick: Put damp sponges in resealable plastic bags and toss them in the freezer. These are excellent for injuries and are reusable.
- An assortment of bandages and gauze
- An elastic bandage
- Knee and elbow pads
- Antibacterial cream
- Scissors

Emergency Procedures

- An emergency number for immediate medical attention. 911 is the standard emergency system, but you might want the numbers of private ambulances and hospitals as well.

⚕ The names and numbers of the authorities to notify or who can offer additional assistance. These might be the security guard, the studio manager, or the chair of the department.

⚕ The institution's insurance rules and regulations should clearly state guidelines for the teacher to follow in case of injury.

⚕ Insurance forms should be readily available.

⚕ If no one at your school is certified in CPR, take a course. A CPR poster should be hung in the studio for reminders.

⚕ A poster about common acute and chronic injuries and systemic conditions and their symptoms should be posted on a bulletin board for quick reference.

Acute Injuries

An injury in class, whether major or minor, is generally acute; that is, it has a sudden onset. A fall can lead to a broken bone; a stretch can result in a pulled muscle. The first order of business is to assess the seriousness of the injury. Any injury eliciting a scream or a fall warrants stopping class, rushing to the scene, and calling 911. If a student has any trouble moving any joint, they should see a doctor immediately. Being overly cautious is prudent in these situations. Insurance policies at many schools prohibit a teacher from touching an injured student. Keep the student warm and focus on breathing until help arrives. Make arrangements for someone to travel with the student to be their advocate. No one should face the hospital alone.

Inflammation accompanies most acute injuries. It is the body's natural defense system sending fluids to the site to help; swelling, warmth, redness, pain, and dysfunction are the results. Pain is included in nature's plan, particularly for those people who have no common sense. Doctors generally recommend rest, ice, compression, and elevation (RICE) for any injuries with inflammation. Once a student has had a medical evaluation, these simple tactics prevent further damage to the site and promote the body's own healing systems. Even though the student might want to come back the next day and take class, *rest* is the first order of business.

Chronic Injuries

Chronic injuries sneak up over time as the result of improper alignment, inadequate conditioning, overuse of a particular muscle group, or environmental stresses such as bad floors or cold studios. Chronic injuries can be triggered by acute injuries, especially if a student does not attend to proper rehabilitation. Attach *-itis,* which means inflammation, to a part of the body and you get chronic injuries such as tendinitis, bursitis, and fascitis, to name a few.

Although they're not nearly as dramatic as acute injuries, chronic injuries are psychologically devastating. Students need wise counsel to properly deal with the steady pain and possibly career-ending potential of chronic injuries. The first step is to make sure they get proper medical help. Because these injuries are often due to misalignments, a teacher's trained eye can be instrumental to the healing process.

Health-Care Practitioners

Martina Navratilova traveled with an entourage of masseuses, physical therapists, and bodyworkers. We should all be so lucky. But the rock stars of physical performance have taught us an important lesson: An ongoing relationship with health-care practitioners is essential for better performance and serves as a support system when injuries occur. The local dance community or sports teams are usually an excellent place for references. When it comes to injuries, the dance teacher is an important conduit between student and health-care practitioners. Developing a reference list is an important first step. But more important, this is an opportunity to educate students about the *process* of healing. The broader the knowledge about healing, the more the students can make informed choices about who to see and what to do to further their own healing.

> *The broader the knowledge about healing, the more the students can make informed choices about who to see and what to do to further their own healing.*

Although doctors and teachers are important partners in the dance toward healing, students must learn to take charge of their healing process. Dancers have spent a lifetime learning about their bodies. If validated, this knowledge will serve them well in the healing process. Dancers should be encouraged to ask questions of their doctors and teachers so that they fully understand their injury. They should also listen to and communicate to their doctors the intuitive messages of the body. Reading and research will make them smart healers, allowing them to return to the studio sooner and better than ever expected.

Many dancers don't have access to medical insurance, so besides the trauma of the injury they face the reality of financial disaster. Teachers can offer preventative help on this front by building ongoing relationships with medical schools and organizations. Massage, acupuncture, and chiropractic schools look for patients to practice on. Student health-care workers are supervised by faculty, so excellent care is available. Even better, the institutions can be cajoled to bring their services to the dance studio, where dancers may receive treatments prior to or after performances. Many dancers enter careers in health care because of their involvement with medical professionals during an injury. Dancers who are interested in health care should be counseled to seek jobs in health-care offices, where they not only learn about the field but also receive many perks such as massages and adjustments.

Rehabilitation

Performances, dreams, and treasured goals are altered, sometimes drastically, when an injury occurs. While it does not always fit into the neatly outlined plans, rehabilitation of acute and chronic injuries is crucial to longevity in a dance career. Rehabilitation for dancers should link physical therapy and dance training. Liederbach says,

"When one considers the etiologic factors associated with dance injuries, it is easier to see why style-specific, multifactorial, staged rehabilitation programs are needed in order to fully restore function to a dancer and safely return him or her to pre-injury level of participation." She suggests four stages of rehabilitation that incorporate easing back into dance training: restricted, restoration, reacquisition, and refinement. At the beginning, the restricted phase incorporates somatic and mental imagery. The restoration phase concentrates on alignment and stability, perhaps with a return to a beginning-level dance class. The goal of the reacquisition phase is the return to the original class with some limitations. As the dancer return to normal schedule in the refinement phase, he is coached in preventative strategies. (Liederbach 2000, 59-60)

The Boston Ballet began a transition class taught by both a physical therapist and a dance teacher. "The transition class is structured to help dancers maintain conditioning and technique while recovering from an injury, layoff, or illness. The class combines therapeutic exercises and dance technique in order to meet both artistic and rehabilitative goals. The class allows for close supervision of each dancer." (Cassella, Ploski, Sullivan, and Micheli 1999, 139-143)

An injured dancer observing.

I would rather watch the power of a dancer nourished by life rather than one diminished by it.

Watching dance classes is one way of keeping an injured dancer involved, although many find this depressing. Teachers can ease this stress by involving the injured student in educational experiences, such as assisting in comments and corrections or coaching students privately from the sidelines. If watching class is too depressing, perhaps the student can use the time for physical therapy or counseling.

Who am I, if not a dancer? An injury forces us to take a deep look into ourselves. One study reports that the more limited a person's sense of self, the more difficult the process of rehabilitation. A teacher must guide the student to develop other aspects of self by encouraging contemplative hobbies such as reading, writing, painting, or gardening. Perhaps a stronger person and artist will emerge by discovering a self not narrowly defined as dancer.

Luckily, research shows that dancers do indeed get better at the healing process. If dancers view an injury as an opportunity to learn, the healing process will create rewarding results. Sometimes this journey may yield surprising results, the new goal may become the desired dream. Health and excellence are indeed dance partners. I would rather watch the power of a dancer nourished by life rather than one diminished by it.

Investigations

1. Write about a moment of fear preceding a performance.
2. Write about perfection. How does it enhance training? How does it get in the way? Write about a perfect performance.
3. Write about the role fatigue plays in the life of a dancer.
4. Which are your obsessions of choice? What is your definition of beauty? What is your body image?
5. Develop an informative poster about eating disorders for the dance studio.
6. Develop a list of telephone help lines for eating disorders, alcohol or drug abuse, sleeping disorders, and smoking.
7. Write about an injury you had. What support system was or was not in place? What did you learn about the healing process during this time?
8. Create a first-aid kit and an injury procedure document.
9. Create a reference list of health-care practitioners in your town.

In-Class Investigations

Watch for signs of dangerous obsessions.

Reflection: NOURISHMENT

The filly is in training for a big race, but she craves orange-filled chocolate rum balls, living the high life, and staying up late listening to jazz in seedy nightclubs.

Dressed in an orange sequined gown, the sleek nightclub singer croons, *"Button up your overcoat, / When the wind is free, / Take good care of yourself, / you belong to me. / Eat an apple every day, / Get to bed by three. / Take good care of yourself, / you belong to me."*

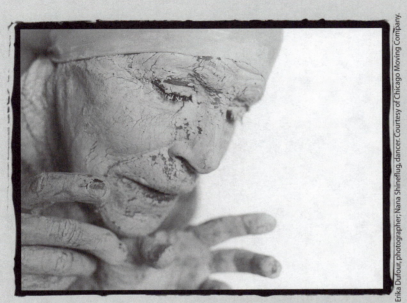

Erika Dufour, photographer; Nana Shineflug, dancer. Courtesy of Chicago Moving Company.

The jazz singer's black, curly hair streaks through air as she mounts the filly. They ride through clouds. Kicking its flanks, her voice sounds shrill as she belts out the song slightly off-key, *"Keep away from bootleg hooch, / when you're on a spree. / Take good care of yourself, / you belong to me."* Getting fat on rum balls, flying fast is becoming a distant dream.

Dressed in an orange polyester jumpsuit, the trainer, with dyed black hair and a smoker's rutted skin, heaves her weight up on the rail as she screams, "You belong to me you sway-backed excuse for a horse, run faster or the glue factory is your next stop."

You belong to no one, dancing, flying, and soaring faster and faster. Flicking flies away, you nourish whom? "Take good care of yourself." I belong to me.

chapter 14

Youth Spinning
V I T A L I T Y

Eagerness, curiosity, discipline, care, bitterness, and determination are all reflected in the way we wear our dance clothes, the way in which we age, the way we make or don't make difficult and courageous choices. Students see the true picture of the inner world through outer manifestation. Rainer Maria

Rilke says "Innerness, what is it? / If not intensified sky / scattered through with birds and deep / from winds of hometurning. – Summer, 1925" (Rilke 1975, 81) Youthful vitality is ours if we are willing to listen to our own advice. This chapter will explore how to meet the challenges of a long teaching career while aging gracefully.

Youthful vitality is ours if we are willing to listen to our own advice.

BODYMIND

Aging is difficult for a dancer, because it signifies the loss of youth, vitality, spring, and resilience. A lifetime of training recedes as the joints lose their spring. Those dancers who segue into teaching continue to place strenuous demands on the body. Little by little, the dancing body becomes an older body, with the residual aches and limitations that result from years of physical stress. But wait. Does it have to be that way? In *A Natural History of the Senses,* Diane Ackerman speaks about the aging of a violin. "Many violinists and violin makers insist that violins grow into their beautiful throaty sounds, and that a violin played exquisitely for a long time eventually contains the exquisite sounds within itself. Somehow the wood keeps track of the robust, lyrical flights. In down-to-earth terms: Certain vibrations made over and over for years, along with all the normal processes of aging, could make microscopic changes in the wood; we perceive those cellular changes as enriched tone. In poetic terms: The wood remembers. Thus, part of a master violinist's duties is to educate a violin for future generations." (Ackerman 1990, 204) Perhaps teachers can think of their bodies as a complex Stradivarius, remembering sensations immensely valuable to the next generation.

Fatigue and Injuries in Dance Teachers

Many teachers live dual lives, performing and teaching. Feelings of loss flourish in professional dancers who stop performing to begin new careers as teachers. There is no longer a master to turn to; there is no time for their own bodies, and everyone seems so needy. Feelings of loss and grief can turn to bitterness, which can lead new teachers to unhealthy patterns such as focusing on themselves instead of the students or winging every class to save time. Teachers need to find healthy, effective ways to battle the stress and fatigue of their careers.

Most dance teachers have rigorous schedules. Those who are still dancing run from teaching to rehearsals. The body endures tremendous stress when a teacher jumps in to demonstrate without adequate warm-up, stands for hours on inadequate floors, or demonstrates jumps in the fifth hour of rigorous teaching. Many teachers freelance, driving to and from different studios and running out into the cold air after leaving a warm, humid studio. Fatigue develops and injuries can follow.

Healing

Injuries and aging wear out even the most elegant of dancers, but dancers possess an advantage: a lifetime's knowledge about the body. When a computer crashes, a smart computer geek can maneuver the hard drive into behaving, returning it to its original splendor without losing valued applications and programs. The amateur tends to lose everything while trying to fix the problem. An Alexander Technique teacher once said, "When injured, the body returns to its original blueprint to heal." Using this metaphor, a wise professional can coax the body toward its original blueprint, inviting efficiency.

Maintenance

Seeking out activities that give physical balance to teaching is crucial. As silly as it sounds, teachers need to exercise. Counteracting the years of overuse from dance training and performing, lavishing attention on one's own body is an essential part of that balance. Teaching does not provide sustained cardiovascular activity, and cardiorespiratory health is vital, especially as one ages. Swimming is an ideal exercise for dancers; it is opposite in every way to the rigors of dance: aerobic, repetitive, meditative, upper-body based, non-weight bearing. While running might be satisfying to some, dancers are often too flexible to withstand the long-term impact on the joints. Biking or cross-country skiing provides aerobic activity and a chance to be outdoors without tremendous stress on the joints. But whatever the activity, it must provide joy or it won't be done.

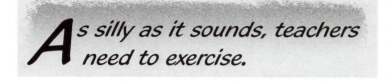

As silly as it sounds, teachers need to exercise.

Teachers are also susceptible to injuries resulting from overuse, so an activity that uses the joints in a different manner than dance is crucial to functional longevity. Yoga can wring out the joints and make them fresh again. The gentle flow of energy in tai chi chuan is an ideal counter to the stresses of teaching for both the mind and body. Learning somatic practices or other movement forms can not only heal the teacher's body but also inspire new ideas for teaching. Body-Mind Centering teaches one to explore the "mind-set of the bones" or the "mind-set of the organs." By utilizing different systems, teachers can shift systems in class and save energy. Alexander Technique promotes personal alignment and offers new information about making corrections.

Choices

Time is the culprit in a stressed life; there is just not enough of it. But time is about choices, hard choices. Having it all is a choice. A great job, a loving family, artistic projects, and a community are all worthwhile endeavors, but being physically broken is not worth having it all. Prioritizing is hard, but ultimately physical health is the winner. What is needed to maintain physical health? What has to be let go in order to maintain mental clarity? Dance teachers must use their creativity to protect their own health. Vacations are ideal times to pamper oneself, moving only for movement's sake. A grant to study a new discipline might afford needed time away. A bike ride to the studio offers aerobic exercise and a chance to be outside. A personal warm-up before class is a worthwhile indulgence, much like a warm bath. For many teachers, a healthy body is not only a barometer of life but also the breadwinner. A broken body spells disaster in more ways than one. The Stradivarius is an expensive investment worthy of elaborate care.

MINDBODY

There is an old story in Zen literature. A young student comes to a master's home and asks to study with him. As they are drinking tea, the student tries to impress the master with how much he knows. The master begins filling his cup with tea and does not stop when the cup is full. The student yells in exasperation, "Stop filling the cup! Tea is running all over the table!" The Zen master says, "You are not ready to study with me; your cup is too full." As teachers, we are supposed to be experts, full of information; yet too much knowledge leads to static solutions and unyielding advice. How do we maintain an empty cup?

Lifetime Learners

A beginner's mind is cultivated when teaching and learning are circular. In *Zen in the Art of Archery*, Eugen Herrigel speaks of this circle, "…it is necessary for the archer to become, in spite of himself, an unmoved center. Then comes the supreme and ultimate miracle: art becomes "artless," shooting becomes not-shooting, a shooting without bow and arrow; the teacher becomes a pupil again, the Master a beginner, the end a beginning, and the beginning perfection." (Herrigel 1989, 5)

Who is the teacher and who is the learner? Curiosity leads the dialogue. Michele Root-Bernstein writes about the importance of maintaining cross-disciplinary interests. "Evidence suggests that successful individuals are almost invariably multiply gifted. Writers paint, painters sculpt, sculptors dance, dancers write. Nor do the multiply gifted necessarily respect conventional divides between the arts, sciences, and technologies. Many of the best artists were and are advanced in their studies of anatomy, medicine, chemistry, mathematics, and other sciences. Many of the best scientists were and are excellent amateur musicians, artists, poets. Indeed, among scientists and other professionals as well, the very fact of an intellectually stimulating hobby itself predicts success in the primary career."(Root-Bernstein 2001, 134)

Monet built elaborate gardens, thus inspiring his paintings. John Cage was a noted expert on mushrooms. Louise Nevelson complemented her work in sculpture by studying eurhythmics. Isadora Duncan was fascinated by Greek culture. If pliés and tendus become the sole focus of a worldview, creativity is stifled and distress and disease flourish.

A teacher must also remain contemporary. The style of dancing is different today than it was twenty years ago, even five years ago. Dancemakers are continually evolving new ways of moving. Teachers must relinquish practices that are no longer relevant. Sorting out fads and revolutions, new trends, and new movement is crucial to understanding the immediacy of the field. Learning a few new tricks might even freshen old bones.

Rest

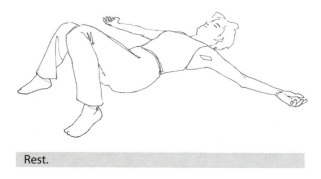

Rest.

Doing something over and over leads to staleness. No matter how fascinating a subject is, a break is needed. Whether or not a sabbatical is built into the system, teachers must take breaks from their work. Tempting though it may be to take on one more class over the summer, imagine the luxury of not teaching, of restoring and rejuvenating. It is a different kind of money in the bank. A brand-new sofa is less important than the ability to sit down.

Sharing With Colleagues

Even though dance is a social art form, teachers often feel isolated. In *The Courage to Teach,* Parker Palmer says, "Though we teach in front of students, we almost always teach solo, out of collegial sight—as contrasted with surgeons or trial lawyers, who work in the presence of others who know their craft well. Lawyers argue cases in front of other lawyers, where gaps in their skill and knowledge are clear for all to see. Surgeons operate under the gaze of specialists who notice if a hand trembles, making malpractice less likely. But teachers can lose sponges or amputate the wrong limb with no witnesses except the victim." (Palmer 1998, 142) If the art form and its instruction are to progress, dance teachers must learn to create a dialogue about teaching practices. Observing each other's classes is an effective conversation starter. Allowing such scrutiny takes a willingness to be vulnerable, but the reward is a true discussion about art and teaching. The teacher to be observed should write a list of questions for her colleagues, thereby directing the focus to real concerns: "Do the rhythms support the movement? Is the pacing too fast, too slow? I am struggling with lackluster energy from the students; any ideas on how I might elicit a different type of energy?" Another way to create discussion is to co-teach a class —not always practical in a world run by economic concerns, but nonetheless a phenomenal experience. Watching another mind wrestle with the same problems you face is at times awe-inspiring and at other times downright comforting. Faculty discussions may be dominated by administrative trivia, but hallways should be filled with dialogues about teaching, students, and learning. Only we can make this happen. (See appendix E).

SPIRITENERGY

In *Zen Mind, Beginner's Mind,* Shunryu Suzuki talks about the relationship between student and teacher. "Through the teaching we may understand our human nature. But the teaching is not we ourselves; it is some explanation of ourselves. So if you are attached to the teaching, or to the teacher, that is a big mistake. The moment you meet a teacher, you should leave the teacher, and you should be independent. You need a teacher so that you can become independent. If you are not attached to him, the teacher will show you the way to yourself. You have a teacher for yourself, not for the teacher." (Suzuki 1970, 77)

Detachment

At times we may need students to boost our egos, but ultimately, we must learn to let go of these attachments, because they create dependence.

I was asked to teach a movement class to a group of junior-high-school boys during a gym class. Completely engaged, these boys passionately rolled, jumped, leaped, ran, and giggled. Then one day they walked in, sat down, and refused to move. "What's wrong?" I asked. They replied, "The other guys said we were *dancing.* We don't want to dance; that's for sissies." Peer pressure raised the ugly head of homophobia. I tried everything to get them back—we talked; we discussed gender roles, prejudice, and peer pressure. Nothing worked. There is no happy ending. I had to let go. All I could hold onto was the knowledge that the boys had reveled in soaring, jumping, and flying, and the hope that perhaps later in life, they would rediscover the dance of their youth. I would not have the pleasure of knowing or seeing this happen.

In *Teaching a Stone to Talk: Expeditions and Encounters,* Annie Dillard says of the stars, "You do not have to sit outside in the dark. If, however, you want to look at the stars, you will find that darkness is necessary. But the stars neither require nor demand it." (Dillard 1982, 43)

Rapture

So we go out into the dark and stare at the stars. But unlike the stars, each human being needs another to guide him toward pinpricks of light. The wind swirls and reminds us that this is it. This is our chance to offer the world a gift, and what greater gift is there than to shine a flashlight on the blood, muscles, and bones of someone discovering himself? We probe with our beam of light, demanding that the secret corners be revealed. And what do teachers receive in return? We get front row seats to flashes of discovery, and starry eyes when students enter stage right. Giddy with excitement, we pass down from generation to generation, as the philosopher Joseph Campbell says, "the rapture of being alive." If technique is a harness, then its straps and ropes and sails are carefully woven from the rapturous threads of a teacher's sturdy heart.

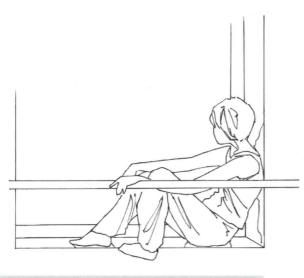

Letting go.

Investigations

1. Find five minutes in your day, every day, for a moment alone.
2. Leave the studio or building every day for a short walk. Write about it in your journal.
3. Schedule a massage once a month or once a week. (Massage schools often need people to practice on—start a relationship between a massage school and your dance institution.)
4. Cultivate the curiosity of a child. Learn something new.
5. Teachers: Create a partnership with another teacher. Observe each other's classes. Create a list of questions for each other that address important issues about teaching.
6. Teachers: Spend a faculty meeting discussing, "critical moments…one in which a learning opportunity for students will open up, or shut down—depending, in part, on how the teacher handles it." (Palmer 1998, 145) This might be the first question, the first time a student challenges your rules, or the breakthrough moment.

Reflection: RENEWAL

My colleague falls onto the couch in my office, exhausted from a day of bending unwilling bodies. We decide to go to a Tina Turner concert.

Courtesy of Erika Dufour, photographer; Suet May Ho, dancer.

Twenty thousand people fill the sports stadium, now reconfigured into a performance space. With 60 years of life behind her, Tina, decked out in a sequined miniskirt and patent-leather spiked heels, belts out songs and jumps and gyrates for two and a half hours. Her energy increases as the show progresses.

Flashback: Two young, awkward dance students dressed in miniskirts, fringed vests, and go-go boots enter an Ike and Tina concert. They are unaware at the time that they will fulfill their dreams. Fragile and uncertain, they slip into Tina's vortex of energy. Tina is yelling and screaming with a voice both fragile and powerful. The young hippie women, full of flower-power hopefulness, let out a whimper of compassion when Tina falls into a heap at the end of the show.

Tonight Tina is harnessing the energy of 20,000 people. Winding down the crowd by riding up and down the scales of a ballad, Tina carefully sculpts the ebb and flow of the evening. The quiet calm feeds the coming momentum that will burst wildly forward once again. Tina enjoys the raspiness of her voice and the power of her lioness-like body, lighting a fire under anyone who might doubt her.

Dressed in their finest city-slick, black leather miniskirts, the colleagues are screaming and bouncing in the aisles well past their bedtime. Tomorrow they will *keep on rolling* with fire in their hearts because the next generation with tattoos and piercings have unending dreams waiting to be fulfilled and there is a ballad to sing and dance.

Appendix A
THE DANCE CENTER OF COLUMBIA COLLEGE CHICAGO MODERN DANCE TECHNIQUE SYLLABUS

Developed by the Dance Center of Columbia College Chicago Faculty:
Bonnie Brooks, Jan Erkert, Dardi McGinley-Gallivan, Shirley Mordine,
Deborah Siegel, Eduardo Vilaro, and Richard Woodbury

RATIONALE

Modern dance technique heightens awareness of the body; builds physical, aesthetic, and performance skills; and develops appreciation for the art form of dance. The daily practice of these skills is essential to the development of a skilled contemporary dancer. Throughout the training process, students will study the fundamental principles, practices, and vocabulary common to a variety of modern dance styles, which the students will be exposed to throughout their technical training at the Dance Center. Modern technique prepares the student to perform with clarity and artistry, cultivate personal presence, and withstand the physical rigors of a career in dance.

DESCRIPTION

The modern dance technique class consists of a series of technical exercises that increase skills of coordination and alignment while building strength, flexibility, and endurance. Class begins with warm-up exercises and progresses to rhythmic movement patterns that travel through space, building rhythmic, spatial, and dynamic skills. Live musicians accompany all modern classes.

OBJECTIVES

Dance is a continuum of learning. Each level of technique will address an increasing complexity of dance skills as well as increased expectations of performance. A skilled contemporary dancer will have the ability to perform dance and exhibit the following qualities:

- **Coordination:** The ability to efficiently link movement patterning
- **Alignment:** The ability to maintain correct musculoskeletal positioning in movement or stillness
- **Conditioning:** The ability to demonstrate balanced flexibility, strength, and endurance
- **Clarity:** The ability to accurately and consistently execute intended movements
- **Adaptability:** The ability to employ physical and performance skills for a variety of choreographic intentions
- **Artistry:** The ability to integrate technical skills with intuition and personal presence

TOPICS

- Breath support
- Movement coordination
- Dynamic alignment
- Centering (exploring dynamic balance both on and off center)
- Movement retention
- Relationship of the body with gravity and weight
- Spatial patterning and directions
- Movement in and out of the floor
- Speed, rhythm, musicality, and phrasing
- Inner connectivity and outer expressivity
- Movement intent
- Dance vocabulary
- Class etiquette (listening skills, self-discipline, spatial awareness, proper attire)

COURSE REQUIREMENTS AND GRADES

The purpose of this class is to develop cognitive, intuitive, physical, and performance skills. To move to the next level, you must achieve the objectives listed in the level-placement guide. While you work toward these skills, your grades will be based on the following two points.

Demonstrated Improvement (50 percent)

The fundamental concern of this course is your growth as a dancer. Success in this area will be determined by semester-long improvement in the six course objectives: coordination, alignment, conditioning, clarity, adaptability, and artistry.

Quality of Effort (50 percent)

The quality and consistency of your efforts are crucial to increased physical skills. This portion of the grade will be based on self-discipline, understanding of class etiquette, level of concentration, consistency of work habits, self-confidence, and demonstrated responsiveness to the instructions of the instructor. Lackluster effort will have a negative effect on your success in this course, whereas consistently enthusiastic and focused performance of class materials will positively affect your final grade.

Tardy Policy

Students are expected to attend every class and to be dressed and ready to move on time. *No one* will be admitted to class after the class begins. Students who do arrive late may observe class, write their observations, and turn them in to the teacher. This will be counted as half an absence. If you are late and do not turn in observations, you will receive a full absence.

Attendance Policy

Missed classes can seriously affect your grade. When illness or crises cause absence from class, a limited number of makeup classes are allowed (one for a once-weekly class; two for a twice-weekly class). Students should discuss absences or tardies with the instructor to demonstrate that they are handling the course responsibly. Attendance is figured into a grade once a teacher arrives at a grade for demonstrated improvement and quality of effort.

MIDTERM EVALUATIONS

Near the middle of the semester all students will receive notice of their current standing. Whether presented verbally or in written form, the notice will indicate your grade to date. This will include a grade for quality of effort, a grade for demonstrated improvement, and the number of absences or tardies. This is an important time to discuss with your teacher what you can do to improve by the end of the semester. Students are encouraged to discuss their progress with their instructor throughout the semester whenever they have a question, problem, or concern.

GRADING SCALE FOR TECHNIQUE COURSES

Excellence (A): *Excellence* is for students who show a hunger to know, a passion for learning, and a willingness to take movement risks and integrate corrections. Excellence means striving for the best at all times and demonstrating exceptional growth toward the objectives of this course. An A student is capable of running, jumping, and leaping at a substantially higher level than when the semester began. The A student goes after the best, consistently, day after day.

Good (B): *Good* is for students who do their work with uniform solidity. Showing dedication, a willingness to take new steps, concentration, and consistent work habits, a B student demonstrates increased accomplishment of some skills during the semester. The B student is solid beyond reproach.

Average (C): *Average* is for students who do their work and actively participate in class but lack the energy or will it takes to push to new heights. Even though present in class, a C student does not command to be seen. The student has accomplished some skills during the semester, but both student and teacher know that it could be better. Work habits are inconsistent. A C student can accomplish more.

Poor (D): *Poor* is for students who have not done their work regularly. Lacking the necessary energy or passion for dance, the D student has shown very little improvement. Consistently leaving class early or coming late, D students are not interested in passing or improving their dancing.

Failing (F): *Failing* is for the student who has missed so many classes, been tardy, or left class so much that there is no base from which to grade. Try again next semester!

Reprinted, by permission, from L. Lehrer, B. Brooks, R. Woodbury, S. Mordine, D. Siegel, E. Vilaro, D. McGinley, and J. Erkert, The Dance Center of Columbia College Chicago. From *Harnessing the Wind* by Jan Erkert, 2003, Champaign, IL: Human Kinetics.

Appendix B

THE DANCE CENTER OF COLUMBIA COLLEGE CHICAGO LEVEL PLACEMENT GUIDE

Developed by The Dance Center of Columbia College Chicago Faculty:
Bonnie Brooks, Jan Erkert, Dardi McGinley-Gallivan, Shirley Mordine,
Deborah Siegel, Eduardo Vilaro, and Richard Woodbury

MODERN DANCE TECHNIQUE I - EXPECTATIONS FOR ENTRY INTO MODERN II

Modern I students will spend a majority of their time working on *coordination, alignment,* and *conditioning.* A student who is ready to move to Modern II should show accomplishments in these areas and be ready to concentrate on *clarity.*

1. **Adagio:** Simple, low leg extension coordinated with arm movements. The student should be able to

   ► clearly replicate forms in space;
   ► articulate legs and arms with awareness of proper pelvic, spinal, and scapular alignment;
   ► articulate the spine; and
   ► demonstrate a general sense of balance, strength, and flexibility.

2. **Locomotor:** A traveling sequence that links two or three locomotor movements (for example, triplets, slides, skips) in simple rhythmic patterns (six, eight, three). The student should be able to

   ► move consistently on the beat;
   ► coordinate movement patterning;
   ► maintain torso alignment while moving;
   ► recognize personal body tensions while moving; and
   ► move through space with focus.

3. **Movement combination:** A short movement sequence composed of simple rhythmic phrases (one or two phrases of eight counts) that incorporates changes of direction and level (to and from the floor). The student should be able to

- learn the movement sequence accurately and be able to repeat consistently;
- demonstrate at least one or two pathways to and from the floor;
- demonstrate proper use of weight and momentum in relationship to gravity; and
- sustain concentration.

4. **Simple jumps in place:** A simple jump exercise (at least 16 counts long). The student should be able to

- jump without undue strain; and
- hold spinal alignment, articulate feet, or keep shoulders down (ability to accomplish generally one or more of these).

MODERN DANCE TECHNIQUE II - EXPECTATIONS FOR ENTRY INTO MODERN III

Modern II students will spend a majority of their time working on *coordination* and *alignment* with a special emphasis on *clarity* of rhythm, form, and energy. A student ready to move on to Modern III should have the skills necessary to address *adaptability* and *artistry*.

1. **Adagio:** A slow sequence that moves through spatial forms that are challenging to range and balance. The student should be able to

- clearly replicate forms in space;
- perform with a sense of spatial intent;
- maintain dynamic alignment;
- articulate spine, legs, arms, and feet; and
- sustain balance and flow of movement.

2. **Locomotor:** A traveling sequence that links two or three locomotor movements (triplets, slides, skips, and turns) with one or two direction changes. The student should be able to

- demonstrate rhythmic clarity;
- coordinate movement patterning;
- maintain torso alignment while moving;
- articulate smaller details consistently;
- move through space with commitment; and
- move in space with awareness of self and others.

3. **Movement combination:** A moderately long (two or three phrases of eight counts) movement sequence in mixed meter that incorporates changes of direction and level (in and out of the floor). The student should be able to

- pick up the sequence quickly (after being shown the movement three or four times);
- accurately perform movement qualities; and
- demonstrate clarity of focus, intent, and internal commitment.

4. **Run-run-leap:** A very simple run-run-leap. The student should be able to
   - ► maintain focus (spatial intent, sense of self, no undue strain);
   - ► achieve adequate height in the leap while maintaining dynamic alignment and joint articulation; and
   - ► demonstrate rhythmic accuracy.

MODERN DANCE TECHNIQUE III - EXPECTATIONS FOR ENTRY INTO MODERN IV OR FOR GRADUATION WITH A BACHELOR OF ARTS DEGREE IN DANCE

Modern III students will spend a majority of their time on *clarity* and *adaptability*. A student ready to move on to Modern IV should have the skills necessary to concentrate on *artistry*.

1. **Adagio:** A sculptural adagio that moves through spatial forms that are challenging to range and balance. The student should be able to
   - ► demonstrate clarity of spatial intent;
   - ► maintain dynamic alignment while articulating extremities; and
   - ► maintain breath and sustained flow of movement.
2. **Locomotor:** A traveling sequence that links three or four locomotor movements (triplets, slides, skips, and turns) with two to three direction changes. The student should be able to
   - ► demonstrate rhythmic clarity;
   - ► coordinate movement with ease and smoothly link transitions;
   - ► maintain dynamic alignment and articulate smaller details while moving;
   - ► move through space with confidence; and
   - ► move in space with awareness of self and others.
3. **Movement combination:** A long (three or four phrases of eight counts) movement sequence in mixed meter and/or syncopated rhythms that incorporates change of directions and level (to and from the floor). The student should be able to
   - ► pick up sequence and all details quickly (after being shown two or three times);
   - ► create phrases with dynamic shifts using knowledge of weight, momentum, and the body's relationship to gravity; and
   - ► perform with internal commitment and external awareness.
4. **Run-run-leap:** A leap pattern with arm patterns or direction changes. The student should be able to
   - ► demonstrate connectivity;
   - ► achieve height in the leap while maintaining dynamic alignment and joint articulation, and land efficiently; and
   - ► demonstrate rhythmic accuracy.

MODERN DANCE TECHNIQUE IV - EXPECTATIONS FOR GRADUATION WITH A BACHELOR OF FINE ARTS DEGREE

The Modern IV student will spend a majority of time on *adaptability* and *artistry*. A student ready for graduation should be ready to integrate technical skills with personal presence.

1. **Adagio:** A sculptural adagio that moves through spatial forms that are challenging to range, balance, and dynamics. The student should be able to
   - demonstrate a sculptural approach to form;
   - maintain dynamic alignment while articulating extremities;
   - maintain breath and sustained flow of movement; and
   - shape the movement into phrases.

2. **Locomotor:** A traveling sequence that links three or four locomotor movements (triplets, slides, skips, and turns) with two or three direction changes. The student should be able to
   - perform with rhythmic clarity with attention to accent, meter, and phrasing;
   - coordinate movement with ease and presence;
   - maintain dynamic alignment while moving and articulating details;
   - move through space with command; and
   - move in space with awareness of self and others.

3. **Movement combination:** A long (three or four phrases of eight counts) movement sequence in complex rhythmic patterns that incorporates changes of direction and level (to and from the floor). The student should be able to
   - pick up sequence and all details quickly (after being shown one or two times);
   - create phrases with dynamic shifts using knowledge of weight, momentum, and the body's relationship to gravity;
   - shape rhythmic phrasing; and
   - bring a sense of self to the movement.

4. **Run-run-leap:** A leap pattern with arm patterning and direction changes. The student should be able to
   - perform with connectivity and ease;
   - achieve height in the leap while maintaining dynamic alignment and joint articulation;
   - land efficiently and smoothly; and
   - demonstrate rhythmic accuracy.

Appendix C
Pre- and Post-Assessment in the Performing Arts

Neil Pagano, Richard Woodbury, and Jan Erkert at Columbia College Chicago

Assessing student achievement in performing arts programs presents a number of challenges. First, the judgments we make are inherently subjective given the subjective nature of the performing arts. In addition, the performances we are attempting to assess are, quite literally in the case of dance students, moving targets. Finally, closing the feedback loop can be difficult if there is little agreement concerning assessment criteria and if there is the steadfast belief that one cannot remove the subjectivity associated with assessment.

As daunting as these challenges are, the Dance Department at Columbia College Chicago has addressed them and crafted an approach to academic assessment that accomplishes its two major purposes: to affirm student achievement and to make informed curricular decisions.

Columbia College Chicago is a private arts and communications college in Chicago's South Loop. Total undergraduate student population is approximately 8,500. The Dance Department offers both a bachelor of fine arts degree and a bachelor of arts degree. One of the most important aspects of the dance program is that it, like the college, is an open-admissions institution, so admission to the dance program is based on student desire and not on ability.

When the movement to develop a systematic approach to assessment came to the college in the mid-1990s, one of the first steps the Dance Department took was to develop objectives for the bachelor of arts degree program. (The bachelor of fine arts degree was introduced in 2001.)

The program objectives were as follows:
Graduates of the dance program at Columbia College will

1. possess a coordinated, conditioned, articulate, and aligned instrument (their body, mind, spirit) that is responsive to direction, accurate in execution, and capable of integrated expressive performance;

2. choreograph dances that display originality and the application of compositional principles;

3. understand the fundamental elements, theories, and aesthetics of contemporary modern dance within the context of a diverse world of dance practices, and be informed by historical/cultural perspectives and dance's relationships to other fields; and

4. demonstrate the attitudinal and behavioral attributes of effective participation in dance, including openness to new experiences and challenges, willingness to take risks, the ability to work collaboratively, facility in creative problem solving, self-discipline, and self-directed curiosity.

In order to systematically assess many aspects of these objectives, Primary Trait Analysis (PTA) rubrics were developed. PTA (Walvoord and Anderson 1998) is a widely accepted assessment approach where student work is evaluated using an agreed-on rubric that contains criteria directly related to an assignment, project, or performance. In the case of dance students, these criteria had already been articulated in many of the performing areas, since they were the criteria used to place and pass students in the different course levels.

During the 1998-99 academic year, the department was presented with an excellent opportunity for assessing program change: Contact hours for the modern dance technique courses increased three-fold. Under the former curriculum, one credit hour of dance technique equaled one contact hour in the studio. Under the revised curriculum, one credit hour equals three contact hours in the studio.

In addition, even though there is a series of three modern dance technique courses (I, II, and III), the only technique requirement under the former curriculum was that students complete 7 hours in Technique III. The new curriculum lengthened this requirement, mandating that all students go through the three-course series and eventually complete 24 hours. In short, the contact hours increased and the required sequence was lengthened for every student.

During the 1998-99 academic year, class performances from students in Modern Technique II were videotaped in the fall and in the spring. (It should be noted that since students typically spend more than one semester in each of the technique courses, the composition of these classes was largely the same.) A faculty panel of three assessed student performances, and in each area, students made substantial gains.

In terms of assessing what Astin (1993) refers to as "talent development," this assessment activity suggests the students grew as performing artists as a result of their experiences in Modern Dance II specifically and in the dance program in general.

In addition, it gave the faculty the opportunity to reflect on the curricular changes regarding increased contact hours and lengthening the sequence. The entire process —the tapes, the panel review, and the subsequent discussions —prompted some profound comments on the performances of the students and how these reflect the curriculum, the program, and departmental pedagogy.

The faculty comments and conclusions can be categorized into four areas: strengths, weaknesses, curricular implications, and pedagogical implications.

Table C.1 Assessment of Student Performance

Modern dance technique II	Fall 1998 (n = 28)	Spring 1999 (n = 25)	Gain
Body as skilled instrument			
Musculature	2.00	3.17	1.17
Alignment	2.17	3.00	0.83
Physical isolations	1.83	2.83	1.00
Neuro-muscular coordination	1.83	3.00	1.17
Movement memory	1.83	3.00	1.17
Ability to pick up new material	1.67	3.00	1.33
Average	**1.89**	**3.00**	**1.11**
Performance qualities			
Concentration	2.50	3.00	0.50
Dynamic phrasing	2.00	3.00	1.00
Musical awareness	1.67	3.00	1.33
Rhythmic accuracy	1.67	3.00	1.33
Spatial intent	2.17	2.67	0.50
Focus	2.00	2.83	0.83
Overall artistry	2.00	2.83	0.83
Average	**2.00**	**2.90**	**0.90**

I. STUDENT STRENGTHS

The students showed marked improvement between semesters. They were much stronger, more conditioned, and more centered. They demonstrated better awareness of alignment, primarily in standing and stationary work. They were much more accurate with spatial forms, demonstrating patterns with more clarity. Their technical skills were good. Overall, they seemed cleaner, clearer, stronger, and more confident with movement material.

II. STUDENT WEAKNESSES

The students' weaknesses seemed to be in qualitative performance aspects. While they were clear with spatial forms, they lacked a sense of spatial intent and a three-dimensionality and sculptural sense of their body in space. Rhythmic work was weak. While they were more "on the beat" by the second semester, they lacked phrasing. They seemed more robotic than musical. A sense of dynamic flow was missing; they did not understand the relationship of weight, gravity, and flow. While these seem to be huge gaps, the students are where they should be. Modern Technique III (the next course in the sequence) should be more weighted toward performance and qualitative work.

The panel noted that as the concentration and commitment of the students to learning has grown, there has been less questioning of teachers. They ask less about the "whys" and "hows." Because of this, the students are less disruptive in class. They are serious and working hard, so there is less temptation to slow the class down with unnecessary questions. However, this can be a dangerous slope for the faculty since we emphasize rigor and discipline. We must keep rigor and curiosity in balance, so we encourage healthy curiosity. We recommend that faculty assign at least a day of nonmoving classes, when the students and teachers can discuss training, including style, history, philosophy, and goal setting.

III. CURRICULAR IMPLICATIONS

Being in class consistently has greatly enhanced the students' technical strengths and skills. The faculty panel felt that this progress validates the dance program's increased technique requirements. The faculty noted that student strengths reflected the strengths of the particular instructor in those courses and that a conscious rotation of assignments based on matching faculty strengths with observed student need would be advisable. Although students had made notable progress with physical skills, they needed improvement in refined or nuanced performance. It was noted that that was to be expected in Modern Technique II, and that advanced performance skills are developed at the Modern Technique III level.

The students' concentration, alertness, and enthusiasm were significantly higher than they were three years ago. They were thinking faster and knew that it was their job to do so. They were taking their learning more seriously. Two of the panelists noted that our senior-level students are more skilled than our alumni.

IV. PEDAGOGICAL IMPLICATIONS

Teacher evaluations reveal that many students have been frustrated by the lack of individual attention. Our classes are getting larger. We suggest that we begin teaching students how to take class constructively—how to get the most out of any correction. In our fall meeting, we would like to stress student "ownership" of taking class at each level, which may help minimize frustration and make our students better learners.

For many years there have been attitude problems in the Modern II level. This level is difficult, close to adolescence. Often, they have a hard time valuing repetition, and yet that is exactly what they need. It might be worth holding some faculty workshops to discuss repetition versus new material in the struggle to gain technique.

We noted that the strength of our technical program has been the confidence we instill in students and the individuality and performance nuance of each dancer. (They are not cookie cutters.) As we begin to see more technical strength and clarity, we must not lose the aesthetic and performance qualities that we value as most important.

We recommend moving technique teachers to different levels. Spring would be the ideal time to make the changes. All students would change teachers when they move to a new level, then return to a previous teacher in spring. The movement would allow the varied strengths of our faculty to influence all the levels, creating more balance between technical skills and performance.

In summary, effective assessment programs are faculty driven, present critical and honest insights into student performance, suggest potentially effective ways to change the curriculum, and offer meaningful evaluation of changes. The creativity and commitment of the faculty in the Dance Department at Columbia College Chicago have made assessment a worthwhile and valuable undertaking.

REFERENCES

Astin, A. 1993. *Assessment for Excellence.* Phoenix: Oryx.

Walvoord, B., and V. Anderson. 1998. *Effective Grading.* San Francisco: Jossey-Bass.

Reprinted, by permission, from L. Lehrer, B. Brooks, R. Woodbury, S. Mordine, D. Siegel, E. Vilaro, D. McGinley, N. Pagano, and J. Erkert, The Dance Center of Columbia College Chicago. From *Harnessing the Wind* by Jan Erkert, 2003, Champaign, IL: Human Kinetics.

Appendix D
The Dance Center of Columbia College Chicago Course Evaluation—Student

Developed by The Dance Center of Columbia College Chicago Faculty
Bonnie Brooks, Jan Erkert, Dardi McGinley-Gallivan, Shirley Mordine,
Deborah Siegel, Eduardo Vilaro, and Richard Woodbury

This content is to be used as a guideline for teachers to develop their own evaluations.

A. Please rate the instructor/course according to the criteria below:

	Excellent	Very good	Good	Fair	Poor
1. Clarity of goals	_____	_____	_____	_____	_____
2. Clarity of demonstration	_____	_____	_____	_____	_____
3. Knowledge of subject	_____	_____	_____	_____	_____
4. Thoroughness of warm-up	_____	_____	_____	_____	_____
5. Challenge of material	_____	_____	_____	_____	_____
6. Pacing of class	_____	_____	_____	_____	_____
7. Clarity of corrections	_____	_____	_____	_____	_____
8. Ability to work with each student individually	_____	_____	_____	_____	_____
9. Sense of engagement	_____	_____	_____	_____	_____
10. Value of accompanist to class	_____	_____	_____	_____	_____

B. Please rate your participation in the class.

1. How well prepared were you for the course?

   a. very well prepared   b. adequately prepared   c. had to struggle

2. How would you evaluate your participation in the course?

   a. above average   b. average   c. less than average

C. Please rate the difficulty of the course:

   a. too hard   b. challenging   c. hard   d. average   e. easy

   1. What did you like most about this class or the teacher's approach to the material? Why?

   _____

   _____

   _____

   _____

   2. What did you like least about this class or the teacher's approach to the material? Why?

   _____

   _____

   _____

   _____

   3. Do you have any suggestions for changes you would make?

   _____

   _____

   _____

   _____

   4. Do you feel that you have improved as a dancer in any way as a result of this course? If so, comment on what you gained.

   _____

   _____

   _____

   _____

   5. Would you recommend this class to other students? Why or why not?

   _____

   _____

   _____

   _____

Reprinted, by permission, from L. Lehrer, B. Brooks, R. Woodbury, S. Mordine, D. Siegel, E. Vilaro, D. McGinley, and J. Erkert, The Dance Center of Columbia College Chicago. From *Harnessing the Wind* by Jan Erkert, 2003, Champaign, IL: Human Kinetics.

Appendix E
The Dance Center of Columbia College Chicago Instructor Evaluation

Developed by The Dance Center of Columbia College Chicago Faculty
Bonnie Brooks, Jan Erkert, Dardi McGinley-Gallivan, Shirley Mordine,
Deborah Siegel, Eduardo Vilaro, and Richard Woodbury

This content is to be used as a guideline for teachers to develop their own evaluations.

CLASS CONTENT

1. Were movement principles being taught?

_____
_____
_____
_____

2. Were the goals clear and were there strategies to arrive at the goals?

_____
_____
_____
_____

3. Was the material appropriate for the level?

_____
_____
_____
_____

STRUCTURE

1. Were exercises sequenced effectively?

_____

_____

_____

_____

2. Was the warm-up thorough and safe?

_____

_____

_____

_____

TEACHER

1. Preparation and organization

_____

_____

_____

_____

2. Spontaneity

_____

_____

_____

_____

3. Pacing

_____

_____

_____

_____

4. Corrections

_____

_____

_____

_____

5. Images

_____
_____
_____
_____

6. Communication

_____
_____
_____
_____

7. Rhythm

_____
_____
_____
_____

8. Demonstration

_____
_____
_____
_____

9. Relationship with the accompanist

_____
_____
_____
_____

STUDENT

1. Did students feel a sense of involvement in the class?

_____
_____
_____
_____

2. Did students understand class rules and etiquette?

_____

_____

_____

_____

FINAL EVALUATION

1. Strengths

_____

_____

_____

_____

2. Challenges

_____

_____

_____

_____

Bibliography

Ackerman, D. 1990. *A Natural History of the Senses*. New York: Vintage Books, a division of Random House.

Alexander, R. M. 1994. *Bones: The Unity of Form and Function*. New York: Macmillan.

Allison, N. 1999. *The Illustrated Encyclopedia of Body-Mind Disciplines*. New York: Rosen Publishing Group.

Alter, M. 1996. *Science of Flexibility*. Champaign, IL: Human Kinetics.

Bartenieff, I., and D. Lewis. 1980. *Body Movement: Coping With the Environment*. New York: Gordon and Breach Science Publishers.

Bateson, M.C. 1989. *Composing a Life*. New York: Grove Press.

Cardone, A. 2002. Killing the body ego, dance research with Min Tanaka at Body Weather Farm, Japan. *Contact Quarterly* 27(1): 16.

Cassella, M., C. Ploski, E. Sullivan, and L. Micheli. 1999. Transition dance class: Rehabilitation through dance. *Journal of Dance Medicine & Science* 3(4): 139-143.

Chatwin, B. 1987. *The Songlines*. New York: Penguin Books.

Clark, G.A., M.D. Day, and W.D. Greer. 1987. Discipline-based art education: Becoming students of art. *Journal of Aesthetic Education* 21(2): 130-193.

Cohen, B.B. 1993. *Sensing, Feeling, and Action: The Experiential Anatomy of Body-Mind Centering*. Northampton, MA: Contact Editions.

Cooper, R., and A. Sawaf. 1997. *Executive EQ: Emotional Intelligence in Leadership and Organizations*. New York: The Berkley Publishing Group.

Csikszentmihalyi, M. 1996. *Creativity, Flow, and the Psychology of Discovery and Invention*. New York: HarperCollins Publishers, Inc.

Csikszentmihalyi, M. 1997. *Finding Flow: The Psychology of Engagement With Everyday Life*. New York: Basic Books.

Dillard, A. 1982. *Teaching a Stone to Talk: Expeditions and Encounters*. New York: HarperCollins Publishers, Inc.

Dowd, I. 1995. *Taking Root to Fly: Articles on Functional Anatomy*. New York: Irene Dowd.

Eakin, E. 2002. Penetrating the mind by metaphor. *The New York Times,* 23 February, A17

Erdrich, L. 2001. *The Last Report on the Miracles at Little No Horse*. New York: HarperCollins Publishers, Inc.

Farhi, D. 2000. *Yoga Mind, Body, & Spirit: A Return to Wholeness*. New York: Henry Holt and Company.

Fitt, S.S. 1996. *Dance Kinesiology*. New York: Schirmer Books.

Fox, H.N. 1990. *A Primal Spirit: Ten Contemporary Japanese Sculptors*. Los Angeles: Los Angeles County Museum of Art.

Franklin, E. 1996. *Dynamic Alignment Through Imagery*. Champaign, IL: Human Kinetics.

Gardner, H. 1983. *Frames of Mind: The Theory of Multiple Intelligences*. New York: Basic Books, Inc.

H'Doubler, M. 1968. *Dance: A Creative Art Experience*. Madison, WI: University of Wisconsin Press.

Hackney, P. 1998. *Making Connections: Total Body Integration Through Bartenieff Fundamentals*. Amsterdam, The Netherlands: Gordon and Breach Publishers.

Hartley, L. 1995. *Wisdom of the Body Moving*. Berkeley, CA: North Atlantic Books.

Hawking, S.W. 2002. *The Theory of Everything*. Beverly Hills, CA: New Millennium Press.

Hay, D. 2000. *My Body, the Buddhist*. Hanover, NH: University of New England Press.

Herrigel, E. 1989. *Zen in the Art of Archery*. New York: Vintage Book Edition.

Homans, J. 2002. Where is the heartbeat in the Balanchine legacy? *The New York Times,* 26 May, Arts and Leisure, 22.

Humphrey, D. 1959. *The Art of Making Dances.* New York: Grove Press, Inc.

Hurston, Z.N. 1937. *Their Eyes Were Watching God.* New York: Harper & Row.

Isozaki, A. *Ma: Space-Time in Japan.* Chicago: Art Institute of Chicago.

Jowitt, D. 2001. *Not Just Any Body: Advancing Health, Well-being and Excellence in Dance and Dancers.* Ontario: The Ginger Press.

Koch, L. 1997. *The Psoas Book.* Felton, CA: Guinea Pig Publications.

Krasnow, D., L. Mainwaring, and G. Kerr. 1999. Injury, stress, and perfectionism in young dancers and gymnasts. *Journal of Dance Medicine & Science* 3(2): 51-58.

Kriesberg, M. 2002. A composer thinking globally, acting locally. *The New York Times,* 26 May, Arts and Leisure, 26.

Lepkoff, D. 2001. Steve Paxton: Extraordinarily ordinary and ordinarily extraordinary. *Contact Quarterly* 26(1): 37.

Liederbach, M., and J.M. Compagno. 2001. Psychological aspects of fatigue-related injuries in dancers. *Journal of Dance Medicine & Science* 5(4): 116-120.

Liederbach, M. 2000. General considerations for guiding dance injury rehabilitation. *Journal of Dance Medicine & Science* 4(2): 54-65.

Mainwaring L., D. Krasnow, and G. Kerr. 2001. And the dance goes on: Psychological impact of injury. *Journal of Dance Medicine & Science* 5(4): 105-115.

Michaels, A. 1996. *Fugitive Pieces.* New York: Vintage Books.

Moyers, B. 1993. *Healing and the Mind.* New York: Bantam Books, Inc.

Netter, F.H. 1997. *Atlas of Human Anatomy.* East Hanover, NJ: Novartis Medical Education.

Olsen, A. 1991. *BodyStories: A Guide to Experiential Anatomy.* Barrytown, NY: Station Hill Press.

Overby, L.Y. 1990. The use of imagery by dance teachers: Development and implementation of two research instruments. *Physical Education, Recreation and Dance* 61(February): 24-27.

Palmer, P.J. 1998. *The Courage to Teach: Exploring the Inner Landscape of a Teacher's Life.* San Francisco: Jossey-Bass.

Paskevska, A. 1992. *Both Sides of the Mirror: The Science and Art of Ballet.* Hightstown, NJ: Princeton Book Company.

Paz, O. 1976. *Eagle or Sun?* Translated by Eliot Weinberger. New York: New Directions Publishing Company.

Pierce, E., and M. Daleng. 2002. Exercise dependence in elite female dancers. *Journal of Dance Medicine & Science* 6(1): 4-6.

Read, H. 1961. *The Art of Sculpture.* New York: Pantheon Books.

Remen, R.N. 1996. *Kitchen Table Wisdom.* New York: Riverhead Books, distributed by The Berkley Publishing Group, a division of Penguin Putnam Inc.

Rilke, R.M., 1975. *Rilke On Love and Other Difficulties.* New York: W.W. Norton & Company, Inc.

Root-Bernstein, M. 2001. Abstracting bulls: A dancing words/writing dance workshop. *Journal of Dance Education* 1(4): 134-141.

Schlaich, J., and B. DuPont. 1993. *The Art of Teaching Dance Technique.* Reston, VA: American Alliance for Health, Physical Education, Recreation and Dance.

Senge, P.M. 1990 *The Fifth Discipline: The Art and Practice of the Learning Organization.* New York: Doubleday.

Sennett, R. 2001. Resistance. Edited by Ian Jack. *Granta, The Magazine of New Writing/ 76 Music,* 31-36. London, England: Granta Publications.

Shah, I. 1970. *Tales of the Dervishes.* New York: Dutton.

Shlain, L. 1991. *Art & Physics: Parallel Visions in Space, Time, & Light.* New York: Morrow.

Skura, S. 1990. Interview with Joan Skinner. *Contact Quarterly* 15(3): 12-13.

Slater, L. 2002. The trouble with self-esteem. *New York Times Magazine,* 3 February, section 6.

Stinson, S. 2001. Choreographing a life: reflections on curriculum design, consciousness, and possibility. *Journal of Dance Education* 1(1): 31.

Suzuki, S. 1970. *Zen Mind, Beginner's Mind.* New York: John Weatherhill, Inc.

Sweigard, L. 1974. *Human Movement Potential: Its Ideokinetic Facilitation.* New York: Harper & Row.

Teck, K. 1990. *Movement to Music: Musicians in the Dance Studio.* Westport, CT: Greenwood Publishing Group, Inc.

Thomas, L. 1986. *The Medusa and the Snail.* New York: Bantam Books, Inc.

Todd, M.E. 1929. *The Balancing of Forces in the Human Being: Its Application to Postural Patterns.* CE: Mable Ellsworth Todd.

Todd, M.E. 1937. *The Thinking Body.* New York: Paul B. Hoeber, Inc. Reprint, Dance Horizons, Inc.

Vermeersch, P. 2002. About butoh: In research for its origin and actual meaning, an interview with Min Tanaka. *Contact Quarterly* 27(1): 22-23.

Volianitis, S., Y. Koutedakis, and R. Carson. 2001. Warm-up: A brief review. *Journal of Dance Medicine & Science* 5(3): 75-81.

Voss, D., M. Ionta, and B. Myers. 1985. *Proprioceptive Neuromuscular Facilitation: Patterns and Techniques.* Philadelphia: Harper & Row.

Whitehouse, M.S. 2002. Movement experience: The raw material of dance (1958*). Contact Quarterly* 27 (2): 22.

Wilson, J. 1999. Abstracts from the ninth annual meeting of the International Association for Dance Medicine & Science *Journal of Dance Medicine & Science* 3(4): 162.

Winterson, J. 1991. *Sexing the Cherry.* New York: Vintage International.

Zaporah, R. 2002. What's on my mind now: Frames, listening, and expression. *Contact Quarterly* 27(1): 51.

About the Author

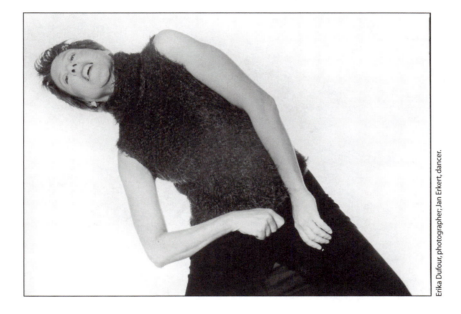

Erika Dufour, photographer; Jan Erkert, dancer.

Jan Erkert is a dance artist, leader, and builder in contemporary dance. As artistic director of Jan Erkert & Dancers from 1979 to 2000, she presented her work throughout the United States as well as in Germany, Mexico, Taiwan, Japan, Uruguay, and Israel. Erkert and the company have been honored with numerous awards including fellowships from the National Endowment for the Arts and the Illinois Arts Council, collaborative grants with Mexico and Japan, a CalArts Alpert Award nomination, a Fulbright Award, and seven Ruth Page Awards for choreography and performance. Erkert has served on panels for Fulbright and McKnight Foundation Awards.

Erkert is currently a professor at the Dance Center of Columbia College Chicago, where she teaches modern dance technique, pedagogy, anatomy, kinesiology, improvisation, and composition. She recently received the prestigious Excellence in Teaching Award from the college. She conducts training workshops at major dance departments to help faculty, teaching assistants, and dance majors learn how to teach modern dance more effectively. Erkert is known throughout the United States and internationally as a master teacher, inspiring people with her intense, honest approach that interweaves scientific principles with the artistic drive for excellence.

In her free time, Erkert likes to spend time outdoors hiking, swimming, gardening, bicycling, and traveling. She also enjoys sewing, cooking, and practicing Ashtanga yoga. Erkert and her husband, Bernt Lewy, live in Chicago.

For more information about Jan Erkert's training workshops and performances, write to erkertdance@aol.com.

About the Contributors

Erika Dufour (photographer)

Erika Dufour earned a bachelor's degree in photography from Columbia College. Along with her degree, she has had training in dance and has used those skills for her photography. She now lives and works in Chicago, where she continues to photograph dance in addition to doing fine art and editorial work.

Contact Information

Web address: www.erikadufour.com

William Frederking (photographer)

William Frederking lives in Oak Park, Illinois, and has taught in the photography department of Columbia College Chicago for 19 years. He began photographing Chicago-area dance in 1989, and his dance photographs have been published in newspapers and periodicals nationally and internationally.

Contact Information

E-mail address: bfrederking@earthlink.net

John Matthews (illustrator)

John Matthews was born and raised in Oklahoma. He received a bachelor's of fine art degree in painting and drawing at Oklahoma State University and a master's of fine art degree at the University of Illinois, Urbana-Champaign. He now lives and works as a draftsman and illustrator in Chicago, Illinois.

Contact Information

E-mail address: armsakimbo@hotmail.com

*You'll find
other outstanding
dance resources at*

www   etics.com

47-4457

.... 08 8277 1555
.... 800-465-7301
.... +44 (0) 113 255 5665
.... 09-523-3462

IETICS

ublisher for Sports & Fitness
• Champaign, IL 61825-5076 USA